Aging Famously

Praise for *Aging Famously*
Follow Those You Admire to Living Long and Well

"Here it is! What everyone really wants to know but is too superstitious to ask about. These are wonderful lives, masterfully written about."
— Liz Smith, syndicated columnist *New York Social Diary*

"Some mentors teach us specific skills; others teach us major life lessons. Elizabeth Howard gives the reader the opportunity to learn from an impressive group of wise and experienced elders, beginning with her own father."
— Dr. Margery Hutter Silver, co-author *Living to 100*, retired Assistant Professor in Psychology at Harvard Medical School

"The author, Elizabeth Howard, expresses the essence of this book which reveals that 'living is giving.'"
— Carol Channing, actress/comedienne

"This collection reminds us of how evergreen the subject of aging always remains. So much to say, so little time, yet the many beguiling and inspiring essays in Elizabeth Howard's book all celebrate exploring every last drop of life. You'll feel younger by the page."
— Jane Barnes, author of *Falling in Love With Joseph Smith*

"Whether it's work (Walter Cronkite), love (Carol Channing) or good education, good health and learning how to rest (Rosa Parks), we hear gems from heroes and lesser known, but equally wise, experts on aging, all inspiring us to live fully and joyfully."
— Kathryn Erskine, author of *Mockingbird*, National Book Award winner for young people's literature

Aging Famously

Follow Those You Admire to Living Long and Well

Elizabeth Meade Howard

Jefferson Park Press
Charlottesville, Virginia

Interior book design by Jon Marken, jmarken@lamppostpublicity.com
Cover photo by Susan Kalargis, http://www.sbkphoto.com/contact/
Cover design by Mary Murray, mary@mmurraydesign.com

Publisher's Cataloging-In-Publication Data
(Prepared by The Donohue Group, Inc.)

Names: Howard, Elizabeth Meade.
Title: Aging famously : follow those you admire to living long and well /
    Elizabeth Meade Howard.
Description: Charlottesville, VA : Jefferson Park Press, [2017]
Identifiers: ISBN 978-0-9849921-3-3
Subjects: LCSH: Older people--Interviews. | Celebrities--Interviews. |
    Aging. | Old age. | Well-being--Age factors. | Happiness in old age. |
    Self-help techniques.
Classification: LCC HQ1061 .H68 2017 | DDC 305.26--dc23

ISBN: 978-0-9849921-3-3

Jefferson Park Press
Charlottesville, Virginia

In memory of Everard and Virginia Meade,
parents who knew how to live

To Johnny, for sharing the journey

CONTENTS

FAITH. HOPE. LOVE.   255

ACKNOWLEDGMENTS

FIRST THERE WAS THE INSPIRATION of my father. After his death, I began my book as a mourning project and was urged to proceed by writers Donna Lucey and Henry Wiencek. It was a long time coming and through the slog, I'm most grateful for encouragement and helpful contributions from Karen Kostyal, Jane Barnes, Mariflo Stephens, Kathy Pond, Jodie Allen, Amy Entelis, Claudia Jessup, Ann Satterthwaite and Tess Taylor.

Thanks too to Jon Marken, Josef Beery, Lisa Marshall, Lile Deinard, Courtney Nicole Fears, Anne Hulecki and Brandon Butler.

Without the patient support of my husband, John, *Aging Famously* would not have passed muster. Without the experience of Mary Cail and Hilary Holladay, I would not have made it to the finish line. Thank you all.

PROLOGUE

With Love to My Father

MY FATHER TAUGHT ME TO LOOK to the stars: the Big and Little Dippers, and Orion the Hunter, whose belt shines three lights in a row. He taught me to love laughter — as well as Virginia Woolf, haiku, butterflies, Broadway, old movies, and the streets of New York. He taught me to work every day at something I believe in. To eat what is put in front of me. To say "thank you" and "I'm sorry" and mean it. To be on time and never to go to bed angry. To walk the beach in summer and winter. To save bees and bats and anything that lives. He taught me to keep going when he no longer could.

In 1981, my father, Everard Wilson Meade, was 71 when my mother died suddenly in her sleep. She was 72.

My father, a would-be actor, claimed heritage from Episcopal ministers with meager bank accounts. My mother inherited writer genes from her traveling journalist father, also a man of modest means, who met my grandmother while working in Virginia. My parents, amidst parental protest due to their youth, married on a dream and a dime. They were sophomores at the University of Virginia which my mother attended as a special student of a staff daughter. They had few professional prospects. It was 1931, the heart of the Depression.

On graduation, they headed for New York's Greenwich Village. My father packed his rave college acting notices and newspaper columns, my mother her local book reviews and general reporting. My father, bound for Broadway, went to theater auditions that didn't pan out. My mother found a one-room rental on Eighth Street over a Japanese restaurant. She briefly taught at the Arthur Murray Dance Studio and gave Shimi, the restaurant owner, dance lessons in exchange for noodles and sukiyaki. She also got a job in Gimbel's toy department.

When my father applied for an office-boy job in the mailroom at Benton and Bowles advertising agency, he was told they were only hiring Ivy League graduates. "I feel a University of Virginia grad can lick stamps as well as any Yale or Harvard man," asserted my father. He was hired. And thus began his long and fortuitous career in advertising.

Ad agencies in the early days worked hand in hand with their clients' publicity and on-air material. My father grabbed chances to contribute to radio scripts for comedian Fred Allen, and later in Los Angeles and New York, rose in the ranks as a writer and radio producer for Jack Benny, Al Jolson, Fred Astaire, and George Burns and Gracie Allen.

My father's advertising career peaked when he was named vice president of radio and television at Young and Rubicam and, later, at Ogilvy and Mather. When his office-boy pal, Pat Weaver (soon to gain fame as father of Sigourney), was named president of NBC, he offered my father a top position. Instead, at the tender age of 43, my father "retired" to Charlottesville, where he would write and teach for the next three decades at UVA's Darden School of Business.

Throughout their marriage, my mother backed my father's ambitions, kept accounts, made nests and guided his decisions with good nature and bold, clear-eyed counsel. She'd restored a burnt-up apartment in Gramercy Park, and saved with my father to build their home in Virginia that she decorated handsomely with family antiques and flea-market finds. She led us on adventurous, bargain travels, boarding a freighter for France or a vintage train from

Charlottesville through Texas to the wilds of Mexico. My parents were still planning trips even as he booked the Ritz and she the Ramada. They remained best friends.

My father said my mother's death felt like "a black hole in space." Her death left him alone in the house they'd designed together. At first he said, "It's your mother's house. I don't feel I should move a thing." But in time — favored with good health and the affection of family, friends and even lovers — he found ways to comfortably rearrange the house and to move forward. He adapted to his losses, and although he had no apparent master plan for successful aging, his instinctive solutions served him well. He was my hero and a role model with wise steps to follow.

He left complaints at home and brought good humor to the table.

He vowed not to worry about anything for more than three days.

Every morning, dressed neatly and well groomed, he put his papers in his briefcase and headed out to teach and write at the Darden School. When he reached 70, the age of mandatory retirement, he kept going to Darden and writing for the School's alumni magazine. He also sent out manuscripts of action thrillers he drafted in long hand. Four were published. The year after my mother died, my father wrote and published *The Dragonfly*, a novella about her childhood. Writing remained his first and last defense against aging.

He volunteered his publicity and acting talents to The Recording for the Blind and Dyslexic.

He reread Ian Fleming, Shakespeare, Nabokov and Virginia Woolf.

He drew whimsical cartoons for all holidays and family birthdays.

He called old friends, and sought friendships with junior colleagues. When his younger friends started families, he wrote letters welcoming their new babies to the world. Many of his letters were framed as keepsakes.

My father joined a group trip to England, his first journey without my mother. There he made new friends and returned to visit them during many subsequent springs. One year he took his granddaughter, Virginia, with him. Another summer, he and his grandson, Jamie, flew to Maui where they bought flowered shirts and viewed volcanoes.

He stood straight and tall, swam, walked, and did daily chin-ups on the bathroom door.

In his late 80s, my father had several small car wrecks; when approached by my husband, John, he agreed to stop driving. It was a tough loss of mobility and freedom that could have cloistered him at home. Instead, he asked his housekeeper to drive him to the grocery store and to the Darden School library where he drafted new stories, lunched with faculty and read the *New York Times*. When friends asked his whereabouts, he replied impatiently, "At work!"

On Sundays, my father took a taxi to the early service and sang off-key at St. Paul's Episcopal Church.

At home, he let the paint peel and the roof leak.

He said, "Take it" to anyone who complimented something in his home. And when he said, "I love you," they were easy words to return.

He often volunteered, "I'm a happy man."

While my father fought retirement and remained relatively strong, I eventually became concerned about his living alone, however much he professed independence. I was relieved when he accepted my prodding to have a university student rent a back room, even though their paths would scarcely cross.

I worried that he ate less and slept more; he dismissed cataracts and late-developing diabetes. When he was 88, I saw signs of mini strokes and forgetfulness. He increased his efforts to mask changes with good-natured reassurances and an unusually rich vocabulary.

I remember that late January afternoon. My father walked me to my car in the cold. I patted his blowing hair and red Shetland sweater. We hugged and said good-bye.

The next morning, the housekeeper called in a panic. My father had collapsed at the dining room table while a friend was helping him pay bills. I raced to his house as medics strapped my father to a gurney, sped him to the hospital and into intensive care. Twenty-four hours later, he was diagnosed with viral encephalitis, a rare and aggressive attack to the brain. For a month, he lay near consciousness. I came to see him every day, and every day I feared would be his last.

Incredibly, my father fought his way back. He left the hospital only to spend months at a nursing home before returning to his house and around-the-clock care. His doctor, a hospice specialist who sensitively guided his medical treatment said, "Your father is amazing. Most men half his age would not have lived."

I learned that my father's will to live was indeed amazing. I saw a man much reduced, sometimes bewildered, but by nature still gallant, dignified and fighting the fates with humor. When a visiting friend asked how he spent his day at the nursing home, my father replied, "I get out of bed and put my feet on the floor. Then I take my pulse. If I have one, I shave. If not, why bother?"

On returning home, my father asked his housekeeper to drive him back to the Darden library one more time. Work was still the staff by which he stood.

It would be his last visit to the university he loved. When soon confined to home, my father seemed to decide that life, albeit compromised, was still worth living. On my arrival each morning, he rose out of bed, tied on his striped bathrobe and asked the news. When I said that I was working on a documentary about a 107-year-old local lady, he smiled and asked, "Does she date?"

Other days he struggled with confusion. He reported seeing white tigers loose in the yard. He believed he'd piloted the *Enola Gay* with the atom bomb aboard and begged me to apologize to the women and children of Japan.

Even in his confusion, my father remained courteous and put pleasure before pain. He enjoyed the summer's heat and memories of diving together through the waves at Virginia Beach. Now we sat beside the cracked 1950s pool, eating tomato sandwiches lathered in mayonnaise. In the fall, we drove the country back roads as he flattered the trees for their rich colors. We listened to tapes of Bing Crosby, Strauss, Mozart and Garrison Keillor. I read him nature haiku as well as his own spare poems of London pigeons, swans and whale songs. His last poems — "Only Now" and "The Cost of Living" — were scrawled in pencil. My father asked me who had written them.

Sometimes my father said he felt like he was 100. However weary and worn, he held on until Christmas 2000. We opened a few presents at his bedside. That night, he sank into a deep sleep that lingered for more than a week. My father lived until January 5, seeming to have willed himself into the new century and three days past his 90th birthday. I was thankful for his many years, but when they ended, even 90 felt too few.

PHOTO BY PAM PERUGI MARRACCINI

My father and I, 1997

LOSS

"Set yourself some objectives and be sure you get them."
From my father's letter on my 21st birthday

NINETY YEARS ARE MORE than most are given. I was grateful for my father's long, well-lived life. He'd always been a loving parent, friend, mentor and role model. But still his loss was rough to bear. His death and my abrupt elevation to family elder marked a critical turning point for me. I needed time to mourn and, after a year's vigil at my father's side, to find new direction and purpose.

I started reading. Donna Schuurman wrote in *Never the Same: Coming to Terms with the Death of a Parent.* "Our society tends to say, put (death) behind you. But people can't put it behind them. People want to maintain a relationship with the dead. In a society that says, 'Forget it, move on,' rituals are a way to keep the value of that person's life alive. It is clearer from the research that people who have some context of a religious belief fare better. It doesn't seem to matter what the religious belief is, but a spiritual context is key."

My father had requested a "not too religious" funeral that did, however, provide us a reverent, communal setting and ritual with which to honor his life. Coming together in ceremony, we acknowledged his valor and grace, his dignified decline and death, and anticipated a necessary time of grieving.

I sympathized when I heard Jean Michel Cousteau, the son of oceanic explorer Jacques Cousteau, say in an interview after his father's death, that he kept diving into the deepest seas, because it made him feel nearest to his father "in their shared cathedral under water."

Photographer Annie Leibovitz lost her father and her companion, writer Susan Sontag, within six weeks of each other. She said that she felt fortunate to have taken photographs of her loved ones and to have photography as her refuge. "When you lose someone," she said, "you go to what you know."

After my father died, I too went to the familiar. Each morning I repeated the routine I'd established during his last year and drove to his house. It was a sanctuary that provided me a reassuring illusion of permanence. The front door, never locked in the past, was now bolted. I turned the brass skeleton key and welcomed its click in the lock. I tiptoed from room to room, finding toast crumbs on the dining room table, brushes and combs clogged with fine gray hairs. I half expected to see my father sleeping in his four-poster bed. Surely any minute I would greet his nurse and hear news of his wakeful hours in the night.

As my father had decreed after my mother's death in 1981, I too wanted nothing in the house yet to be altered. After all, my father had lived there for almost 50 years. He and my mother had carefully saved to build the house, so when they moved to Charlottesville from Manhattan — with the future uncertain — their home would be secure. This house represented success, especially to my father.

I was 13 when we headed south. I was sad to leave New York but excited to have new friends and a rose-papered bedroom. This was the room where my best friend and I would laugh and whisper and where, one day, I would be buttoned into my wedding dress.

Shortly before my mother died, she was gearing up for the house's overdue refurbishing. By then, the rose wallpaper had faded, the rugs were worn and paint had chipped in the kitchen and bathrooms. Taking no notice, my father often volunteered, "I love this house. Isn't this a beautiful house?" He hoped that after he died, I would live there too.

Now in my father's bedroom, I folded his shirts, sheets and towels onto the bed. I dusted off the suede shoes he'd bought in England. I put away photo albums that we'd scanned while retelling family stories with their predictable endings.

Sitting cross-legged beside my father's bed, I opened a box of his letters written from my childhood on. Through the years, he never missed a birthday. I read one sent on my twenty-first birthday when he was 50 and already longing for longevity.

Dearest Elizabeth,

Now that you are about to be 21, I don't quite know what merry words to send you. I imagine by now you brush your teeth every night and say your prayers and spell cat without a "k." I hope you are careful crossing streets and never have dates with escaped convicts. If you haven't sense to come in out of the rain, it's my fault. I like to walk in it myself. If I could start again slim and shiny as you are, I would most likely end up as fat and dusty with the journey as I am. (Actually the present is the best time for me, waist and hairlines not withstanding). One thing I would like to develop on a second try would be a habit of setting myself objectives and learning to reach them.

In your case, each summer you emerged from college determined to read this and that and write this and that until summer distractions rob you of your intentions. This year, full grown as a six-inch chipmunk, set yourself some objectives and be sure you get them. I won't presume to say what they should be. I would only hope one is a short story.

As you must know, behind my false front of "cheerio pappy" lives a person who would like to live an extra 100 years — just to watch his child spend her time on earth. You, at the moment, can do without the 100 years — as long as you survive exams. So that's why I write: to wish you luck, to remind you you're not a half-wit, to send you my love.

Daddy

There on the bedroom floor in my parents' house, once my center of gravity, I felt the seismic shift from adult child to family elder. I felt the force of my father's death, and the not-so-simple truths he'd taught me.

In those early weeks, while sorting through my father's things, I found peace and proximity in his house, but I also yearned for companions — those who knew and loved him best — to keep his presence alive. My parents and I were all only children, so my relatives were few; and my children, who'd adored their grandfather, were also grieving.

Jamie returned to work in New York, following his grandfather's footsteps as a copywriter in advertising. Virginia and her husband, David, lived nearby and found comfort in the Catholic church. John and I retold funny Papa Meade stories even as he propelled me through floods of legal papers and cooked dinners that we ate by the fire.

I joined a hospice support group and signed up for a grief study being conducted by the University of Virginia's School of Nursing. At hospice, we were assigned *Understanding Your Grief*, a guide through grief's inevitable stages. Its useful exercises included keeping a journal and writing letters to the deceased.

During our meetings, we told our stories sitting in a circle. I waited to speak, feeling that the loss of a parent must somehow be less than that of a spouse. It helped to hear others' stories. An antiques dealer and father of nine felt bereft without his wife; a policeman could not yet speak his wife's name. An English widow said she didn't want to drive her husband's van but couldn't bear to sell it. She'd brought his photograph, ashamed, she said, to still be crying every day. A daughter, once estranged from her mother, clung to her mother's sewing box of buttons and thread, tokens of the hours that still stitched them together.

Sharing the starkness of others' grief, I admitted how I resisted letting go of my father, his house and belongings. But I was also thankful that I'd been able to carry out his last wishes for "no extraordinary measures," thus allowing him a peaceful death at home. Sharing my feelings and listening to others, I felt glad to be accepted.

Still, questions lingered: What did it mean "to let go?" How and when should I balance feelings of devotion to my father, our family's past and a need to look ahead? What was my new family role? Had I suddenly become "old?"

In the university grief study, I was assigned a counselor — a big-hearted Bavarian damsel with whom I met informally for several months. The study's director observed that mourners who healed and recovered most quickly were the ones who were able to tell and retell their stories, gradually integrating them into a series of events with a clear beginning, middle, and ending.

And so I would begin a journey to fit the pieces of my father's final chapter into a narrative — one to help me comprehend and accept his loss while aging with reason, awareness and hopeful expectations.

I wanted mentors and role models for the journey.

I remembered the reassuring presence of "Grandpog," my father's father, who died when I was only four, but not before giving me his patient and tender attention.

"Nanny," my maternal grandmother, was widowed at 48 after the death of her journalist husband. Although my grandmother had a nine-year-old daughter and had never worked outside her home, she marched to the University of Virginia and presented her innate counseling services to the YMCA. She was soon officially on staff where she would advise and befriend students and faculty into her late 80s.

She read me Bible stories and *Pollyanna* (not a favorite); snipped doilies into paper dolls; taught me Canasta and scolded me for smoking my first — and last — cigarette. She candidly critiqued my boyfriends. She drove under the speed limit, kept up with the news and never missed a chance to vote. She stayed independent, even opening the door of her apartment for her doctor minutes before having a fatal heart attack.

Given Nanny's example, I now longed to talk to men and women who'd recently weathered the losses of aging — the deaths of loved ones; the decline of health and vigor; their retirement, loss of status and uncertain futures. Where should I start? Who would answer my questions?

I kept reading. And, as a journalist, I started asking the experts questions. In *Somewhere Towards the End*, British editor and author Diana Athill, looked forward at age 89: "So here I go," she wrote, "into advanced old age, towards my inevitable and no longer distant end, without the 'support' of religion and having to face the prospect ahead in all its bald reality. What are my feelings about that? I turn for enlightenment to the people I know who have gone ahead of me."

Writer, director and radio producer Norman Corwin wrote in *The Ageless Spirit*, "You reach instinctively for those models of successful old age like Verdi, Shaw, and Michelangelo who lived to a good ripe age — you hold onto those models."

"We all need models for how to live from retirement to past 80 — with joy," wrote George Vaillant, M.D. in *Aging Well: Surprising Guideposts to a Happier Life From the Landmark Harvard Study of Adult Development.*

In *A Sociology of Death and Dying*, Michael C. Kearl, sociology professor at Trinity University, touted the reward of older role models in an era when norms for aging are less defined. Interested in his thesis, I gave Professor Kearl a call. "There no longer is consensus about the social clocks that mark our biographical progression, such as the best age to get married; when one becomes an adult, middle aged, or old; or when to disengage from the labor force," said Kearl. "The absence of such markers produces a sociological equivalent of sensory deprivation: a disoriented existence without benchmarks or frames of reference.

"Role models provide such benchmarks, particularly in old age. They create criteria for self-evaluation, biographical strategies for negotiating this life stage, and examples of what is possible. Further, given the increasing rate of social change, these old role models need to be updated continuously to reveal new life opportunities.

"We're always in process of being old, but there's no one to instruct us in the process," added Kearl. "Someone may not have been the biggest winner in school or in the labor force but can be in retirement."

Kearl asked his students where they'd found older mentors and role models. "Television nowadays is certainly void of models. There are so few public examples of older role models. The only agreed upon personage in my class was Jimmy Carter.

"Where *are* our older role models? We're starving for role models. They're models of hope. Their existence brings hope, not only for the old but to the young as well, who need to know the quality and meaningfulness of life does not have to decline with the years."

Kearl grouped "admired older individuals," or role models, into six distinct categories:

1. The Workers retain a deep-seated work ethic. They remain in the same career their entire adult life or venture into a new field late in life.

2. The Civics give "direct service" to their communities or are generous benefactors.

3. The Continuously Growing value self-development and new learning.

4. The Wise are esteemed for their experienced dealings with past and present.

5. The Leisured travel and relish their noncommercial pleasures.

6. The Survivors have overcome personal adversities and adapt with grace.

I was interested that Margery Hutter Silver, Ed.D., co-author of *Living to 100* and Associate Director of the New England Centenarian Study, had found centenarians productive role models worth emulating. We met and talked in her Boston office. "I think of the centenarians as being explorers, exploring the boundaries of the life cycle. Life is an adventure," said Silver. "They are people who when faced with tragedy and hardship, pick themselves up and keep on going with optimism. This optimism implies a kind of risk taking. If you look at the world as generally positive, you do take more risks.

"We also found that many centenarians had a sense of humor. There's much research on humor and the good effects of laughter on health. Psychologically, humor is really cognitive therapy — taking something and 'reframing,' shifting the focus so it looks different. One person falls off the dock into the water and talks of avoiding pneumonia; someone else falls off the dock and tells a funny story. It's a way of looking at the world and giving hardship a different perspective."

When I met Dr. Robert Butler, author of the Pulitzer Prize text *Why Survive? Being Old in America,* he was the Executive Director of the International Longevity Center in New York. He emphasized the importance of older role models. "I've always had mentors," he said. "In fact, I had no father — he just disappeared when I was a couple of months old. So for me, I had to recruit my own fathers, and I successfully did all my life.

"They were all great. I've had have scientific fathers as well as two political fathers. All the men were marvelous people, like fathers to me. Wonderful teachers, mentors. And they kept right on working until the bitter end, all of them."

An athletic runner at 80, Dr. Butler had reaped the benefits of being a mentor himself. "On the other side, I've had wonderful mentees, without whom I would never have been any success whatsoever. You learn from others and others learn from you. I've been especially blessed, in both directions."

Dr. Richard Lindsay, Professor Emeritus of Internal Medicine at the University of Virginia and a former president of the American Geriatrics Society, named Dr. Butler as one of his mentors along with his own father. "My father was a country family doctor who taught me the most important part of relating to older patients is to respect and listen to them. He said that his patients' personal stories were better than reading any book and made practicing geriatric medicine exciting and enjoyable.

"I have been teaching medical students and students in related disciplines for 50 years, and I always stress to them the importance of choosing mentors. I tell them so much of who they will become professionally will be due to mentoring. Mentoring, beginning with one's parents and continuing with senior physicians, experienced nurses and older patients, results in the transfer of experiential wisdom that will make them better parents, citizens and physicians. It pays off in our later years."

I wanted answers from the masters — productive and creative, older men and women whom I admired. I was drawn to those with whom I had common interests — the arts, film, writing, journalism, photography, politics and religion, seekers of all persuasions.

I began my journey for mentors and role models close to home and gradually widened my "circle of wise elders" to others I'd respected from afar. Some were well known.

Our conversations took place where I spent the most time — at home in Charlottesville, Virginia, in New York City, my childhood home, and during winter visits to Key West, Florida.

Some role models were a decade or less ahead, and if not always physically fit, they were emotionally strong and resilient. Accepting their limitations and using their particular gifts, they demonstrated how to effectively make peace with loss, adversity and aging. They did so with candor and courage, perseverance and humor.

My first role models turned sorrow into healing. They had lost spouses, siblings, or other loved ones. They learned how to grieve and how to begin again. Some adjusted to loss by converting solitude into freedom and creative expression. "At the deepest level, the creative process and the healing process arise from a single source," wrote Rachel Naomi Remen, M.D., in *Kitchen Table Wisdom: Stories That Heal*.

Secondly, I found people once past their immediate mourning thriving on confident resolve and innovative purpose, building on experience and testing new talents. Others pledged their time to a mission or community concerns.

Finally, I found role models upheld by their beliefs and loving relationships, men and women enriched by their convictions, affections, and gratitude. Each knew heartache, fear and struggle and yet persevered with desire and undeniable valor, the virtue I would come to realize was so crucial to the very end.

Many mentors turned out to be children of immigrants propelled by their parents' drive and sense of exploration. They tapped previously undiscovered inner resources and took what might seem to be risks to accomplish their late-in-life goals. They were not fighting fear but acting on innate confidence and tenacity. Each demonstrated curiosity, readiness for discovery and life's ambiguities. They wrestled against their own trials to inspire benevolence and better the world.

If some felt fame hard to relinquish, all were ambitious, determined to challenge their losses and to stay engaged in their last decades. They didn't age passively. They learned how to do more with less. They were keenly aware of time's passage and their own infirmities yet reconciled to their ills and kept growing. Their resilience, rather than trapping them in loss, was grounded in acceptance and what was still left to them. They planned and made the most of their later lives, all the while sharing their stories, experiences and essential examples. They gave me companionship, showing what it takes to live long and well, one willing step at a time. They gave me a chance to walk in their shoes.

I offer their stories to readers who have also worried and wondered about old age and dying, and desire the counsel of wise elders. I urge you to look to your own older role models as well.

In the years I've worked on this book, most of these admirable people have inevitably died. While saddened, I felt their later lives not only demonstrated how to unflinchingly prepare for dying, but their passing increased their lasting legacies and lessons: persevere as bravely as you can to remain active, adapt to aging with creativity; reject regrets, salute your strengths and challenges and you will be rewarded with fulfilling later years. As theologian Bishop John Shelby Spong observed, "To me, the way you prepare for dying is that you learn how to *live*."

PHOTO BY ELIZABETH HOWARD

Hartwell Wyse Priest, Artist

It was good to escape to the work. A part of me was waiting to be developed until I got over the shock and the grief.

1

Easing Grief with Creativity

THERE WAS HARTWELL RIGHT NEXT DOOR. I remembered her call many winters ago when I'd rushed to meet her on the terrace. "Marianna died," she said simply. Her eyes blurred with tears and we hugged in the wind. Hartwell Priest's only daughter, Marianna, a gentle 48 year-old who'd taught third grade and adult religious education, had died of breast cancer. Four years earlier, Hartwell's husband, A.J. had died of pneumonia. He was 81, she was 77.

Together, Hartwell, an accomplished painter and printmaker, and Albert Jackson Gustin, a feisty University of Virginia law professor, had collaborated on their yearly Christmas cards; she produced a print and he a witty poem. When she finished a painting or etching, she gave it to A.J. to name. With A.J, she attended the Unitarian church, played piano duets, joined the peace movement and every day walked through our adjoining woods.

I hoped to meet Hartwell on the lane, binoculars in hand, watching for familiar birds, ferns and wildflowers. I dropped by her studio, drawn to her easy empathy as well as the smell of turpentine, linseed oil and paints mixed on a palette since childhood.

Once weighted with the loss of her husband and daughter, Hartwell returned each summer to her place of solace and renewal — a small island in Canada's Georgian Bay. She and A.J. had bought the island in 1929 for 300 dollars. Their remote refuge was still only accessible by boat, and communication was by ship-to-shore ("over and out") radio with the mainland. Here on the island, she kept painting its ancient rocks, pines and birches, nurtured by the creative cures of art and nature.

"Being in the woods calls forth something you don't feel anywhere else," she said. "There's a kind of freedom about it. Being on the island gives me strength for the coming winter. Each year when I return and see our island coming into view, a very great thrill comes over me.

"After Marianna and A.J. died, I worked more intensely than ever. Making prints is a natural escape into a creative activity that I needed. It is good to escape to the work. A part of me was waiting to be developed until I got over the shock and the grief."

In July 1990, I flew north to shoot a short documentary about Hartwell in her restorative setting. Her son Paul, an English professor living in London, his sons, and Marianna's daughter also would be visiting. Hartwell met me in a motorboat on the dock at Pointe-au-Baril beside the Hangdog Camp and General Store. She steered us back to the island, salt spray dousing our way.

Each morning, Hartwell was first up, heading over rocks into the woods with her easel and paints to catch the early light. Her poodle, Alouette, striding ahead. She drew tree stumps with sharpened pastels; she painted Precambrian boulders in the mist and late, shadowed sunsets. In her studio by the bay, Hartwell wiped the copper plate clean to begin a new etching. She pulled finished prints from the press, pleased with the serendipitous results.

Even as she'd waited for her shock and grief to subside, Hartwell started new work. "Being an artist," she said, "gives me something

I'm really interested in doing and thinking about. I'm always noticing colors and shapes and their relationships. You carry the thoughts wherever you are, at night or driving the car.

"You're always subject to possible inspirations wherever you happen to be — the island's trees and rocks or the mountains in Virginia. A picture might begin with the shape of a branch or an ancient rock. Line starts movement and direction and you build on it. Only you know what you want to do about it. It's an independent, risky thing. It's still very satisfying. It's what you want to do more than anything else."

Hartwell kept experimenting, motivated by her mother, also an artist who never stopped working. "My mother was just naturally an artist, a portrait and landscape painter. She started me with paints when I was about four. So I thought that's what you did in life — go out in the woods with your mother and paint," said the youngest of four children.

"We grew up (near Toronto and in Salem, Massachusetts) with art around us all the time. But it wasn't until her children were married and gone that my mother felt free to then develop her own work. My mother did some of her best work when she was 80. She never stopped painting. She went to Mexico alone the last year of her life at 94.

"My mother was always anxious to go ahead with what's exciting in life. 'Go through the open door,' she'd say. 'Enjoy being alive and doing what you really want to do.' I remember her saying, 'If you have inspiration every day, you're living for your joy in life.' She was never depressed. She always had more to do than she had time for.

"And my mother never paid any attention to age. She believed you're as old as you think you are. I think that's true. Youth is an attitude. You don't consider your interest is going to be any different. You just go on doing it as much as you can."

Her own interest in art unabated, Hartwell had studied painting at Smith College, and after graduation, apprenticed with modernist

Andre L'Hote at the Atelier in 1930s' Paris, and later took courses at the Art Students League in New York. In her fifties, Hartwell was a student of abstract expressionist Hans Hoffman, melding his "free, vigorous, semi-abstract realism" with her own naturalistic style.

Only reluctantly did Hartwell leave Hoffman's instruction and the vibrant New York art scene of 1953 to move to Charlottesville. A.J. had traded in his law practice to become a professor at the University of Virginia Law School.

Hartwell adopted her new surroundings by setting up a home studio and finding fresh subjects — Virginia's woods and Blue Ridge Mountains. Her etchings, lithographs, oil paintings and murals would become part of many permanent collections including the Virginia Museum, Carnegie Mellon University and the Library of Congress.

Hartwell proceeded into her late nineties still in pace with her mother's lead and her own timeline. "An old artist once gave me three suggestions: 'Feel intensely, vividly and control precisely.' That's what I try to do."

At age 98, she worked full-time towards a one-woman show at the McGuffey Art Center in Charlottesville as well as an exhibit at New York's Pen and Brush Society.

I remember an afternoon with late sun slanting on canvases of rocks and trees she'd carried from the island for finishing. Hartwell stepped to the canvas with a palette knife and a brush. She studied the peak of jagged rocks mirrored in water. Something was lacking. With intentional, even strokes, she dabbed her brush in Prussian blue to reflect the light. She added just what was missing, still surprised by possibilities.

Hartwell's sense of discovery, purpose and good humor, along with her encouragement and openness without judgment, attracted me and many younger artists. She set no demarcation between generations; we were all explorers together.

Hartwell's granddaughter, Susannah, a college student painter and musician, spoke of her grandmother's influence that summer on the island. "I've learned new art forms from my grandmother," she said. "My grandmother is always looking for new ways to do her paintings. That inspires me to do the same with my art, my life. It's a good way to be."

Paul, a poet, looked to his mother's inspiration as well. "She's interested in all the arts for the insight they can give into deeper truth." He added that Hartwell played the cello and loved poets Yeats and Wordsworth. "As a painter, the meaning of it for Mother is bringing out the spirit of things. Rocks and trees have a spiritual existence; this is what she is trying to express in her pictures. The inner life; the signature of God."

While her engineer father was a Christian Scientist and Hartwell a practicing Unitarian, she did not speak specifically of beliefs. Before leaving the island, she led me to a concealed grove where flat rocks fanned down to dark blue water. We sat side by side, the breeze sighing in the cedars and white pines. "Marianna and I used to sit here and watch the children swim." Her voice broke, a hairline fracture. "When Marianna died, we let these trees be a chapel for her ashes."

We watched the waves slowly spill in and out. Years later, I remembered this moment when reading Hartwell's letter to an artist after her sister's death:

> After my experience with Marianna, I have such a strong conviction that there is no death.... I think we will know the answers some time, and find our loved ones again. I am very sure that life goes on with enhancement of our interests and powers. I felt her presence and that she wanted us to know she is with us....
>
> I realize this may not really ease the sense of loss and separation when people have been as close as you were.

You will feel her presence with you and she will be glad
you know she isn't far away. She too will be missing you
and sending you her comfort and love.... And as life goes
on, one becomes even more and more grateful to have the
inspiration of our art. (It is somehow life itself.) You will
understand what I mean.

If art for Hartwell was "somehow life itself," she kept to its creativity, driven by curiosity and what might be; boredom, she believed,
was the price of too much leisure. "People think they're going to retire
and have a wonderful time doing nothing," said a printmaker whose
heavy work required her to still stand for hours.

"It's not happy to do nothing. If they don't have something creative to do, they're not content. A lot of people as they get older just
don't know what to do with themselves. They haven't a particular
interest and they're not very happy. They feel that life is over and
their children are gone. If you have something you want to do more
than anything else, that's a great, great help."

At the end of my documentary, Hartwell emerged from the
woods, Alouette still at her side. She'd left her easel on the rocks,
the true colors drying after a day's work. "Some work lifts you up.
And sometimes you think, 'Oh dear, this is a mess,' and you have to
throw things away," she said. "Everything isn't successful. But you
just come up to the top again and go on."

And on Hartwell went. When a black bear clawed open the island
cabin's porch door, she shooed him away by banging her frying pan.
When the yearly hatch of Canadian goslings were born on her home
pond, she pushed off her rowboat to feed them corn. When arthritis
slowed her daily walk to the mailbox, she rested in garden chairs
stationed along the path.

On her 100th birthday, four generations of Hartwell's family and
friends gathered to celebrate with "Newie," Hartwell's nickname for

having been born in Brantford, Ontario, on New Year's Day 1901. She wore a shamrock green pantsuit and shaded her eyes from bright sunlight not forecast when we hugged on her terrace that now-distant winter morning. "How does it feel to be 100?" I asked. She tilted her head with a familiar, teasing smile. "I don't feel any different. Why should I?"

A fellow artist asked Hartwell, "What words of wisdom do you have for us?"

"Isn't enthusiasm the energy of life?" Hartwell answered, perhaps recalling Henry David Thoreau's observation, "None are so old as those who have outlived enthusiasm."

Hartwell Wyse Priest died at home in Charlottesville, Virginia on August 14, 2004. She was 103.

PHOTO BY ELIZABETH HOWARD

Mary Lee Settle, Author

*To be alone by choice is one of the great
luxuries of the world.*

2

Converting Solitude to Creative Freedom

WHEN WIDOWED, VIRGINIA WRITER MARY LEE SETTLE reportedly said to her old friend cabaret singer Bobby Short, "I don't play widow. That's over now. Let's go on to the next stage." If Settle refused to dwell on her loss, she was quick to hold to her "enthusiasms" and redefine her unsought solitude in terms of work, creativity and freedom.

In 1978, the year Mary Lee was 60 and won the National Book Award for fiction, she married William ("Widdy") Tazewell, journalist and lecturer at the University of Virginia. For 20 years, they wrote, traveled and raised Dalmatians. Then Widdy, 14 years her junior, contracted lung cancer and Mary Lee became his wholehearted nurse. He died in April 1998.

After Widdy's death, Mary Lee, then 80, moved from Charlottesville to Vermont to be closer to her son Christopher. Mary Lee had married Christopher's father, Rodney Weathersbee in 1939; they divorced after seven years. In 1946, she married Douglas Newton and they divorced in 1956. Both men were British.

Virginia soon tugged Mary Lee back to the village of Kinsale on the Rappahannock River. I was glad to see this family friend who had given me my first interview as a young reporter. She remained the disciplined, outspoken, challenging writer willing to share her experience some 40 years later on a lazy Sunday in June.

Canadian geese honked high above as Mary Lee arrived on the path with Desmond, her golden retriever and sole companion. They led into the airy studio where Mary Lee had reduced her possessions to the essentials: double bed, desk, sofa, dining room table, and bookshelves crammed with Proust, Conrad, Faulkner and Shakespeare. Light glinted from a blown glass bowl. A Chinese gilded horse, his hoof lifted, was reflected in the picture window.

"I wanted to get rid of everything I owned," said Mary Lee, "I wanted to live in one room and be by the ocean or the bay. You don't have to bother with a lot of stuff. Look, it's all here. My books, my golden horse." I was curious that this often stormy lady had chosen such peaceful isolation — her setting against the back and forth of birdsong, and the wide Rappahannock, curving within walking distance, running to the Potomac, on to the Chesapeake Bay and out to sea.

Desmond sniffed and stretched as the sun spread on the knotty pine dining table. Mary Lee poured the chilled chardonnay and served steamed, garden asparagus and broiled chicken. She remembered Widdy's last months. "He had to have a blood transfusion every week, and we would go places mostly to get him out of Charlottesville. I would take these jobs with travel magazines to keep him from being bored, although Widdy never got really bored. It was depressing to know you were going to die, damn it."

She glanced at a photo of Widdy hugging one of their favorite Dalmatians. "He never showed depression very much. It wasn't an unhappy time. You're very close and you're very happy. The day might be the last one, so let's make it a goody. So when we were stuck out in Ivy, (near Charlottesville) we decided to paint the living room red."

Never one to mince words, Mary Lee knew her antidote. "It's work that has meant more than anything else. Widdy understood that. I still consider every day as a work day," said the author of over 20 books as well as numerous personal essays and travel articles. She had also taught fiction writing at Bard College and the University of Virginia, and had founded the annual PEN/Faulkner Award for fiction.

Mary Lee won the 1978 National Book Award for *Blood Tie*, an epic examining the invasion of American and British expatriates into an ancient Turkish coastal town, characters laden with Western ideas "who seek to steal from the city what they cannot find in themselves." She lived in Turkey from 1972 to 1974.

She was honored as the author of *The Beulah Quintet: The Price of Freedom*, five family sagas spanning the history of her native West Virginia from the 1750s to the present. The novels, written between 1956 and 1982, explore the evolution of the American principle of personal freedom; she used characters from the 17th century landing of former English prisoners in West Virginia's Kanawha Valley and fictionalized as Beulah Land.

Mary Lee passed me a slice of brie on a crisp baguette. It was ripe, rich as butter. "I'm still following my obsession that runs through every book — the price of freedom. I want to recognize and define how we came to have a democracy, a new form of government that's balanced between the constant pull of the right and the left. It's quite miraculous that democracy survives against its critics and cynics, people who use it as a power. I'm still obsessed with the balancing point of democracy."

On this windless, summer day, Mary Lee was writing *Spanish Reflections* — a complement to *Turkish Reflections* — a dramatic study of the clash between Christian and Muslim cultures. Her computer idled under a giant map of Spain. Far from exiled in this protected place, she approached widowhood as a challenge, invigorated by work and plans to soon travel abroad for further research.

Born on July 29, 1918 in Charleston, West Virginia, Mary Lee seemed delivered with restless, inquisitive, and sometimes combative genes that now stood her in strong stead. Her great-grandfather came to the Kanawha River in 1844 to build his home, "Cedar Grove." Her father, a civil engineer in charge of worker safety in the coal mines, moved his family often during the decline of coal mining before the Great Depression. They settled in Charleston when Mary Lee was 10 years old.

Perhaps Mary Lee's restive nature propelled her career path and eventual recognition as "a master of historical fiction." She left Sweet Briar College after two years, impatient to try her talents as a fashion model and actress in New York. She even auditioned for the role of Scarlett O'Hara in *Gone With The Wind*, her raven hair and rebellious beauty a match for black sheep Rhett Butler.

During World War II, Mary Lee joined the British Women's Auxiliary Air Force and later worked for the Office of War Information, the experience documented in her memoir *All the Brave Promises: Memories of Aircraft Woman Second Class 2146391*.

After the war, Mary Lee returned to New York and worked briefly as an editor at *Harper's Bazaar*. While finishing a fashion layout based on *Wuthering Heights*, she realized that Emily Brontë had died at age 30, and that instant, decided it was time to start writing her own books. She walked into her boss' office and resigned.

Nine years later in 1954, Mary Lee published her first book, *The Love Eaters*. And after a half century of myriad accomplishments, she, like Hartwell Priest, only wanted to keep working at her creative craft. At 83, she published *I, Roger Williams*, a novel based on the life of Rhode Island's founder. She'd outlined another memoir and made notes for *Tom: An Appreciation of Thomas Jefferson* based on the third President's boyhood.

"My writing day is like that of an athlete in training." Mary Lee cleared the table. "I get up at seven with the dog, have coffee, sit down at the computer, meditate for 10 minutes, then work until I'm exhausted which is usually about an hour. I can write as much as a thousand words. I'm a quarter horse. I nap. Work in the garden. I have a glass of wine at lunch and, around six o'clock, one drink with my neighbors, and that's it. It helps me rest in the afternoon." She believed her stamina was due to the Alexander Technique — movements to balance the body and release unwanted tensions — which she'd practiced for over 50 years. Her mother lived to 92.

"I think in terms of living. 'Living long and well' is hard work," she said. "I had uterine cancer in 1987. Then I knew my body could make a cancer, and it may be rough crossing the River Styx." Until then, Mary Lee had been a cigarillos chain smoker.

"In April 1997, I was at a Pen/Faulkner reading when I started to sweat. Later, sitting for a portrait, I began sweating again. Suddenly a mule kicked me in the chest. I was having a heart attack. I was basically very healthy, and it didn't do any permanent damage. The only change I've noticed is that I get tired more quickly. So colors became a bit brighter and days become a bit more important."

Desmond stirred in his sleep as Mary Lee stroked his head. "Work still means more than anything else to me. What do you do when you retire? 'Retire' means go to bed at night for me. My great hero — outside of Conrad — was Proust. Proust died writing his book. It's like Madame DuBarry's words on the guillotine: 'Un autre moment, Monsieur Executioner.'

"I don't think of age," she said. "There's not a spiritual, an intellectual, a physical self. There's a whole self. I converted to Catholicism in the late 80s, but my religion is asking questions. When they took Jesus to the temple, he was found asking questions. Any writer who keeps on writing is in the position of Jacob and the angel, wrestling for answers. I often write to know why.

"To me, it's a risk not listening to your soul. I've been very lucky that I've listened. You know that people with the best will in the world will try and keep you from risk. You cannot know the future; you cannot change the past. Your job is to take the next step and the next step is always into the dark. It's always a walk into the unknown."

However sequestered, Mary Lee, naturally given to risk, dared the dark. Now low tide on the Rappahannock, the blue herons swooped for prey in the marshes. I headed home, well fed and wrestling for answers.

Mary Lee didn't disappoint. In 2004 at her first reading of *Spanish Recognitions: The Roads to the Present*, she stood without a podium at Charlottesville's New Dominion Bookshop, backlit against tall windows, an abundance of gold chains accenting her periwinkle pantsuit. Her sometimes raspy voice remained vibrant, her animation at 86 swelled as she read, engaged and amused.

She'd taken her risks into the unknown and restated her bracing declaration of independence on page one: "To be alone by choice is one of the great luxuries of the world."

Traveling solo at her own speed, Mary Lee invited us along, she at the wheel of her stick shift Real on the back roads of Spain. I rode shotgun, steered by writers and change makers that Mary Lee revered: poet and playwright Garcia Lorca to Granada; novelist Miguel de Cervantes to Seville; sixteenth century reformer Saint Teresa to Avila; and Juana La Loca, Queen of Castile and Aragon, to Tordesillas, "the last place where Juana had smelled and tasted the terrors of freedom."

"There was no one to say 'Turn here; turn there. Are you tired? Time to stop,'" said Mary Lee, still rollicking forth, taking notes, asking questions, relishing her freedom and last rebellion. "I drove lickity split all over that damn country. I was told not to drive through the mountains. It was very dangerous. As a West Virginian, I said, 'goody, goody.'

"I thought I'd better do it before I lost my driver's license. I also walked seven or eight miles a day, taking it all in like a seismograph. As an 82-year-old grownup, I didn't want to be tied down to that deadening word, 'itinerary,' I was looking forward to discovery."

Mary Lee Settle died at home in Charlottesville, Virginia, on September 27, 2005. She was 87.

PHOTO BY MERCEDES TAYLOR

Eleanor Ross Taylor, Poet

Love is the most important thing, isn't it?

3

Savoring Life Alone

WHILE WIDOWHOOD GAVE MARY LEE SETTLE license to travel to distant lands, it provided poet Eleanor Ross Taylor a safe retreat, the renewed contentment of staying close to home, writing and reading, a time of review and reflection.

Eleanor was widowed in 1994 at the age of 74. Her husband, Peter Taylor — a distinguished novelist and short story writer — had taught literature and fiction writing at the University of Virginia and in 1987 he had won the Pulitzer Prize for his novel, *A Summons to Memphis*.

Although Eleanor was a poet of deserved standing, her husband's work was more widely read and acclaimed. She'd published her first poetry collection, *A Wilderness of Ladies*, in 1960 at age 40. Her fifth collection, *Late Leisure*, was awarded the Poetry Society of America's 1988 Shelley Memorial Prize, which honored one or two poets each year "with reference to genius and need."

It seemed especially cruel that Peter — unsparing, garrulous, and amusing — suffered a stroke at 75 that compromised his southern cadence but not his charm. He died two years later. In 2001, Eleanor's daughter Katie died of ovarian cancer. Katie lived in North Carolina and Eleanor had not seen her daughter for some years, a separation she blamed on giving Peter priority, and a loss she couldn't reconcile. She remained close to her son Ross, his wife Elizabeth, and their daughter, Mercedes, who lived in Falls Church, Virginia.

I looked forward to time with Eleanor whom I knew to be intensely private. I'd first met the Taylors in 1970 when they enrolled Ross in The Tandem School, the co-educational high school John and a friend had recently co-founded in Charlottesville.

Five years later, we took the Taylors' advice and drove to Key West for a winter break, our introduction to the renegade island where we would often return. Together, we explored the flats, traded books and ate cheap and tangy Cuban dinners at El Siboney and The Fourth of July. We talked easily around the table with Peter's stories getting an animated run before being put to paper. Eleanor, abstemious and restrained to his ebullience and conviviality, never missed the bull's eye, aiming her own nimble salvos into every conversation.

Now many years later, I found quiet comfort sitting beside Eleanor on the slip-covered sofa under the window picturing her tangled garden. A portrait of young Peter in white linen suit — reminiscent of F. Scott Fitzgerald — was mounted above the fireplace and felt an abiding presence. Dark bookshelves, musty with valuable collections, reached to the ceiling.

Eleanor offered me tea or water but didn't drink anything herself. Dainty glass bowls overflowed with peppermints and chocolate kisses. Card tables were neatly arranged with writing projects, and Eleanor's family photos, those of children reading as evidence of its early appeal. One of young Mercedes pictured her reading under the Christmas tree; she was now a student at Amherst College.

Although decades apart, our ages seemed to come closer as we talked freely of marriage, children and writing still to be done. At 87, Eleanor mentored even as she sought consolation; she confided and retreated, struggling through unfinished dialogues with her husband and daughter. She replayed conversations she wished she'd had with Katie, blaming herself for distance never bridged.

I had hoped that *Late Leisure* — published five years after Peter's death — would include poems of reconciliation or healing insights into Eleanor's marriage and Katie's death. I found none. Instead, Eleanor reread old journals, searching for new understanding of matrimony and her own literary years.

She studied notes from long ago summers with writers Caroline Gordon and her husband, poet Allen Tate, as well as years when Katie was a baby, and she and Peter lived in a duplex near critic and poet Randall Jarrell and his wife, Mackie. Eleanor and Peter's literary circle also included writers Robert Lowell, Robert Penn Warren and John Crowe Ransom.

Eleanor had encouraging mentors in Tate and Gordon when she was their student at the Woman's College, now the University of North Carolina at Greensboro. "They were wonderful to students, and Caroline particularly always said, 'You owe it to young writers to help them.' And she did," Eleanor said in a 2002 *Blackbird* interview.

Allen Tate also taught at Vanderbilt where Eleanor had attended graduate school, and he introduced her to his friend Peter Taylor at his home in Monteagle, Tennessee. Eleanor and Peter married in 1943.

Later, living in Greensboro, Eleanor asked Peter to introduce her to Jarrell, a poet on the Greensboro faculty whom she looked up to. Jarrell read her work, identified her talent, and urged Eleanor to write and publish her first poems, however torn she evidently felt between writing and raising two young children. She recalled her mentor's prophetic words in a 1977 *Southern Review* interview: "Randall used to come and say, 'Do you have any poems?' and when I didn't, he'd say, 'You'll be sorry. God will make you sorry.'"

When *A Wilderness of Ladies* was published in 1960, Allen Tate's introduction noted Eleanor's poems of "violent emotion" stemming from a restrained life. Jarrell, Tate and other teachers' confidence in her work inevitably persuaded Eleanor to keep producing poems. "I think that the continuing influence of people who believe in you can help," she said in the *Southern Review*. She benefited from the tutelage of poet Frank Bidart while living in Cambridge, Massachusetts, when Peter taught at Harvard. "Frank taught me how to choreograph a poem. He would talk for a long time about where he'd prefer to put a comma."

However willingly or reluctantly, Eleanor contained her writing career in favor of Peter's and being wife and mother, her poems only grew. They showed the influence of other poets characterized for their restrained and controlled emotional powers — Emily Dickinson, Elizabeth Bishop and Marianne Moore. "I also read Edna St. Vincent Millay as a teenager and fell in love with her poetry," said Eleanor, perhaps exposing her own controlled passions.

Eleanor was nine when her first poem was published in *The Norwood News* and earned her a dollar prize. The youngest of four, she was born on June 30, 1920, in Norwood, North Carolina. Eleanor and her sister, Jean Justice, widow of poet Donald Justice, were the family survivors. Her brothers James and Fred were writers, too, and in Norwood, the siblings were affectionately dubbed "the writing Rosses."

The daughter of a righteous Methodist, and a Sunday school teacher, Eleanor, in her late eighties, still deferred to their authority. "I look at photographs of my grandparents, and sometimes feel I'm going forth for them. My parents were simple dirt farmers. They went to church and my father read to us from the Bible every night before we went to bed. We were on our knees at the table, or beside the fire. My two older brothers had to be called from upstairs, and one sometimes refused to come down. Prayers were part of our daily routine and I found it comforting."

Did Eleanor, a source of comfort herself, still find consolation in prayer? Was prayer magical thinking or a source of peace and genuine healing? "I keep a hymnal by my bed, and in the night read the hymns and marvel at the depths of the beliefs that fostered them.

The people who wrote those wonderful hymns were believers and there must be something if they could find that inspiration."

Eleanor was also reading William James' 1902 canon, *The Varieties of Religious Experience*. "I can almost believe now," she said, "but the older I get, I don't understand faith. At 87 it's hard to think humans live and then it's all over. So much is unexplained. Wonders. ESP. Things like that. And the Bible is about love — a loving God. Don't you think? Love is the most important thing, isn't it? Don't you think sadness and depression in life comes from being unloved?"

I do. And so I watched Eleanor probe the past for intimations of loss and love in all its array. She recognized youthful yearnings, perhaps a refrain from articulating what she'd always felt but rarely spoke. One afternoon, she invited me and a dozen other women to tea. Among us was a woman in her twenties trying to launch her writing career. Eleanor, demure in a gray cashmere sweater, commented mostly to herself: "We start our careers, then sex becomes the most powerful thing in your life and you get married. It confuses everything." She passed the chocolate cookies to stunned silence.

Another afternoon, I brought my father's doctor to meet Eleanor after discovering that he'd also been one of Peter's physicians and was a promising poet. He and Eleanor talked of poets that they both admired, and soon Eleanor, infatuated, became his mentor too.

Ever pithy and missing no nuance, Eleanor still restricted whom she would see, preferring to consider the world without apology within her own confines, the later years a time to enjoy contemplation as much as action. "Solitude without loneliness," as wrote her friend poet Adrienne Rich.

Eleanor had uncovered bits of "doggerel" that made her want to write more. "It's been a long time since I've written a poem. But when one hits me, I write a line down. In poetry, I think something comes out of you, your inner self, that can't be expressed in other ways. Don't you think? Something you're reaching for and give exposure to…. Art is like religion in that way, reaching out — an empathy you're not aware of…."

If "art is like religion," Eleanor implied that poetry and faith could provide us empathy" and reconnection when needed most. "This morning I reread Gray's 'Elegy in a Country Churchyard.' I can understand it now," she said. "I've seen everybody die. I can identify too with the country people. They remind me of people I grew up with. Gray was only 55 when he died. At my age, you don't know if you have a year, nine years, or with people living so long, maybe more." Now at home with the shutters fastened, Eleanor worked on her memories and politely resisted entreaties for hired help, a live-in companion or move to a "retirement community."

Then Eleanor surprised me. She called in late January 2008 just before we left for Key West, saying she had the flu but wanted to say goodbye because she might soon move to an apartment in Falls Church near Ross. I didn't believe she would ever leave the home where she felt safe and free from observation.

Small and half hidden in her Christmas-red bathrobe, Eleanor waved from behind the front door. She formally accepted a hug and then watched as I drove away. When I returned from Key West, I counted on seeing Eleanor open the door, but found her house dark. She had made her move.

Eleanor celebrated her ninetieth birthday in 2010. That year she was a finalist for the 2009 National Book Critics Award, and winner of the William Carlos Williams award for *Captive Voices: New and Selected Poems, 1960–2008.* In 2010, Eleanor won the prestigious Ruth Lilly Poetry Prize for lifetime achievement. The prize for her collection came with $100,000 and much more accolades than she'd ever known before.

In presenting the award, *Poetry* editor Christian Wiman commended Eleanor's work for its "sober and clear-eyed serenity." He said, "We live in a time when poetic styles seem to become more antic and frantic by the day, and Taylor's voice has been muted from the start. *Muted*, not quiet. You can't read these poems without feeling the pent-up energy in them, the focused, even frustrated compression, and then the occasional clear lyric fury. And yet you can't read them without feeling, as well, a bracing sense of spiritual largesse and some great inner liberty."

If such wanted recognition came late to Eleanor Ross Taylor, she — muted without being maudlin, a realist not without a streak of romance — still put forth her testimony to seclusion, life in the present, self-sufficient and rust-free.

Always Reclusive

I'm constructing my own brierpatch. True,
I'm still bleeding from the first canes I dug in;
thorns fight off cultivation, cut both ways;
they like barbwiring things in
as much as battling guests; that's useful;
I won't try getting out too soon, say for a
tipsy fruit, or reckless stroll. What I don't spend
on tickets I'll apply to long-distance calls.

Hunters will come and shake my fence, dogs panting,
paws pointing. I'll like that. I'll cuddle up
and turn the page.

"The blackberry, permitted its own way,
is an unmanageable plant." Here's a
variety called *Taylor*: "Season late,
bush vigorous, hardy ... free from rust.'
That's it. Don't let my brierpatch rust."

("Always Reclusive" was first published in *The Paris Review*, issue 142, spring 1997, and is included in *Captive Voices*.)

Eleanor Ross Taylor died on December 30, 2011, in Falls Church, Virginia. She was 91.

PHOTO BY STEPHANIE GROSS

Stanley Kunitz, Poet

I have found this gift of poetry to be life-sustaining, life-enhancing, and absolutely unpredictable...poetry is for the sake of life.

4

Ensuring Solace

IF ELEANOR TAYLOR FOUND POSSIBLE EMPATHY in poetry, poet Stanley Kunitz in *Passing Through: The Later Poems New and Selected*, proposed that poetry, in fact, can provide enduring potency: "The poem comes in the form of a blessing — 'like rapture breaking on the mind' as I tried to phrase it in my youth. Through the years, I have found this gift of poetry to be life sustaining, life enhancing, and absolutely unpredictable. Does one live, therefore, for the sake of poetry? No, the reverse is true: poetry is for the sake of life."

Did Kunitz, at age 96, our country's oldest elected Poet Laureate, still feel poetry to be life sustaining, life enhancing?

Hoping for his response, I arrived early on a spring evening in 2001 to hear Kunitz read his poetry at the University of Virginia.

He stepped on stage, slightly stooped, wearing a brown shirt, tweed jacket and yellow tie. Poet Gregory Orr introduced his friend, Stanley, the son of Lithuanian Jewish immigrants. Harvard graduate. Reporter. Editor. Translator. Columbia University professor. Author of a dozen volumes of poetry. Winner of the National Book Award. Leader of the Poets Against the (Vietnam) War. Recipient of the 1993 National

Medal of the Arts presented by President Clinton at the White House. And twice Poet Laureate, his last appointment in 2000 at age 95.

"Thirty years ago, I came to New York and he was my teacher," said Orr. "He was a door opening on a whole world of understanding what it is to be a human being whose journey, whose spiritual and emotional path through life takes them through language and imagination. Stanley was that guide, that mentor."

"Kunitz is aware of his mandate as a role model for older artists," wrote Mark Matousek in a 2001 *Modern Maturity* profile. "He took the poet laureate job, in part, 'to make clear that age itself should not be treated as an incapacity for serving great ends' and that 'the accumulation of experience can be a value factor — and not necessarily a debt — that society must pay for.'"

"I think it takes tremendous courage to live well, and that holds true at any age in life," Kunitz said at 83. "The courage comes out of knowing that if you don't persist, you fail. The courage to be is the courage to dare." He advised younger poets in *The Collected Poems*: "Persevere — be explorers all your life." Over a decade later, Kunitz, like Mary Lee, was still accepting the dare.

At 90, Kunitz confirmed his lasting fire in "*The Round*."

I can scarcely wait till tomorrow
when a new life begins for me,
as it does each day,
as it does each day.

Kunitz folded his hands on the lectern and stared into the dark. The house hushed. He opened *The Collected Poems*, seeming to grow taller. His voice, grating and dry, lightened and rose as he remembered *Halley's Comet* and the night the world didn't end.

Look for me, Father, on the roof
of the red brick building

at the foot of Green Street —
that's where we live, you know, on the top floor.
I'm the boy in the white flannel gown
sprawled on this coarse gravel bed
searching the starry sky,
waiting for the world to end.

"Look for me, Father," implored the son to his father still a wish away, a dress manufacturer who committed suicide by drinking carbolic acid six weeks before Stanley Jasspon Kunitz was born on July 29, 1905, in Worchester, Massachusetts. Stanley, the youngest of three, was raised by his two older sisters and a mother who ran a dry goods store to support them.

"My belief that poetry is ultimately rooted in mythology began when I realized that my work is inseparable from the quest for my father, and that led to my other quest, my quest for community," Kunitz told author Nicholas Basbanes in 1995. Kunitz's commitment to community — and especially the promotion of younger artists — deepened as teacher and editor of *The Yale Series of Younger Poets*, and as founder of The Fine Arts Work Center in Provincetown, Massachusetts, and Poets House in New York City.

While Kunitz found healing in community, his perpetual quest for his father was seeded in his early recognition of life and death intertwined. "Years ago I came to the realization that the most poignant of all lyric tensions stems from the awareness that we are living and dying at once," he wrote in *The Collected Poems*.

Perhaps no place unearthed Kunitz's lyric tension more for him than his Provincetown garden, ground reclaimed from a sandy hillside. "I think of gardening in mythic terms," he wrote. "It's a very good solution for my problems. To me, it is the process of death and resurrection. That's a wonderful, exhilarating thought."

In the 2002 documentary *The Secret Life of the Brain*, Kunitz stepped carefully along flowered paths, his abundant, terraced slopes rich with roses, anemones, daylilies, hydrangea and lavender. He was also filmed cooking for his third wife of more than 40 years, poet and painter Elise Asher. He wrote poems longhand and walked the evening shallows at low tide.

On stage, Kunitz next read "Touch Me," a sensuous tribute to Elise before an approaching storm. Published when Kunitz was 90, the poem begins:

> Summer is late, my heart.
> Words plucked out of the air
> some forty years ago
> when I was wild with love

There in the darkness, Kunitz kindled his passion, and ours anew, asking: "What makes the engine go?" He answered:

> Desire, desire, desire.
> The longing for the dance
> stirs in the buried life.
> Darling, do you remember
> the man you married? Touch me,
> remind me who I am.

Kunitz ended his reading with "The Layers," promising his listeners continued transformation.

> How shall the heart be reconciled
> to its feast of losses?
> "Live in the layers,
> not on the litter."
> Though I lack the art
> to decipher it,

no doubt the next chapter
in my book of transformations
is already written.
I am not done with my changes.

The stage lights stayed low. Kunitz hesitated at the podium. He folded his glasses into his breast pocket, tucked his poems under his arm and waved a closing salute.

I wanted to linger, listening in the dark. I wanted more time with this impassioned soul still stirring and soothing the spirit.

Poet Richard Wilbur said of his mentor and teacher: "An extraordinary thing about Stanley is that since his earliest years, he's been an insomniac and he sleeps on the average of four hours a night. And here he is in his nineties and all this time he's been living each day longer than the rest of us!"

In May 2004, Kunitz kindly agreed to my visit to his apartment on West 12th Street in Greenwich Village. His wife, Elise Asher, had died in March of complications from pneumonia. She was 92, and he 99, and by then, the couple had been married 46 years.

I hoped Kunitz was holding to his promise, "I am not done with my changes."

I found Stanley, cushioned and sunk into a gold velvet armchair within reach of his walker and books — *Remembering Trees of the World, Geons, Black Holes and Quantum Foam: A Life in Physics.* Here, too, were volumes by poets Rainer Maria Rilke, Wallace Stevens and Marianne Moore.

His bibles of sorts recalled a 1997 *American Poet* interview: "I do not subscribe to any organized religion, yet I think of myself as a religious person, and that's independent of any kind of faith or practice, or belief in God. While I was still in college, I fastened onto the phrase 'the holiness of the heart's affections' in one of Keats's letters, and it has stayed with me ever since. To me, that's religion. 'I am certain of nothing,' he quoted Keats, 'but the holiness of the heart's affections and the truth of imagination.' Though I am in no danger of conversion, the poets you mention as early influences — Herbert, Donne, Blake, Hopkins — still speak to me and light the way."

Kunitz's white hair had now grown long; several days' stubble fuzzed his cheeks. He raised his eyes, receiving me and my condolences and yellow roses with a cozy curiosity. "Sad," he said, his gaze gone to a painting of a lissome nude floating at sea in a crimson sunset. Asher's painting was prompted by Stanley's poem, "The Long Boat," which ends, "He loved the earth so much/he wanted to stay forever."

Asher's abstracts framed the doorway; others hung beside paintings by friends Philip Guston, Franz Kline and Robert Motherwell. Her collection of music boxes, miniature mandolins and glass paperweights lined the piano and tabletops. I imagined Elise tuning her music boxes, the lamps low, while she and Stanley talked late into the city night.

I remembered my father's hesitation to move any object after my mother's death. I mentioned to Kunitz that my young parents had lived in a walk-up down the street where my mother had traded ballroom dancing lessons for take-out from the Japanese restaurant owner downstairs. Meanwhile, my father — new to city attractions — attended Broadway burlesque shows between auditions for acting roles.

Kunitz smiled, recalling his own first New York apartment on 9th Street. "I discovered, after a few noisy nights, that my door opened to a speakeasy. I went in and had drinks on the house. We all became great friends." Apparently Stanley had a reputation for shaking a great martini himself.

Genine Lentine, a young friend, poet, reader and literary assistant, carried in my roses in a china vase. She and Stanley had met when she came to clean his Cape Cod house and she'd stayed to help in his garden. Genine recollected an "idyllic afternoon" in which she and Stanley had inspected his plants for the newest blooms, slowly watered and pruned back the lavender hedge. In Stanley, said Genine, she'd found a mentor capable of "deep attention. A listening canyon."

Genine and a caretaker planned to accompany Kunitz to Provincetown that summer so he could tend his garden again.

In 2005, Genine and Stanley would write *The Wild Braid, A Poet Reflects on a Century in the Garden*. "A garden," he wrote, "is capable of bringing the world back to another kind of reality."

If Kunitz's constant passion for gardening brought him "a kind of reality," then did poetry, once promised "to be life sustaining, life enhancing, and absolutely unpredictable" now bring solace?

"Nothing helps," Kunitz said. Then he slowly reconsidered, still engaged. "Poetry is as good a medication as many for keeping one's senses alive. And not only the senses but the mind, the affections. It's very important to feel one's self as part of the world you live in, and to care about others as well as your own being. Poetry becomes so much a part of your life. I'm afraid to separate it from life itself."

Life itself now seemed distilled to a tender essence in Stanley Kunitz. He sat still as if anticipating an arrival. He kept steady watch, waiting and perhaps connecting past and present, replaying a recurring harmony, composing a new poem, listening like a canyon.

Stanley Kunitz died at home in New York City on May 14, 2006. He was 100.

PHOTO BY ARLINE KATZ

Alma Halbert Bond, Psychoanalyst/Author

*Everything one does in life is a risk, even
getting married and having children.
Follow your impulses, and ignore the 'shoulds'....*

5

Risking Another Desired Pursuit

AFTER MY FATHER'S FUNERAL, John and I took time out in Key West. At a friend's request, I'd lent my father's house to Alma Bond, a Key West resident attending the Virginia Festival of the Book. Although we hadn't met, I liked thinking of someone in my father's house, the lights back on, the tea kettle boiling, his books being read once more.

When Alma returned to Key West, she arrived at "Duffy's" on Simonton Street wearing a purple running suit and red sneakers, jogging in place. "I couldn't believe it," she said, first thing. "Your father had so many books by Virginia Woolf. She's my favorite author. I wish I'd known your dad."

I wished so, too. I felt an immediate affinity with Alma, maybe because she'd just come from my father's house and appreciated his presence as others no longer would. Or because Alma, like Stanley Kunitz, was so open and attentive on first acquaintance. Her direct dark eyes and empathetic nature certainly enhanced 37 years as a successful New York psychotherapist.

Alma chose an end booth facing away from the crowd. We both ordered BLTs and started swapping stories faster than tag sale steals. We talked until the lunch crowd had gone and the waiter had refilled our water glasses more often than most. We split the check and made a date to meet soon again.

Many a tropical afternoon, we talked together in Alma's air-conditioned and immaculate townhouse filled with her books and infectious energy. I learned of her losses, as well as her willingness to take chances, change direction and reinvent herself.

As a teenager, Alma dreamed of an acting career. "At 16, I wanted to be an actress like Bette Davis and Barbara Stanwyck. Bette Davis lit up the screen. I fantasized that Barbara Stanwyck was my mother," she said. "One day I came downstairs and asked my father, 'Can I go to college to learn acting?'

"'I will sell my shirt to send you,'" said her Polish immigrant father who had established a profitable chain of dry cleaning stores in Philadelphia. Alma's mother, a dressmaker, had emigrated from Rumania.

Alma began studying at Temple University, and tried out for a part at the Neighborhood Theater in Philadelphia. She was paired with fellow actor Rudy Bond. "I was emoting about love with Rudy's head in my lap. He looked up and winked. That started it." Alma could still blush.

It was 1946; Rudy was 34, Alma only 23. Their fine romance carried on when Rudy enrolled in Elia Kazan's Actors Studio in New York, and she at American Theater Wing and won a walk-on, Broadway part. "I was the good screamer." She laughed. Rudy soon appeared on Broadway to top reviews in the original cast of *A Streetcar Named Desire*. An oversized *Streetcar* poster of Rudy, forever burly, mustached and full of vigor, hung on the landing.

Rudy went on to play memorable character roles on Broadway as well as in Hollywood films, *On The Waterfront* and *The Godfather* among them.

"Rudy was one of those larger-than-life people. He took up more space than anybody else in the room," she said. Alma and Rudy were married in 1948. Their friends included actors Karl Malden, Marlon Brando, Anthony Quinn and Kim Hunter.

Instead of furthering her own acting career, however, Alma decided to earn a Ph.D in Development Psychology at Columbia University, and later completed post-doctoral study in psychoanalysis at the Freudian Society. "I was drawn to people's complexities and the chance to help in their pursuits. In analysis, people find themselves and grow when they have an interested, objective listener with no ax to grind. I thought of it as *life*, not listening to troubles. Generally it was the creative people who came. You helped them live happier lives. I wasn't bogged down by it all. It made me very happy."

And Alma's happiness was more so for marrying Rudy, a man who understood and nurtured her ambitions. "A friend once said, 'Alma isn't the first liberated woman. Rudy is the first liberated man.' When we had the twins, Janet and Jonathan, we would be up all night, each rocking a baby. Rudy helped me with them and later when Zane was born. He took the kids to the park when I was working. I couldn't have managed without his help." Alma conveniently saw patients in an office downstairs in their apartment building on the Upper West Side.

"I'm a rather moody person but there was no day of eight or 10 hours with patients when something didn't happen that made me happy. I guess I thought I was helping. It was really an honor to be allowed to do that work, to be taken intimately into people's lives.

"I told Rudy he should have married someone like my sister, a more normal housewife. He said, "I'd be bored.' So I was lucky Rudy and my family always encouraged me to do or be what I wanted to be. Some people's children are not at all accepting of their mother's work, but my kids loved it and my husband too.

"Rudy also said he wouldn't be an actor if it weren't for my help.

I helped him because I supported the family in a much better style than an actor would have been able to. He always appreciated it.

"We both lived from the heart on an intellectual level and we let each other be. I always said it was a devout, mental marriage. It was different from other marriages."

Then after 34 years, Alma's give-and-take marriage suddenly ended. "In 1982," she said, her memory safely distanced, "Rudy was in Colorado to open the lead in *Babe* [Ruth]. He had a heart attack. They called me that night, but Rudy died soon after.

"Rudy was 70, a lot older than I. He had his first heart attack at 47. He ate whatever he wanted and gained weight. He didn't exercise. He didn't take care, which is maybe one reason I do." Alma restricted herself to a low-fat diet with daily doses of vitamins and exercise.

"It made sense, but it's always a shock. I think he could have lived if he'd taken better care of himself. I don't know if he'd still be here but ...."

Alma was 59 when Rudy died. Although she retained her busy practice, Alma deeply missed Rudy, his dynamic and affectionate rapport and reliable cheerleading.

"Four years after Rudy died, I was coming home from jogging in Central Park and a nutty taxi driver came around the bend and hit me. I went 20 feet in the air, came down and hit a pole. I was in a coma and had seven broken bones. They didn't think I was going to live.

"When I came out of the coma, I thought, 'I'm very lucky to be here. I've really had a good life, done everything; had a good career as a psychotherapist; a nice family and husband. Traveled all over the world. But one thing I have not done — and I've wanted to do all my life — I have not written.' I'd had professional articles published, but I hadn't written the way I wanted to write. Full-time."

So in her early sixties when many people consider retirement or full-time grand-parenting, Alma bet on a big dream. "Over two years I gave up a very prestigious, well-paying practice in Manhattan to take a chance on being a writer and not making a nickel. I came to Key West to a literary seminar and knew I wanted to stay," said Alma, pleased by her bold decision. "I love to write. It's exactly right for me. I want to write as long as I live."

In an office minimized to professional degrees, computer, two printers, a scanner, copier, and fax machine, Alma kept to a strict schedule sometimes writing eight hours a day. "I could paper a room with the rejections. But becoming a writer is still the best decision I ever made. In fact, I should have done it earlier, but then I would have missed out on another very rich part of my life which *helps* me write."

Instead of ending a career, Alma ventured a new one. Over 20 years she would publish 22 books. She delved into her experience as an analyst to explore psychological perspectives and characters' inner lives as only a trained and perceptive professional could do. Her titles ranged from *Who Killed Virginia Woolf?*, a psychobiography, to *Is There Life After Analysis?* In *The Autobiography of Maria Callas: A Novel,"* Callas spoke with insight into her past. "I don't believe I could have done it if I weren't an analyst," said Alma.

In her novel, *Camille Claudel*, she analyzed Claude Rodin's model, "the great sculptor who worked with Rodin but stole all her thunder," and how, at the end of her life, she came to terms with memories both bitter and sweet. Claudel, in turn, prompted Alma to sculpt her own appealing miniature figures, artfully arranged on an oval glass table.

Banking on her professional past, Bond began an engrossing analytic series: *Marilyn Monroe: On the Couch; Jackie O: On the Couch: Lady Macbeth: On the Couch. Hillary Clinton: On the Couch* and finally, *Michelle Obama: A Biography*, a fresh look at the background that shaped the First Lady.

In 1992 Alma collaborated with Lucy Freeman to write *America's First Woman Warrior: The Courage of Deborah Sampson* — the story of a woman impersonating a man to serve in the Continental Army during the Revolutionary War. Freeman, a former *New York Times* reporter who extensively covered mental health issues, was Alma's senior by six years, and a significant mentor until her death at 88.

In *Death is a Terminal Disease*, Alma considered the loss of another close friend. "Growing old is a new role for me and there's much about it I don't understand. I don't mind getting older," she said, her voice less certain. "I only mind the idea that apparently I don't have much time left. I'm angry about it. I'm going to do everything I can to stay well, healthy and happy as long as I can. My son says I'm going to live to 107. Knock on wood."

When Alma was hit by a New York taxi and ended up in a coma, she allowed that she'd also had a consoling "near death experience." "I felt drawn to a light at the end of the tunnel, and I discovered that dying isn't so bad." In facing death, she felt it easier to accept the inevitable and gain from "better health, less daily conflict and the likelihood of a fuller, richer life."

Alma Halbert Bond was born in 1923, the second of three children, and now the only one still alive. While prodigious in her writing, how had Alma overcome the loneliness of a writing career after so many years in contact with patients and a loving husband and family?

"When you write, you're never alone. I *lived* with Maria Callas for years writing her story. But," she added, "I had an easier time than most widows because I'm an independent, optimistic person, and I was used to living alone a great deal because Rudy was on the road. When I gave birth to my first child, he was on the road. There was a strike and he traveled on a milk train all night, and I was 24 hours in labor. He came in just as the baby was born.

"I also had my own money, my own bank account. I couldn't be dependent on Rudy; he wasn't there. I practically raised myself," said Alma. "I was always a loner and liked my solitude a lot. I adjusted rather easily. It's very interesting, however; the man is supposed to be dead, but he is still with me. Psychologically. I'm always remembering things Rudy said. He seems so much alive. I think that always helps. The kids and I talk about him all the time."

Sure of Rudy's reliable company, Alma also kept in close contact with her three children. "I don't know how people manage without children when they get old. I feel my daughter is my best friend. I love to go to the opera with her. And I love the grandchildren dearly. But I don't think family is enough to live for. For me, it wouldn't be."

At 85, Alma kept striving. "I still want to make the bestseller list. I think maybe that drives me to stay alive, to work at it. I don't want to do anything that doesn't add up. I want to find out if there'a anything I've been avoiding writing about, and do it.

"Everything one does in life is a risk, even getting married and having children. Follow your impulses, and ignore the 'shoulds' as much as is feasible. Doing what you want to do is play. Living alone, you're more likely to follow your impulses. You can't do that if you have to worry about somebody else.

"I try to jump in when I feel it's right and ignore the anxiety. Each impulse you follow gives you a little surge of wellbeing which contributes to mental as well as physical health," said a lady who retained her natural girlish gaiety.

On another summer day in winter, I watched Alma dive into the deep end of her community pool. She came up for air ready for the next lap. "If there's one secret to survival, good health and longevity," she said, "it's follow your bliss. Go where your heart takes you."

And so Alma pursued her bliss, writing one intriguing book after another. We last met in 2008, this time at New York's Key West Diner on 96th and Broadway. Alma was then living in a West side retirement residence. This year's running suit was pale pink. Her dark eyes still shone, now with incredulity. Nine months earlier, her younger son, Zane, had died after years of battling bipolar disease. A coin dealer and numismatics hobbyist, Zane wrote candidly of his "life and death struggle for survival" in *A Prophet Operating at a Loss.*

Alma ordered an omelette and a cup of coffee. "Zane lived in another world but knew himself in depth more than most. He was highly creative and channeled things from the unconscious. His book made a real contribution."

Her coffee cooled. "We had long talks, and we were friends when he died. I asked him if he thought I'd been crazy to give up my 37-year career to start writing. He said, '37 years are enough.'"

I ordered a rich slice of cheesecake with two forks, and again Alma and I let the afternoon take its time leaving. In the glare of the deco diner, Alma slowly anticipated her next book — a biography of child analyst Margaret Mahler with whom she'd once worked. "You have to rest from your grief to another world," she said. "You get to the late stages in life, you do what was left undone and want to do it. Life hangs by a thread.

"I've now written for over 20 years. I'm lucky. If I had to do it over again I'd do the same thing." Alma took the last sip of coffee and carefully set her cup back on its saucer.

PHOTO COURTESY OF STEVE FRIEDMAN

Walter Cronkite, Broadcast Journalist

*I'm curious about everything. I don't read a piece in
the paper that doesn't make me want to know more.*

6

Informing and Staying Informed

LIVING HIS LIFE OVER, Walter Cronkite would certainly choose to report again from the frontlines of history.

I can still hear the catch in his voice: "President Kennedy died at one p.m. Central Standard Time, two o'clock Eastern Standard Time." He checked the studio clock. "Some 38 minutes ago." He removed his dark-framed glasses and broke the news, swallowing hard, sharing his disbelief and grief. Then he cleared his throat, and although shaken, calmly continued.

In silence, we watched Cronkite, in tie and shirt sleeves, report the marathon events the rest of that November day. It was 1963, just after lunch at Episcopal High School, the boys' boarding school in Alexandria, Virginia where John taught English and art and we lived on campus. We'd only been married six months. I was 24, and John 28, but we suddenly felt much older.

The night of the assassination, we drove into Washington to a friend's previously planned party. The streets were empty, storefronts shuttered; in every window, posters of our fallen President. At the small supper, no one mentioned Kennedy; it was too unspeakable.

Three days later, John chose a long walk in the woods, while I waited with hushed crowds watching the flag-covered casket drawn by white horses and flanked by soldiers, sailors and Marines marching to Arlington National Cemetery. It was cold and cloudless as brass bands played and drums rolled. Jets soared overhead. Finally, taps tolled and a choir sang the Navy hymn, "Eternal Father, strong to save...."

Through those solemn days Cronkite's confident, penetrating voice became our reliable source of reason. We trusted his predictable presence and above suspicion reports. As a young journalist, I looked up to Cronkite, the newsman who had set the bar high and would forever define the face of the no-frills, responsible reporter.

And over the years, we kept turning to our media mentor for reassurance, to understand the news, bad and good: the assassinations of Robert Kennedy and the Reverend Martin Luther King, Jr., the shootings at Kent State; the Watergate and Iranian hostage crises. In 1962, Cronkite captivated the thrill of live space coverage as over 100 million viewers tuned in to his 10-hour commentary of John Glenn's orbit of the earth, the first by an American astronaut. Cronkite's fervor was even more contagious throughout his marathon reporting of the 1970 Apollo moon landing as he cheered, "Wow! Go baby, go!"

Cronkite also showed on-the-ground outrage at the Tet Offensive and termed the war an "insoluble quandary" in his 1968 "Report from Vietnam." His report allegedly led to President Johnson's pronouncement, "If I've lost Cronkite, I've lost the country," and Johnson's subsequent decision not to run for re-election.

Crossing the line from journalism to politics, Cronkite's diplomatic efforts in implementing Egyptian President Anwar Sadat's 1977 peace mission to Israel earned him the 1981 Medal of Freedom from President Jimmy Carter. Cronkite's clout mattered.

We came to count on Cronkite. In fact, we expected him to always anchor the CBS *Evening News*, signing off "And that's the way it is." He'd accepted the role at age 46, recruited in 1962 by the network's legendary broadcaster Edward R. Murrow.

We expected Cronkite to present perspective, fair and balanced coverage, to narrate our times and, when needed, to be our avuncular sage. We certainly never expected him to age.

Then, in 1981, having stated that he would step down at the mandatory age of 65, Cronkite retired from his managing editor and anchor post. He was succeeded by Dan Rather whom Cronkite later characterized as only "playing the role of newsman."

Although he retained a CBS contract affiliation, and talked of sailing around the world with his wife Betsy, Cronkite's departure according to biographer Douglas Brinkley, was reluctant and unprepared for. "He had quit too soon," Brinkley wrote in *Cronkite*. "He had never felt more hopeless. He had a partial interest in everything, without a sharp sense of mission about any one thing."

I thought of Cronkite waking, eyeing the East River from his U.N. Plaza apartment, reading the *New York Times* and *Washington Post*, and then dressed for work, at odds where to put his considerable energy, curiosity and nose for news. He'd honed his inquiring talents as a young United Press reporter in Kansas City and gone on to cover World War II. An aviation enthusiast, Cronkite was turned down for the military because of color-blindness, only to be embedded as a reporter in bombing runs with the Eighth Air Force over Germany and to report on the Battle of the Bulge. After the war, he headed UP bureaus in Amsterdam, Brussels and Moscow.

Cronkite had dropped out of the University of Texas to begin his beat as a news and sports reporter with the *Houston Press*. In *A Reporter's Life*, he credited his subsequent career to his Houston high school journalism instructor and mentor, Fred Birney, "an inspired teacher who directed the course of my life." Cronkite would be nicknamed "Old Ironpants" for his stamina, dogged and meticulous fact-finding and zest for information, and himself become a role model and mentor to younger journalists Bernard Shaw and Connie Chung. He vied with Barbara Walters for top rated interviews. If in his mid-sixties he felt lost without a mission, demoted by age and retirement, it was a harsh finality even for the world famous, "most trusted man in America." He too would have to rethink his future and adjust to change.

As a celebrity, Cronkite had more expectations — and more resources — than most. He still had clout and credibility, and he knew how to use them. He set about building on his exalted journalism career, soon hosting special CBS reports and the weekly science program, "Universe." He contributed to over 50 books including *The Events That Shaped Our Lives: The Hindenburg Explosion* to the Attacks of September 11. In 1993, he co-founded the Cronkite-Ward Company and produced numerous historical documentaries including *Cronkite Remembers*. In 1996, he authored *A Reporter's Life*, and in his 80s, wrote weekly columns and *Huffington Post* blogs that left no doubt as to his Democratic political preference: "U.S. Unintelligence," "Telling The Truth About The War on Drugs," "Global Warming," "Why I am Marching."

Cronkite kept competing, writing and voicing his often-liberal opinions. I was curious how, at 87, he maintained his momentum when presented with professional losses.

In the fall of 2003, I arrived early at CBS headquarters on West 52nd Street. I'd twice circled the block and wished for another cup of calming, chamomile tea. I anticipated my interview negotiated by Marlene Adler, Cronkite's former CEO at Cronkite-Ward and his personal chief of staff for 17 years. Classy style from head to toe, Marlene was described by Doug Brinkley as an "organizing influence." She ushered me past locked doors to Cronkite's office foyer on the 19th floor where he retained the coveted corner office nearly a quarter century after his official retirement. Cronkite memorabilia lined the walls: photos of him leading the Mormon Tabernacle

Orchestra; astronauts landing on the moon; NASA's Public Service Medal; a "Cronkite" asteroid; letters of thanks from fans missing his nightly sign-off.

Adler received a call on her headphone. "He's running late," she said. "You'll have to speak up so he can hear you." I just hoped I'd be able to speak. I'd heard that Cronkite could be gruff and impatient. I thought of him as larger than life and framed in a TV screen.

"He's in the building," Adler announced on cue. Cronkite came in and caught his breath. "Sorry I'm late." He extended a firm handshake, persuading me that although he was shorter, more furrowed and less intimidating in living color, he was, in fact, the famous broadcaster with the baby blue eyes, familiar mustache and sententious baritone.

Adler helped Cronkite off with his raincoat, tucked his bifocals and corn pads into his pocket, gently steering her former boss into the inner sanctum. Here, shelved titles chronicled world leaders and the major news events of the second half of the twentieth century: Churchill, Nixon, Margaret Thatcher, Abba Eban. *Decision in Normandy, The Soviets, The Battle of Dienbienphu, America in the World.* Ship models were overshadowed by Atlas and lunar modules, a vintage radio, Kennedy Center honors and Emmy awards, one for lifetime achievement.

Souvenirs also displayed Cronkite's off-camera entertainments. He had a football from Don Shula and a baseball from Nolan Ryan, along with a gong given to him by Mickey Hart after a *Grateful Dead* concert. Cronkite and Hart had been friends for 20 years and they loved to sail and jam on the drums together. Cronkite, also a fan of Big Bands and a pal of Jimmy Buffet's, was known to dance into the night, drink his fill of Maker's Mark while telling racy jokes. Once a wannabe sports car driver, he'd liked to gun it on cross-country runs and occasionally race his Austin Healey and Lotus XL.

Cronkite now more often took to the sea. A watercolor of his 46-foot yacht, *Wintji*, hung between the tall windows just above his illustrated text, *Around America: A Tour of Our Magnificent Coast-line*, that charted his 5,000 mile coastal tour from Maine to Key West from Texas to California. For years, Cronkite, Betsy and their three children had steered *Wintji* south to the Caribbean in winter and back for summer sails out of their homeport, Martha's Vineyard.

I bent forward from my matching green leather chair, trying not to shout. "My father used to work at Y&R across the street from the old CBS. He loved to eat at Louis and Armand's. Did you ever eat there too?"

"Oh yes. Very good. Wonderful restaurant. It was a drinking hole. Did your father have his martinis?"

"No, he didn't. He said he was the only person with a clear head after lunch."

Cronkite laughed readily, the genuinely genial mid-Westerner. "He would have been if he ate at Louis and Armand's."

I relaxed recalling Dan Rather's remark: "Walter Cronkite would talk to a potted plant." And even, it seemed, to an unknown journalist from Virginia.

In a 1996 *Grand Times* interview he'd said he wanted to be remembered as "...a person who tried to give the news as impartially, as factually as possible, and succeeded most of the time." I asked Cronkite why, in his later years, had he sharply voiced his more liberally biased opinions?

"I'm writing and speaking now because I'm concerned about the (George W.) Bush administration." Cronkite's ire was palpable. "It's quite clear that we have an entirely new world with which we must deal, and we must learn how to bring into the family of civilized nations those nations which are susceptible (to terrorism) today because of their deep poverty, their envy for the more economically stable world which they are not even part of. Meanwhile, we have on our hands a war of new dimensions that is challenging our defenses and creating a sense of unease in the rest of the world."

Cronkite's temperature kept rising as he discussed the decline of journalism, the disappearance of newspapers and his worry that 24-hour cable television could erode the accuracy of the news and crowd out in-depth analysis. "Broadcast journalism to me is very, very spotty. With all the profusion of channels, some of the material on cable networks, some is bad and some of it is very good. The news programs on cable networks are called 'talk shows'; they're 'shout shows.' I really intensely dislike the shouting matches. It's quite clear they're not trying to inform; they're trying to entertain. That's a terrible waste of airtime," said the reporter who'd led broadcast news in the era of three major networks and expanded stories in-depth beyond the headlines.

Always "fascinated by politics," Cronkite challenged the networks to use higher reporting standards and provide free airtime to political candidates. Gravitas Cronkite still had. And he wasn't above putting his heft to defending his beliefs, political and religious. As honorary chairman of the Interfaith Alliance — a grassroots organization to protect the separation of church and state and America's diversity of beliefs — he described himself as "a concerned person of faith" and gave reasons for speaking his conscience:

> When I anchored the evening news, I kept my opinions to myself. But now, more than ever, I feel I must speak out.... That's because I am deeply disturbed by the dangerous and growing influence of people like Pat Robertson and James Dobson on our nation's political leaders....

In his youth, Cronkite had served as a church acolyte and even considered the Episcopal ministry. He now regularly attended St. Bartholomew's Episcopal Church on Park Avenue.

Fueled by faith, frustration and the pulpit of fame, Cronkite's desire to be heard remained uncurtailed. If at 65 he'd left his broadcast stage too soon, at 57 he conceded in a 1973 *Playboy* interview, he feared the loss of vigor and becoming a cranky elder, like his father, set in his ways, "as only old people are inclined to be."

Cronkite admitted that he also dreaded becoming "an old fuddy duddy" akin to his father-in-law. "Betsy's family were classical musicians, although amateur for the most part. Her mother played the piano; her father played the violin and cello. They had a little five-piece orchestra of their own.

"When I was courting Betsy, we would listen to the radio and Bing Crosby was a favorite of ours. Every time we'd turn on Bing Crosby, this smooth-voiced crooner, Mr. Maxwell would jump up, go over to the radio, snap it off and say, 'I'm sorry but I can't stand that damn caterwauling!' 'Caterwauling?' My gracious, a phrase that could never be applied, it seemed to me, to Bing Crosby. But today, I hop up and turn off the caterwauling of modern-day musicians." Cronkite backed in his chair laughing. "I began to lose out with the hip wagler (Elvis Presley)."

If Cronkite flinched at becoming a fuddy duddy, his war correspondent and CBS pal Andy Rooney thought it unlikely. "The greatest old master in the art of living is Walter Cronkite," he wrote in a 1986 column. "He works and plays all day long.... If life was fattening, Walter would weigh 500 pounds."

Cronkite was also given his impudent due in Roger Angell's *New Yorker* essay, "This Old Man: Life in the Nineties:" "I don't read Scripture and cling to no life precepts except perhaps to Walter Cronkite's rules for old men, which he did not deliver over the air: *'Never trust a fart. Never pass up a drink. Never ignore an erection.'*"

Walter Leland Cronkite, Jr., was born November 4, 1916, in St. Joseph, Missouri, to Helen Lena Fritsche and Dr. Walter Leland Cronkite, Sr., a dentist. Cronkite's parents of German and Dutch ancestry divorced when he was 16, allegedly because of his father's alcoholism. Walter and his mother were then thrust into the Depression and many sparse years, he wrote, when "our pantry slowly emptied."

Through the worst and best of times, Cronkite always looked up to his mother. "My mother was a role model of a sophisticated,

vidual. She was a housewife and socially active. She
ɔedias. Her social graces were certainly to be com-
ᶜ as much as one gender can learn from another, she
o me. She was very a popular lady right up to the end,

d beautifully. If she got any exercise, it was dancing. She
ain from drinking. And I was never aware of her dieting.
emed to enjoy whatever was served. She was interested in poli-
cs living in Washington, but very seldom seemed to take a political stand on anything. I think she was Republican most of her life.
Nothing that went on seemed to exercise her particularly. Of course
she didn't live in the Bush administration." Cronkite got his laugh.

"I tried to interview my mother but she was so hard of hearing,
and I was getting hard of hearing; it was kind of a strange dance of
the deaf. I'd shout at her and she'd shout at me." He smiled. "We'd
both get disgusted and stop."

When his mother died, Cronkite was 77 and still in good health.
The TV anchor who ended his nightly broadcasts tamping down his
pipe, had long given up smoking but still liked his fill of hamburgers
and hot dogs. He'd undergone a knee replacement and quadruple
bypass surgery. He pointed to his ankle in its gray silk sock, a torn
Achilles tendon yet to heal properly after surgery three years ago.
"I'm beginning to get a little tired of it. I don't expect to get too tired
of it," he mocked, "but you know the saying, 'getting older is not for
sissies.' All the little aches and pains and deficiencies that develop
are annoying.

"One of the phrases that just drives me out of my mind, and is
used both as a compliment and as a warning, is 'for a man your age.'
They take my blood pressure and say, 'That's remarkable for a man
your age' or 'Well you've got to expect that for a man your age.' Expect whatever it is — hearing loss, a new set of glasses — every few
minutes. But as hearing and sight diminish, it's hard to accept."

Cronkite's winning candor allowed a willingness to be vu while resisting his losses. He elected to press on, to keep learnu seeking. "I feel I'm open to new ideas. I'm curious about everyu I don't read a piece in the paper that doesn't make me want to ku more." He'd even asked his doctors to rig up a mirror so he cou witness his own appendectomy.

"Curiosity is the main energy," claimed modernist artist Robert Rauschenberg. Should energy falter, Cronkite counseled, "You have to hang in there as best you can. It's maintaining what you've always done. I don't think you can do any more than try to keep on doing what you're doing. Trying to beat back the infirmities. Try to avoid sinking into inactivity and disinterest in the world around you. Be with your family, your associates."

His tone sobered. "One of the serious dangers [in aging] is losing friends. With every death of a close friend, you lose some of your memory. There's nobody to talk to…about the old days, to reminisce, to laugh, even to cry occasionally. That's what disappears and makes growing older more difficult." He said particularly tough losses were his friend and producer Bud Benjamin and CBS colleague Ed Bradley.

If losing friends meant losing part of your history, Cronkite added that he felt especially fortunate to have shared his life and political opinions with Betsy. The couple met in the late 1930s while both worked as journalists at radio station KCMO in Kansas City. He reported news and sports for newspapers and radio, his on-air role model, journalist and explorer Lowell Thomas.

Walter and Betsy married in 1940. Of their lasting partnership, Cronkite wrote in *A Reporter's Life:* "I attribute the longevity of our marriage to Betsy's extraordinarily keen sense of humor which saw us over many bumps, (mostly of my making), and her tolerance, even support, for the uncertain schedule and wanderings of a newsman."

Cronkite was making plans with Betsy to sail again from Edgartown. Until then, he had speeches to write and engagements to keep. Marlene Adler returned to Cronkite's office tapping her watch. He rose slowly. "Oh my gosh. I'm late already."

I asked broadcasting's senior statesman, the authoritative voice who'd summoned us all to The CBS Evening News, for his parting advice.

"Keep up and don't give in to either the mental or physical deterioration that's bound to happen. Try to beat it back," Cronkite said again, off to his next appointment.

I wished Cronkite well, hoping he'd be free of frailties, somehow spared, be stronger and surer than the rest of us. "Soon as I get this leg cured, I'm back on the tennis courts and onto the water," Cronkite pledged. "You bet!" He waved goodbye.

In March 2005, I read that Betsy Cronkite had died of cancer at 89. Cronkite was also 89. He spoke of Betsy on the CBS Special, *Walter Cronkite at 90.* "I lost my North Star, Betsy. For 65 years, she was hardly out of sight. I miss her every minute." His daughter Kathy recalled her parents together: "They went to bed holding hands." Cronkite's friend, comic Robin Williams, added, "Walter was best with Betsy and one cocktail."

I tried to envision Cronkite, staying his course without his North Star, beating back the infirmities, still asking questions, speaking out and being heard.

While heavy-hearted, Cronkite soon found companionship with another recent widow. In June 2005, he was photographed at a black tie dinner for the Museum of Television and Radio with former opera singer Joanna Simon. Carly Simon's older sister was a neighbor and real estate agent from whom Walter and Betsy had bought their U.N. Plaza apartment.

Together in 2007, Cronkite and Joanna visited his World War II posts of London, Berlin and Nuremberg where he'd reported the Nuremberg Trials as UP's chief correspondent and returned to narrate their personal and historical impact in the documentary, *Legacy of War*. He looked leaner, his voice hoarse; his bow tie straight and his eyes unblinking to the camera.

Despite the relentless years, Cronkite's impact remained real in a fast-changing media world. If tough to walk away from fame, he persisted as an iconic influence, perhaps not as saintly or objective as once perceived, but a candid and unpretentious news warrior still on the front lines contending and practicing his reputable trade.

I'd first admired Walter Cronkite for his trustworthy and up-close reporting. I was later impressed by his readiness to speak up for his beliefs, and when declining, by his desire to still make a difference. Cronkite may have preferred to keep moving rather than reflect. He was someone inclined, and even eager, to meet new people if only to connect for a moment, perhaps because he still could, or because he wanted witnesses with whom to share and report his story and stubborn struggle. He wanted us to remember ... "that's the way it is."

Walter Cronkite died at home in New York on July 17, 2009. He was 93.

PHOTO BY ALEX DI SUVERO

Esther Leeming Tuttle, Actress and Model

I'll go back and try the thing I really love to do ... acting.

7

Taking A Second Chance

ESTHER TUTTLE WAS FEATURED on the front page of a 2010 *New York Times* article above the cutline "Secrets of the Centenarians." Described as "vibrant" and "physically fit," she contributed her secrets as a soon-to-be centenarian: pick the right genes, work at what you love, turn adversity to advantage, "be conscious of your body" and practice moderation in food and drink. She was amused that at 99 people seemed amazed she could still talk, and delightfully so.

I'd met Esther Tuttle almost a decade earlier when she was merely 90, her second and third careers then rising like the early snowdrops in Central Park. She'd just returned to her apartment in the East 60s after yoga and a brisk walk in the park. She wore tailored black slacks and a crisp white shirt. Winter sunlight flooded her living room the color of cranberries. "Call me Faity, everyone does," invited this dynamic widow who'd given up a promising acting career in the 1930s and 40s to marry Ben Tuttle, an insurance executive 10 years her senior.

Faity sat on the silk-striped Victorian sofa beneath her husband's handsome portrait. Before they met, Faity said, she'd debuted off-off

Broadway in *Androcles and the Lion* and *Hay Fever* then moved to Broadway in *The Petrified Forest* with Leslie Howard and Humphrey Bogart. After *Petrified Forest*, Faity played Broadway runs as a Russian drama teacher in *Straw Hat* and a French demi mondaine in *Tapestry in Gray*.

She'd come to New York to be an actress after graduating from Warrenton (Virginia) Country Day School in 1929. "It was the year of the stock market crash. I worked wherever I could — theater groups in different churches or in summer stock up in the country, the WPA Theater. We got paid $99.50 a month and we had to live on it. I landed my first speaking part in summer theater in Wilton, Connecticut, as the harem dancer Azuri, in *The Desert Song*. That's when I realized it doesn't pay to be a shrinking violet." Not a chance.

In her memoir, *No Rocking Chair for Me*, Faity recalled her 1935 run as the Mexican cook in *Petrified Forest*: "It was a wonderful play. That was Bogart's first bad guy. I enjoyed it all so much that I'd have performed for nothing." She laughed, remembering Bogart as an attractive "older guy" in his 40s. "I was in two other Broadway plays; one ran three days, the other, three weeks.

"I was a character actress. I was too big to be an ingénue — even at 18, I was five feet eight and a half. That was tall then. I was broad-shouldered and had a big body so I decided to be a character woman."

To support her budding career, Faity sold books at Macy's, toys at Saks and F.A.O. Schwartz and modeled hats for John Frederick. She also rode in the 1939 World's Fair "Railroads on Parade."

Although Faity might have waited in the wings, she didn't regret giving up her early career for the man she found "witty and brilliant." Together, Faity and Ben had two sons and a daughter, and a fulfilling, urbane life in the city as well as country recreations on a farm bought for a bargain in Kinderhook, New York.

She touched the gold disc on a chain around her neck and translated its engraving in French: "'I love you more than yesterday and less than tomorrow.' Ben put this in the toe of my stocking Christmas 1968." She smiled, eyes straight ahead. "We were married for 48 years. Ben died in 1987 at 86, after 10 years with Parkinson's."

Widowed at 78, Faity had suffered another devastating loss just four years earlier. She pointed to a photograph of a slender young woman sitting side-saddle and wearing a top hat ribboned in tulle. "Our darling daughter, 'Missy' (Mary). She was a librarian at the Emma Willard School where she graduated. She was diagnosed with melanoma, and we thought she was cured. Twelve years later she died." Faity's matter-of-fact manner couldn't hide her lingering loss.

Bereft but not defeated, Faity took stock. "When the children were growing up, I always worked at something," she said. "I think it's important. I was very interested in anything to do with kids and with gardens and almost became a professional volunteer, especially with the Botanical Society." She served on the boards of the Brooklyn Botanic Garden, the Brooklyn Academy of Music and the Girl Scouts as well as her children's PTA.

And Faity kept acting. She'd volunteered with children's theater and performed with the SNARKS Ltd. theater troupe and the Amateur Comedy Club of New York. She remained friends with actresses Helen Hayes, Kitty Carlisle and Celeste Holm.

"After Ben died, I thought, the boys were grown and married, and I'll go back and try the thing I really love — acting. I took lessons in working in the media, and called Actors Equity to rejoin. The guy said, 'How long have you been a member?' I said, '50 years.' He looked me up, and sure enough there was my name. He said, 'Sure, you can rejoin. You left in good standing.'" A half century later, Faity took a second chance on her first career.

"A friend doing photographic modeling also suggested I try it. She said, 'modeling would be good for you because you have a good, strong face.' That's what got me started, and I've been modeling ever since. It helped me [recover] to get back to work and use the discipline I'd known before."

Faity braved new classes and auditions, competed with younger, professional actors and read for unconventional parts even when callbacks didn't result. Her discipline and willingness to return to the fray were ultimately rewarded with numerous roles, highlighted in 1994 when she played Lady Bracknell in *The Importance of Being Earnest* in an off-Broadway production.

What had given Faity the gumption for reinvention after the deaths of her husband and daughter, and the approach of her 80th birthday?

"My parents. Their loss," she said.

Esther Leeming — born July 1, 1911, in New Canaan, Connecticut — grew up as the youngest of four in a privileged homes in New Canaan and New York City. Her father, architect Woodruff Leeming, in 1907 designed the Coty Cosmetics building that became Henri Bendel's on Fifth Avenue. In 1919 during World War I, her father contracted tuberculosis and died at the age of 49. Three years later, Faity's mother died of diabetes at 46. Faity was only 11 when she, her brother and two sisters were orphaned and sent to live with an aunt.

In her memoir, Faity recalled "the subsequent virtue of being orphaned so young.... I don't think anything that's happened to me since then has been as hard or hurt as much as losing my mother.... Looking back I believe that losing my parents so early probably made it easier for me to cope with other tragedies later in life. I think I developed an intuitive understanding that I could survive anything after that. I learned I could be happy again after suffering horrendous losses. I was ready for a stimulating new challenge."

Today Faity, still up for the challenge, slid like a teenager from the sofa to the floor reaching for a pile of videos and magazines of her current ads and commercials. In *Paris Match*, she posed in nun's habit for Brightling watches. In *Elle*, she modeled haute couture. For Hallmark cards, she was outfitted in a granny frock and wire-rimmed glasses. "Modeling is like playing, and I feel playing keeps you young," said Faity, proving her point.

She appeared on *The David Letterman Show* and *Law and Order* and in the movies *Moonstruck* and *Mona Lisa*. She fast-forwarded her sample reel of many dowdy disguises to her most enjoyable — a little old lady slapstick boxing a "gorilla" on Conan O'Brien's *Late Night*. For a Cherokee Jeep commercial, she played a stripper to the tag line, "There's no limit on age." Her great-grandson spotted Faity's ad featuring her as a nurse's patient and exclaimed, "There goes Granny on the back of the bus!"

Did Faity mind playing stereotypes or cartoons of older women?

"I never mind what I look like. If they want me to be a less good-looking older woman, I'll do that," said a woman of smart, casual style.

Whatever the work required, Faity was game. She next wanted to try voice overs for television commercials. "I'm so glad that I'd persisted," she said. "In fact, my (early) experience was a great lesson in the value of persistence — a quality that has helped me overcome setbacks and remain optimistic about life."

Her optimism paid off. "I'm very glad that I had the courage to follow my dream and decide to become a professional actress.... I've also come to believe that it's very important to be flexible about your goals as well as other aspects of life. I've observed that people who never pursue their own special dreams are seldom able to find true happiness."

Faity crossed her still limber legs. True happiness, she said, mixed many crucial parts: Family. Friends. Laughter. A receptive spirit. Useful, community pursuits. Great genes. Mental and physical activity. Everything in moderation.

"When I was in the theater, I smoked but never until the day was over. Then I had one cigarette with a glass of beer. I never went to bed until midnight after I'd unwound a bit. Eat or drink, always in moderation. It helped me be as well as I am." Faity had survived breast cancer 25 years earlier; she now wore a pacemaker, hearing aid and contact lenses.

"Be conscious of your body," she cautioned. "I had to stop driving the horse carriage because of poor vision. I just have the sight of this one eye; the other is very blurry. It's also maddening to have your hearing go.

"I still ride occasionally, which is a risk at my age. You don't have the muscles to hang on with your knees and your legs if the horse does something unexpected. One time, I almost got trapped in a mudslide. I still take care of the horses in the summer. And there are a couple of ponds where I swim when visiting my sons. I'm the last of my siblings. I'm surprised that I've been able to live so long and so enjoy life as much as I do."

Agile, playful and still taking risks, Faity sprung back on her feet. "My sons want me to move to a retirement place near them in the country, but I can walk to everything I need in the city. I can stay active, which is very important at my age. I've always been independent."

Long might Faity hold to her independence, her readiness to tempt failure and vulnerability late in life. She was rewarded with renewed confidence and control. "I think faith in God is very important for peace of mind," she added. "It's helped me cope with losses since my father's death when I was eight. I believe in God firmly but I am not a church religious person. I look up to certain people and nature more than organized religion."

Faity seemed a sturdy oak, taller and more indestructible than most in the woods, even when lightning struck. She buttoned her winter coat, setting out for lunch with French lessons and conversations to follow.

That evening, Esther Leeming Tuttle would rehearse for the SNARKS' production of *The English Teacher* in which she starred as the bold and abiding mother. I assumed good reviews and later to read in the *New York Times* Faity's secrets on how to reach 100.

Esther Leeming Tuttle died in Chatham, New York, on July 9, 2015. She was 104.

IMAGE COLLECT/S. BUKLEY

Nanette Fabray, Actress

I only have one opportunity to be Nanette
Fabray MacDougall on this earth.
I'm going to enjoy it.

8

Singing, Dancing and Having The Last Laugh

VISITING FRIENDS AFTER MY FATHER'S DEATH, I spotted Nanette Fabray's name on the Cape Cod Playhouse marquee. I looked forward to laughter, remembering her live comedy on *Your Show of Shows* and *Caesar's Hour* which I watched with my parents in the '50s. Nanette lit up our seven inch black and white television. She sang, danced and crossed her eyes; she sweet-talked Sid Caesar into buying her a shirred beaver coat, and the two of them pantomimed a high-pitched squabble to *Beethoven's Fifth*.

I snagged a last matinee ticket in the front row balcony. Enter Nanette Fabray, at 82 the slinky lady in sequins with the showgirl legs, and all-or-nothing grin. Between vintage TV clips with Sid Caesar, Carol Burnett and Mary Tyler Moore, Nanette reminisced in song and dance: tart tales of Broadway, Hollywood and MGM movie musicals. She snatched wigs and costumes spilling from a trunk. She threw herself into pratfalls as a latter day rock star. In sapphire satin slit to her thighs, she took the mike into the audience, flirting with a fella more than happy to have Nanette Fabray sit on his lap. She zinged the heartstrings of "By Myself," assuring her audience, "I'm still here!" Whistles drowned the applause.

Nanette's appealing comedy won her three Emmys during decades when she starred on Broadway in a dozen shows from *Bloomer Girl* and *High Button Shoes* to *Make a Wish*. She won a Tony Award for her lead in *Love Life* and a nomination as First Lady Nell Henderson in Irving Berlin's *Mr. President*, her last Broadway musical in 1962. She toured with musicals, among them *Wonderful Town* and *No, No, Nanette*.

Nanette co-starred with Fred Astaire in MGM's 1953 hit *The Band Wagon*. She as one of three toddler "Triplets" dancing into film history. She later clowned it up on variety shows from *Dinah Shore* and *Andy Williams* to *The Hollywood Squares*. Nanette never missed a beat as the 1970s sit-com grandmother, Katherine Romano on *One Day at a Time*, or as wisecracking mother to her real-life niece, Shelley Fabares, in *Coach*.

Backstage, Fabray greeted fans in a peach, silk flowered robe. Gracious and polite, she was petite in person, her hair bronzed, her brown eyes shining. While rushed, she agreed to a phone interview after returning to her secluded home in Pacific Palisades.

Since Nanette delivered the laughs onstage, I supposed many more. I'd learn that much of Fabray's stellar career had been no laughing matter. "I started losing my hearing in my 20s," said Nanette, who debuted on Broadway at 19 playing Bette Davis' lady-in-waiting in *The Private Lives of Elizabeth and Essex*. "I was doing a show in Chicago. I missed some cues and had a hard time hearing the orchestra. I went to an ear doctor who diagnosed otosclerosis (an inner ear disease that progresses to deafness). He told me, 'You're going to lose your hearing, and when you lose your hearing, you lose your speech.' He believed I would be deaf and dumb within a few years.

"It was the '40s, a time when no one wore hearing aids. Everything had to be perfect. You didn't wear glasses. You wore the same hairdo. You wore the same clothes. You followed moral patterns, fashion styles and rules that were laid down by others. You did not admit that you had something the matter with you."

Although young, facing deafness and a career in jeopardy, Nanette balked at accepting a restrictive and dire diagnosis. Instead, she found her own prescription. She starred in Broadway and Hollywood productions while wearing a discreet hearing aid and undergoing a series of surgeries with wire implants that, over time, greatly improved her hearing.

Nanette also spoke out. "I was the very first celebrity ever to stand up and say, 'I have a problem. I don't hear well. I am physically handicapped or disabled.' I felt that one should not be ashamed of having a problem. I didn't say 'Look at me.' I was in my late twenties and I just started talking about it here and there and the press picked it up."

And her press got attention. Nanette testified before Congress on the rights of the handicapped. She was given a presidential appointment in the Eisenhower era and served through the Reagan administration. She also became a founding member of the National Council on the Disabled that in 1992 wrote the Americans with Disabilities Act.

Fabray, with First Lady Pat Nixon, attended the groundbreaking of the Model Secondary School for the Deaf at Gallaudet College. Years later, she established the MacDougall Creative Writing Award at Gallaudet to foster writing careers for deaf students. Nanette knew the opposition to the deaf in the hearing world. In an *Archive for SHE American Television* interview, she remembered appearing on *The Carol Burnett Show*, and her agreement with the star that she would perform "Somewhere Over the Rainbow" a cappella and in sign language. Burnett "wrote it in the script, and it went upstairs to the powers that be — and it came right back down. 'There will be no sign language on television. It's too controversial.'

"But Carol was a smartie and she'd planted someone in the audience. The woman said, 'We hear that Nanette sings a beautiful song in sign language.' 'That's right,' she said. 'Nanette, come on out here and sing your song.' And I did the song. CBS couldn't cut it out. It was a live show." Fabray was still smiling.

"Carol got such an enormous response from that song that the next time I was on, it was the first time ever sign language had been integrated into an entertainment program where hearing singers sing and dancers dance to sign language."

While independently championing the needs of the handicapped, Nanette battled her losses and adversities off stage. In 1951, her four-year marriage to Dave Tebet, a former NBC vice president, ended in divorce.

"I also have been very ill through a lot of my life," she said. "I had breast cancer when one didn't talk about it, 25 or 30 years ago. I was given less than a 50 percent chance of living. I said I would not accept that diagnosis even though I was terrified. I would not accept a mastectomy because I felt it would be disfiguring. I had one of the very first lumpectomies and radiation and survived just fine. Somehow I have good recuperative powers. I think a lot of it is a positive attitude.

"I'm not a Pollyanna," she added firmly, "In the early '70s over a very short period of time, I first lost my father, then my (second) husband (screen writer, director producer Randal MacDougall and father of their son Jamie), then my brother and my mother. My whole family structure just collapsed, disappeared. My son was 14 and all his family was gone except for me.

"I had a mental breakdown. I couldn't cope with the loss of my hearing and the loss of work because I was depressed. I was committed to a hospital for months. Psychotherapy helped me pull back out of it. And I kept going because I had a child to take care of."

Nanette also remembered her mother. "My mother was a feisty, fabulous, fighting person." She described her father, a train conductor, as "a very gentle, passive man." Her parents divorced when Nanette was 10. "My sister, brother and I grew up through all of the

Depression; my mother would not give up, would not give in. We kept boarders; she cooked and cleaned. My god, looking back, I don't know how she did it. She was the fighter in the family. She also had a good time. She was a party girl. She had friends around and gave parties. That was the kind of person she was." A lady a lot like Nanette.

Nanette started out as a singer and dancer, her natural talent as an amusing actress soon discovered. "I'd be hired as a leading lady but I would also be funny. I wasn't really a comedienne until I worked for (Broadway producer and director) George Abbott. He said, 'You are funny. Use that.' I hadn't thought about being funny before he told me that I was.

"Humor is something you either have or you don't have. It's a gift. I can do something and it turns out to be funny, and someone else can do exactly the same thing and it isn't funny. If I knew why I'd be a zillionaire."

Relying on humor, optimism and backbone through the best and worst of times, Fabray also took professional risks, whatever the consequences. In 1978 while shooting *Harper Valley PTA*, she was hospitalized again, this time for a freak accident on the set. "It was bizarre, but I was attacked by an elephant. My neck and head hit the sidewalk. I lost feeling on my left side; my eyes wouldn't track.

"But as I became more aware that I was hospitalized, I said, 'I've absolutely got to get out of here. I have to get well and get back to doing what I know how to do: live a good life, enjoy my son and grandchildren and get on with it.'"

Nanette Fabray — resolute, unshakable and often sunny — got on with it while still practicing what she most enjoyed. "I'm working because I love to work, to be busy. What else would I do? Sit around and look at my fingernails?"

If Nanette was not the clown she played and was sometimes testy and restless, she kept working and cheerfully ensured that her message for the handicapped was still heard. UCLA's Center for Aging gave her the 2001 Icon of the Year Award. I expected her to keep advocating for the disabled and to keep dancing and performing, pratfalls and all. I expected her to defy her birthdays to the last candle.

"It has to do with getting up in the morning; sometimes that isn't easy to do — getting dressed and getting out. Once you're out, you feel better," she said. "I perform my show several times a year. I walk and I still love to tap dance. With tap dancing, you use every part of your body and your brain. Plus, there's the excitement of music and noise. Each new step, each new routine inputs new programming into your mind and into your body. And it changes all the time. I wasn't sure physically I'd be able to do two hour-and-a-half shows back to back. That's very hard for somebody in their teens or twenties. But I feel fine."

So fine that in 2007, Fabray opened at the Whitefire Theater in Sherman Oaks in "The Damsel Dialogue," an original review on work, life, love and loss. She was still hoofing from Pacific Palisades, the West Los Angeles neighborhood where she was once dubbed honorary mayor.

Ruby Bernadette Nanette Fabares was born in San Diego on October 27, 1920. She tap-danced onto the boards at age three as "Miss New Year's Eve 1923" at the Million Dollar Theater. She studied dancing with Bill "Bojangles" Robinson and performed in Vaudeville as "Baby Nanette" and beyond. I saw that toe-tapping girl now turning up the music, and with or without a partner, dancing past dark.

Or maybe with her grandchildren. Her son Jamie and his children lived down the coast highway in Manhattan Beach; her granddaughter loved to dance and her grandson to sing. "He has perfect pitch. It's amazing to hear him."

Nanette laughed. "Maybe the genes are there. I thoroughly enjoy what I do, and I think that makes a big difference. I realize that I only have one opportunity to be Nanette Fabray MacDougall on this earth. I'm going to make the best of it. I'm going to enjoy it."

Nanette Fabray MacDougall died at home in Palos Verdes, California on February 22, 2018. She was 98.

PHOTOGRAPH COURTESY OF THE ESTATE OF JEAN BACH

Jean Bach, Documentary Producer

The Golden Age of Jazz is a world I knew, and I decided that I wanted to share it with people.

9

Focusing Professional Talents to New Purpose

JEAN BACH'S ROWHOUSE IN A MEWS ALLEY near Washington Square, was within earshot of where she once applauded jazz greats late into the New York night. She opened the door in an a la Chanel suit, a pearl choker and gold link bracelets, speed talking, high heels clicking, one sentence nabbing the next.

Like Nanette Fabray, Jean Bach seemed a lady determined to delight in every sunrise. The 85-year-old former producer of *The Arlene Francis Show* advised in her 1960s' paperback, *200 Ways to Conquer the Blues:* "When you're with people, don't wear your depression like a badge. You're going to have to learn to fake cheerfulness." Far from a faker, Jean contributed her considerable good cheer along with a crash course in reinvention.

"That's me and Bob and (gossip columnist) Dorothy Kilgallen; she was on *What's My Line.* We used to go dancing with Dorothy and Dick (at the Stork Club)," said Bach, surrounded by photos of her friends and her second husband, Bob Bach, producer of the 1950s quiz show *What's My Line?*

"Bob got sick. Cancer," said Jean, straight out. "Still, we had that last year. After Bob died, I had nothing to do. I was pining. I still had some drive and wanted to do something new."

So this radio pro at 71, like Mary Lee Settle with no thoughts of retiring, pondered how she might do something new, how she could put her professional past to her long-loved interest — jazz.

"I saw this 1958 *Esquire* photo taken (by Art Kane) of famous jazz stars' reunion on 126th Street." Jean was almost overshadowed on the sofa by the enlarged photograph behind her. "There's Thelonius Monk, very odd; Dizzy Gillespie, utterly adorable; Gene Krupa among the drummers; Count Basie sitting down on the sidewalk; Gerry Mulligan's bleached out so you can hardly see him. Marian McPartland's in front holding a handbag. That's Mary Lou Williams, she's the most historic figure. The greats of jazz. The Old Masters. They're the foundation, the Golden Age of Jazz is a world I knew, and I decided that I wanted to share it with people.

"I wanted to get as many people who were still breathing back together to comment on their life and times. I first thought recordings would go to a library or the Smithsonian for people to learn about how it is. Learn about Monk and all these people. I didn't want them to be forgotten."

Jean dated her own passion as a "jazz groupie" to the night of her 18th birthday, the evening she first heard Duke Ellington play at Chicago's Congress Hotel. It was instant replay. "I met Duke Ellington in 1936, graduation night from prep school. Everybody was in party clothes. My date said, 'Shall we ask Mr. Ellington to come over and have a glass of champagne?' I said, 'I'd love it.' He came over and stood at the table. Very proper. He said, 'What are your plans, Miss Enzinger?' I said, 'I'm going to go to Vassar in the fall.' 'Oh,' he said, 'I live near there. We must get together.' Of course, I followed through!"

Before the first fire drill, Jean took the train from Vassar to New York and knocked on Ellington's door in Harlem's Sugar Hill. She became the brazen kid back on Duke's doorstep. "His father came to the door and looked a little appalled. Out stepped Ellington, sleepy and dressed in a Sulka robe. He said, 'How nice to see you again.'" After an hour's visit, Jean rode back to Poughkeepsie. She and Ellington remained friends until his death in 1974.

Jean's first job in 1930s Chicago included writing record reviews for Hearst newspapers, a chance to sneak in her other early "music enthusiasms." "I heard Billie Holiday at the Grand Terrace night club. I followed her into the ladies' room and she fluffed me off, snorted at me." Jean laughed. "I wanted to come up on the bus and hear Count Basie, but I couldn't find the way."

In 1940, Jean met swing trumpeter Shorty Sherock at The Three Deuces playing with Gene Krupa's band. Three weeks later, Jean and Shorty were married. They traveled on the road with Krupa and other big bands like Jimmy and Tommy Dorsey and Bob Crosby. Later Shorty had his own band that Jean managed. "Shorty was darling and played like Roy Eldridge," she said. "He had the best sense of humor in the world." She and Shorty divorced in 1947, and Jean married Bob Bach a year later.

Jean had her old friend Ellington and other jazz luminaries in mind when primed to produce her first film. "It turns out that everything is a learning experience. Being a radio producer was the perfect background for this film because number one, you had to track people down."

Jean's 24-year stretch producing the *Arlene France Show*, regularly broadcast from Sardi's celebrity restaurant, required finding the right people to interview on air five days a week. If a guest failed to show up, Jean stepped up to the mike and delivered her own intelligent, impromptu observations. "As producer, I met all these wonderful people. A lot of eggheads and political people. I love political scandals; that's one of my passions. We'd go to Washington all the time and tape the nation's lawmakers. I was interested in overthrowing the government." She cracked. "Arlene was my cat's paw. She caught on after a couple of years."

As a 1983 *New Yorker* profile attested, "One of the settlers who have given New York immeasurable passion during the past 35 years is a pretty, witty, quick, indefatigable woman named Jean Bach."

Years later, unflagging Jean was on her passionate search for documentary footage. First she discovered a home movie shot at the same time as the original Harlem photograph. "You see the still photograph in black and white and then it suddenly comes to life; there's blood in their veins. That's what started me.

"Next, I began rounding up people from the photograph and located places where we could film the living musicians. The first two interviews were shot in the Sweet Basil, a nightclub here in the Village that had this photo on the wall. It was in the afternoon.

"No one was in there but the bartender started the Mixmaster. Then he'd bang things, and I was ordering drinks for people and paying for them, but I guess I should have slipped him a big wad in the beginning so he'd pipe down. I hadn't realized that problem, and the noise took a lot of editing. It seemed unsatisfactory so I just gave up, and instead, interviewed a lot of people right here in this living room, in a lot of funny corners so it looks like there were many different locations."

Jean had rearranged Gertrude Vanderbilt Whitney's former studio — complete with a grand piano, skylight, flower embroidered chairs and a Chippendale mirror stretching to the crown molding — into the perfect movie set. She waved her hands, returning the actors to their places. "Dizzy sat in that chair. Sonny Rollins sat there. Marian McPartland was photographed at the piano. It was pretty artful. When people would be a little taciturn or self-conscious, I fell on a trick. I'd mention Thelonious Monk and everybody came to life. Everybody had a Monk story."

Jean made it easy to hear the pepped up stories and music again. She incorporated performance clips and narration by producer Quincy Jones into her film, and her deft, artful vision won rave reviews. *The New Yorker* critiqued *A Great Day in Harlem* as a film "about mortality, loyalty, talent, musical beauty." It also won its producer a 1995 Academy Award nomination.

Jean laughed. "The film still plays all over the world — the U.S. and Canada, South Africa, Australia and Europe. You can't beat it to death with a stick. The year of the Oscar was 1995, but it's still cooking. Its won millions of prizes. This (crystal obelisk) is the first prize it won. In Chicago. I'm still not a filmmaker. I don't know how to do it. It was dumb luck."

Hardly. This gutsy and glamorous lady of a certain age made success look easy, when, in fact, it required professional and financial risks in a highly competitive and unfamiliar field. She was willing to learn, to try and to fail, but not to be defeated or let down those whose jazz talents she was dedicated to document.

"I guess the film was an extension of learning a new skill and new stuff about these great people, most of whom I'd known for a good bit of my life: Sahib Shihab. Blakey, Freeman, Count Basie, Max Kaminsky, Dizzy. So many have died since the film was made.

"I think I've done a little bit to keep the consciousness going. In the film Sonny Rollins says, 'What's the point of living to be 100 if you don't accomplish something?' I gave it a lot of thought." And action.

In 1999, Jean made *The Spitball Story*, a 20-minute postscript film about her friend Dizzy Gillespie. It too won many awards, including top honors at the Chicago International Film Festival. She worked on a documentary about saxophonist Gerry Mulligan and had more film plans in mind.

On her 80th birthday, Jean was honored at her alma mater, Vassar College, with her best friend Bobby Short and his orchestra playing her picks. Short's photo in her powder room showed him decked out in a houndstooth suit and coonskin coat, his polished shoes posed on the Duisenberg running board. His snappy photo hung beside Dylan Thomas' line drawing of "Queen Edith Sitwell and Princess Marianne Moore on their first meeting, executed in the White Horse

Tavern, N.Y. 1952." Johnny Mercer signed his tribute to Jean, "the Perle Mesta of our set and the crown princess of hipsville who introduced me to Ray Charles, Saturday night fish fry and Blossom Dearie, the Peggy Lee of the Village."

According to the *New York Times*, a gossip columnist once quoted Frank Sinatra asking on arrival in the city, "What's happening down at Jean's?"

Oh, to have partied with Manhattan's Pearl Mesta of the 1940s and '50s, foxtrotting into the wee hours at black tie, Duke Ellington dances hosted by Jean and Bob. After Bob died, Jean kept up the tradition with her pal Bobby Short. "Everybody was crazy about Bobby, so we had kind of a distinguished guest list. It was not bad," said Jean, vintage New York sophistication at the spin of the dial. A sentimental photo showed Bobby at the keyboard with friends Jean and jazz clarinetist Artie Shaw.

In 1981, Jean and Bobby celebrated their 40-year friendship. They'd met in 1942 Chicago at the Sherman Hotel soon after Short graduated from high school. Her attraction, Short recalled in a 1983 *New Yorker* interview, was not only Jean's Duke Ellington ardor but that she could sing in perfect sync with Ben Webster, Cootie Williams and Johnny Hodges. "And," said Short, "she *knew* my idol, Ivie Anderson who sang with Ellington's band.... She was by far the most elegant and beautiful and sharply intelligent person I had ever met."

The phone rang while we talked. It was Bobby Short on the line; Jean promised to phone him right back. Jean and Bobby could surely still throw an A-list bash at the first drum roll.

Holding to friends and present pursuits, Jean stayed connected and au courant. "I read four newspapers. The news really grabs me. World affairs still concern me. I'm on the muscle all the time. I want to knock some people's hats off. I guess it's kind of hopeless, but I'm still in there punching. I sat up in bed one night after reading a book I found wonderfully interesting. I was making notes. I suddenly put my pencil down and thought, 'Damn, this is the thing that really gives me bliss — acquiring information.'" Jean's new books included *West Coast Jazz*, Gore Vidal's *Lincoln*, and Chris Hedges' *War Is a Force That Gives Us Meaning*.

Still punching, Jean confided that she also had her quota of aches and pains. "I have arthritis and am tempted to do nothing, but I keep moving, swimming and walking." This vivacious only child was born in 1918 in Milwaukee, Wisconsin, to an advertising executive and "beautiful" mother, both active in the arts. They divorced when Jean was 18.

"My daddy was kind of a playboy, and my mother would get furious. Sometimes she'd find out if he'd sent flowers to somebody else. It was tempestuous. He married four times and died just after age 70. My mother swam every day, winter and summer. She was very healthy and gorgeous to the end. She lived to 94."

Jean retained her beauty and passion for bringing out the best. "In the 80s, I went overboard with French cooking but apparently it didn't do any harm and vegetables are chic now anyway. Look after your health; it's important. I'm still at it. Wish me luck."

Indeed. Jean lapped the field even as she claimed to be "pulling up the drawbridge." Running late for a War Register's League luncheon, she'd also scheduled a jazz concert at the Church of the Heavenly Rest. Jean Bach refused to rest, and doing so, secured her legacy as well as that of many jazz legends.

Jean's own charisma shone through Art Farmer's closing words of her film: "We don't think about people not being here. We don't think, 'Well Count Basie was here, but he's not here anymore. Count Basie is here. Coleman Hawkins is here. Roy Eldridge *is* here. They are *in* us, and they will always be alive."

Jean Bach died at home in New York on May 27, 2013. She was 94.

PHOTO BY ELIZABETH HOWARD

Albert Maysles, Documentary Filmmaker

The moment you begin to control things, you're defying reality. It's very important to let things be, to keep an open heart and mind to discover someone's true nature. Risk — it's everything.

10

Plumbing Your Own Life Story

WHEN I MET AL MAYSLES, he made me want to be a filmmaker. It was 1970 at the University of Virginia's screening of *Salesman*, a documentary of four Boston Bible salesmen whom Al and his younger brother David trailed door to door. Their handheld cameras steadily uncloaked the salesmen's disillusioned stories about their trade. The brothers focused on compelling characters and proved that they didn't need a script to tell their tale.

Hooked, I kept tracking the Maysles brothers' pioneering "direct cinema" teamwork, with Al on camera and David manning sound and editing. The pair produced such groundbreaking films as *What's Happening! The Beatles in the USA*, Academy Award-nominated *Valley Curtain* (about Christo, the artist), and *Gimme Shelter*, the 1970 Rolling Stones' concert film in which a brawl killing by the Hell's Angels was captured on film.

Al and David, sons of Jewish Russian immigrants, shot their first film while motorcycling from Munich to Moscow to document the Polish student revolution of 1956. A year earlier, Al gave up his position teaching psychology at Boston University to film patients in Russian mental hospitals. Once *Psychiatry in Russia* was in the can, Al's career course was set.

I interviewed Al in 1976 for an article on *Grey Gardens* — the Maysles' keyhole peek at an eccentric mother-daughter duo who happened to be Jackie Onassis' aunt and cousin sequestered in their dilapidated East Hampton home. The film would become a cult classic and inspiration for a book, Broadway play, and HBO drama. Soon after our interview, Al invited me to a gathering in the landmark Dakota on Central Park West where he and his wife Gillian, a psychotherapist, lived with their four children. With giddy anticipation, I wound down a spiral staircase into Al's book-lined study to join a circle of young filmmakers, all clamoring for Al's attention. He was our hero and mentor whether he wanted to be or not.

In 1987, I read that David Maysles had died of a stroke. By then, Al and David had shot more than 15 films together. I wondered how one set of eyes could work without the other. How would David's death affect Al's films? How would Al's loss change his creative choices?

Eighteen years after David's death, Al created the non-profit Maysles Institute in Harlem, "dedicated to the exhibition and production of documentary films that inspire dialogue and action." The Institute "extends the Maysles Brothers' principle that the lives and opinions of people not only deserve but demand our attention."

I interviewed Al again in the fall of 2006. He requested that I come early to review recent films made with his new collaborator filmmaker Susan Froemke. The elevator rose slowly to the rooftop offices of Maysles Films West of Broadway. An intern showed me to the screening room and cued *Lalee's Kin: The Legacy of Cotton*, a Mississippi family's passage through unrelenting poverty. The documentary won Maysles Films a 2001 Academy Award nomination as well as the Sundance Film Festival's Cinematography Award for Documentaries. *Letting Go: A Hospice Journey* recorded the peaceful farewell of three terminally ill patients at home. Al, unflinching behind the camera, bore quiet witness to the most private of family dramas, reminding me, of course, of my father's last days.

Al, at 80, arrived intense as ever, taut and wiry, his white hair tousled. His immediate smile and slightly befuddled, affable and curious, low-keyed attention made our reunion feel like we were old friends, even as I wondered if Al actually remembered me.

We settled in a back room away from young staffers answering the phones. Traffic clattered far below. We sat side by side on a sofa wedged between shelves of film canisters and camera equipment. The ceiling light cast pale shadows. I held my tape recorder up close and asked about David.

"David's death [at 54] was unexpected. A terrible loss. It's not the same without him. Never the same. Work helped to get away from the pain," said Al, the realist. "My philosophy hasn't changed. I'm applying the same methods with Susan (Froemke). Recently I've been dilly-dallying, but now I'm making more personal films."

Al was pursuing themes of loss and family identity whether or not linked to David's death. His film in progress, *Scapegoat on Trial*, confronted his Jewish heritage, if circuitously; it told the story of Mendel Beilis, a 1913 Kiev factory foreman falsely accused of murdering a 13-year-old Christian boy. "It's very much linked with persecution, being on trial, what a Jew feels from being Jewish. I'm finally exploring the idea of the outsider as a Jew.

"David and I identified with the outsider. We fought on the Boston streets with Irish kids quick to label Jews 'Christ killers.' *Salesman* was personal for me and David growing up Jewish in Boston. It brought me and my brother closer together with the Irish.

"We also identified with Edie and her mother in *Grey Gardens*. Outsiders. The Bible salesman was also an outsider. In a sense, the housewives we met were outsiders too, outside of the more fulfilling life, just stuck in the house.

"I'm sure one of the things I found so interesting in making *Salesman* was that Paul — like my father — was a poetic kind of guy but in the wrong job. My father could have done better than being a postal clerk."

His father's World War I silver cornet hung on his kitchen wall, but Al said he'd never heard his father play a note. He imagined his father trumpeting when he washed the dishes as *his* father had done before him.

Al also remembered that his father had hit him with a strap and he'd cried afterwards. Al lowered his voice. "He was so sorry for hurting me; it was a moment of intimacy."

If Al understood his father's hurt and lack of fulfillment, he saw his mother stigmatized for being Jewish and fighting for her job as a school teacher. "My mother was always very active in civil rights, rights for women, blacks. When she was dying of cancer, she turned to us and said at the last moment, 'I know what I want on my grave-stone: 'count on me as one who loved my fellow man.' Both my parents were very optimistic, true believers in life."

Al prized photographs of his mother with other young immi-grants, and one of his father as a boy glancing cautiously at the cam-era. "I'm now looking at my own Jewish identity. Sooner or later any serious artist gets closer to his cravings and elements of childhood. Like my parents, I too believe there is good in everybody. I'm looking for it and don't want to let it go by unnoticed.

"I think a documentary filmmaker is at his or her best when there's something in that person's childhood — way back, images, some event — that is somehow related to the film at hand."

Al recalled leaving New York's 125th Street train platform to join the army in World War II in 1944. He was 17. "My family was all lined up on the platform," he said in a film clip for *Index Magazine*. "They couldn't see me, and they looked very serious, thinking, I'm sure, that I might never come back. That image and my inability to talk to them has prevailed all through my life."

The haunting image of his disappearing parents ultimately gen-erated Al's three-decades, unfinished film project, *In Transit*. "I'm now filming fellow passengers, poetic moments, chance encounters, stories and reconciliations as they take place on and off trains world-wide," he said. "The train is a metaphor for life. Margaret Mead said, 'We need to find 'common ground.' If there's a purpose for this film, that's it."

At the Philadelphia train station, he'd filmed a 26-year-old woman reuniting with her mother. She was only three when she'd last seen her mother, and her parents had then divorced. On a train crossing his ancestral Russia, Al met a couple en route to Ukraine with two little boys, sons of the woman's sister who, Al learned, had been brutally murdered by her drunken husband.

Al came closer to his own story in filming his "fellow passengers." "Not long ago, PBS asked me to be the subject of a documentary. I was interested until they suggested a filmmaker for the job. I said, 'If anybody in the world was going to make it, I should. Let's do it as an autobiography.' They refused."

Born on November 26, 1926, Al now sifted through footage and outtakes — old and new — of more than a half century for his own film to be called *Handheld and from the Heart*. His son Philip had written a school essay saying that his "father's worn baby shoes held generations of Jewish history."

Al and Philip, now a visual artist and filmmaker, had recently established documentary training and apprenticeships for youths at the Maysles Institute on Malcolm X Boulevard. The program was formed for youths in Harlem, the South Bronx and north Manhattan, particularly teens with incarcerated parents. Al, in turn, had become a mentor and role model to new generations of filmmakers.

On this late October afternoon, Al Maysles, observer, patient listener, and persuasive mentor, kept teaching and planning future films. "The best films are literally personal or personal in an underlying fashion," he said. "Filming documentaries is a chance to discover as it happens and make it fruitful. You're dealing with random events, the uncontrollable. The moment you begin to control things, you're defying reality. It's very important to let things be, to keep an open heart and mind to discover someone's true nature. Risk — it's everything.

"I try to get an engagement going between the viewer and what's on the screen, an engagement that hopefully transfers the experience of the other person into a lasting memory." Al lowered his voice. I inched closer. It was getting dark.

"I feel there is no greater communicator than one real person to another. You have to get close; use your eyes and empathy to get into the heart and soul of the matter. Making a film is a way of looking at the world, an act of love."

After our interview, I often thought of Al and how he viewed the world with affection and perseverance. In 2009, he worked with director Andrew Jacobs on *Four Seasons Lodge*, documenting an annual summer reunion of Holocaust survivors in the Catskills. *The New York Times* stated that the group gathered "to dance, cook, fight, flirt and celebrate their survival."

On the 10th anniversary of the 9/11 attacks, Maysles chronicled *The Love We Make*, Paul McCartney's concert to honor and reward the first responders of New York.

If survival had become his mainstay, Maysles celebrated it again in *Iris*. His 2014 portrait of 93-year-old interior designer and fashion icon tracked Iris Apfel in her owlish black spectacles on her Seventh Avenue rounds, in and out of her crowded clothes closets and the Florida condo where she and husband Carl collected art and whimsy and celebrated his 100th birthday party.

Perhaps at 88, Al had found a role model in this slightly more senior, lippy, youthful spirit from Queens. She'd traveled the "ends of the earth" discovering antique textiles, bargaining for baubles and collecting enough bold-patterned clothes to stuff two apartments and a special exhibit at the Costume Institute of the Metropolitan Museum. To say nothing of designing and selling jewelry, shoes and handbags for the Home Shopping Network with time out to introduce design students to some off-the-runway realities of the not so glamorous "rag" trade. She often used the word "fun" and jested with "charming" Al on camera.

Iris, a self-proclaimed "geriatric starlet," bore a hint of "Big Edie," the elder eccentric from Al's now iconic *Grey Gardens*. In a *Los Angeles Times* interview however, Al said that while shooting *Iris*, he subconsciously thought more about his kindly, nurturing mother than Edie.

I saw *Iris* in May 1915 at Film Forum in the Village. Afterwards, I read the *New York Times* review in the lobby. The last paragraph reported that the documentary was Al's second to last and *In Transit* was his last. Al had died two months earlier.

Tears started. I remembered my afternoon with Al, his lessons on filmmaking and the importance of looking for what matters. I wanted some final words of consolation. Al's website confirmed what he and David had unfailingly practiced: "As a documentarian, I happily place my fate and faith in reality. It is my caretaker, the provider of subjects, themes, experiences — all endowed with the power of truth and the romance of discovery. And the closer I adhere to reality the more honest and authentic my tales. After all, the knowledge of the real world is exactly what we need to better understand and therefore possibly to love one another. It's my way of making the world a better place."

Albert Maysles died at home in New York on March 5, 2015. He was 89.

PHOTO BY PAM PERUGI MARRACCINI

Rebecca Fuller McGinness, Teacher

*Just remember me as one woman who enjoyed
life ... and gave it back to people ... to youngsters.*

11

Outliving Your Losses

IT WAS AL MAYSLES WHO INSPIRED ME to film Rebecca McGinness, a woman born in 1892, 29 years after the Emancipation Proclamation and three days before the election of Grover Cleveland. This granddaughter and daughter of slaves taught five generations of Charlottesville students, and retired in 1960, four years before President Lyndon Johnson signed the Civil Rights Act officially ending segregation. She never gave up teaching younger generations of African Americans by the book and by her "nobody's fool" example. At 105, Rebecca McGinness had long outlived her family and knew something about survival.

Like Cronkite and Maysles, she bore witness to history. Rebecca had lived the span of the twentieth century and kept contributing past age 100. It would take months and many phone calls before Mrs. McGinness agreed to my visit and to talk on camera.

Mrs. McGinness, slight but substantial, sat tall and proper in her flowered wing chair. She wore a cobalt blue jersey dress with a scoop neck, and pearl and blue bead cluster earrings with a matching necklace. Her dark eyes were intent, her dignity intimidating.

She commanded the camera as she told me what she considered a very old story: Rebecca Fuller was born on November 5, 1892, and named for her grandmother who had seen her daughters sold on the auction block. Rebecca's mother was a laundress, and her father, once freed, became a waiter and butler to a Washington, D.C. judge. Rebecca and her brother and sister attended Charlottesville's segregated Jefferson Elementary School that ended in the eighth grade. Her parents worked overtime to send their eldest daughter to Virginia's Hampton Institute to become a teacher.

Her alma mater awarded Rebecca McGinness an honorary doctorate degree on her 100th birthday. She straightened in her chair. "Training the heart, head and hand. I learned that at Hampton. Make the best of what you have. Turn it to use. That's my philosophy."

After graduating from Hampton in 1915, Rebecca McGinness put her philosophy to work. She returned to the Jefferson School where she taught all subjects to fifth and sixth graders in a school without running water or indoor plumbing. She bought students school supplies and "begged a piano" to teach music. She helped start a soup kitchen, held class devotions and didn't hesitate to raise a ruler to the unruly. She also taught youngsters to honor their African heritage. "They needed to know where they came from to know where they needed to go," said Mrs. McGinness. She now lived only a block from the Jefferson School, herself a key conservator of its heritage.

Rebecca's eyes narrowed in indignation recalling the offenses of the Jim Crow era—the segregation in Charlottesville hospitals, theaters, stores and the University of Virginia. "At a soda fountain, there was a white girl sitting a little above us. They brought her drink in a beautiful glass; they brought mine in a black cup. I asked why mine was different. 'It's what we serve colored folks,' she said. 'If we have to have a different one,' I said, 'then I won't drink from that cup.'"

Mrs. McGinness also stood her ground when told where to sit on the trolley. "There was one vacant seat next to a white gentleman. I sat down and he jumped up. He said, 'You can't sit here.' I said, 'Yes, I can,' and he pushed me off. The driver stopped the trolley. He said to the man, 'Sit quietly or you get off.' I sat down. I thought there was going to be a riot right there on the trolley," said Rebecca McGinness whose protest took place decades before Rosa Parks'. "I can tell you this, whatever good came to us in those years, we had to fight for it."

Mrs. McGinness worked for justice behind the scenes, joining women's clubs and service organizations: the League of Women Voters, the Eastern Star and the NAACP. She also fought for equality as one of an army of resolute African Americans teachers throughout the "Massive Resistance" of the 1950s, years when many black schools in Virginia remained open and white schools closed rather than integrate. After 45 years of teaching, she retired before integration became the law of the land. She was 68.

She left the classroom, but Rebecca McGinness never retired from her lifelong mission — teaching young African Americans the necessity of education and equality. She tutored children at home in her living room and at the kitchen table, holding court with neighbors, friends and former students.

"In large measure, I chose education as a profession because of the strong image of Mrs. McGinness and the other women who taught us," said Alicia Lugo, Rebecca McGinness's next-door neighbor and grade school student. "I remember the stream of students visiting from as far back as when she began her teaching career. That's a sign of a really good teacher when your old students show up to talk to you after 50 years and still have a tremendous respect and outpouring of concern."

Instead of losing status with her years, Mrs. McGinness gained ever more regard. She helped start a neighborhood association and was dubbed "the keeper of the village" without whom the past would be lost.

On her 100th birthday, Mrs. McGinness was applauded from the Hampton podium for "teaching several generations of students …

as master teacher and consummate professional ... and as our oldest living alumna, Rebecca Fuller McGinness continues to be an inspiration to all of us."

And as the years added up, Mrs. McGinness became the revered "mother of the church" at First Baptist Church which her grandparents helped to establish and she faithfully attended. She kept teaching and counseling youth groups. She nurtured friendships with the young.

During one morning's filming, a young white woman dropped by with her son and daughter, children of a man Mrs. McGinness had befriended at church when he was in trouble. At 97, she'd given him a home for six years. Today in her kitchen with fresh coffee brewing, she opened her arms and hugged them all. "Hi darlin. Hey, sugar boy." She laughed. "These are some of my family, part of my good works."

Together we leafed through family albums, creased and curling photos of Mrs. McGinness' other "children." "My Charlie," she said. "My nephew; I raised him. He died at Walter Reed from an injury in Korea. I raised two other boys, too. They called me mother. I was mother to a lot of children but didn't have one of my own."

Rebecca stopped at a sepia photograph of a child in pigtails. "A doctor at the hospital told us there was a little girl who had a heart condition and had been abandoned. He asked us if we'd like to take her in. The doctor said she had five years to live. She asked Mac, 'Will you be my daddy?'

"My husband was so devoted to our child. Virginia was a little angel. She loved the piano. I taught her the keys. We called her 'Piggy.' She had heart problems. I was walking back from the hospital from seeing her, and a few minutes later, they called that she'd died. She was only 20. It was so hard." And her loss still hurt.

Mrs. McGinness held up a photograph of her husband, Mac, a former tailor; he was smoking a cigar beside his rose bushes. "The Bible said 'cling to your husband ... he's part of you.' Your husband becomes part of you. Mac died February 1970 ... some 60 years to-gether." She closed the album. "I felt lost. Lost."

If lost after the deaths of her husband and children, Mrs. McGin-ness never retreated from the world. She opened to new ideas and objectives. "I'm interested in history. I like to ask questions; find out things," she said. "I like to see things, go places. After I retired, I went to Mexico, Canada, all across the country by train and bus. I would go now if I could."

A broken hip might have limited Mrs. McGinness's mobility, but she used her walker and remained self-sufficient by restructuring her dining room into a "bunk house" bedroom and renting upstairs rooms to a mother and daughter. They often stopped in the kitchen to see if she needed anything at the store. "No thank you," said Mrs. McGinness, quick to remind the young girl to "speak up and stand up straight."

Ever the taskmaster, Mrs. McGinness had outlived all of her fam-ily and peers — her brother and sister, her father who died at 95 and her grandmother at 98 — her endurance likely due to a firm will, hardy genes and healthy habits.

"I'm the last of my family; the last loaf of bread on the tray.... I can eat most anything. I love greens. The doctor said I don't need medication. I take one supplement a day," said Mrs. McGinness. An oversized carton of Special K stood on the shelf next to a half-empty bottle of Manischewitz's blackberry wine.

"I like wine, too. I was brought up on wine. We had grapes in our backyard." She smiled. "My grandmother made grape wine and always gave us some, especially when we had a cold. She'd throw us over in the feather bed and let us sweat it out."

I brought a bottle of Manischewitz to our next taping. We opened it as the sun set and slowly sipped the sweetness together. We took our time, letting the day disappear. We talked of how the town had changed, for the worse and for the better.

She'd watch the evening news and maybe a late movie. "I like old movies. John Wayne. I like police stories," she said. "I like to see how the law comes out. About one a.m., I drift off to sleep. I'm lucky I still have my right mind. I can't jump or dance, but I can still walk."

Maybe Rebecca McGinness could no longer jump or dance, but she sang and laughed and never spoke of being old. Initially intrigued by Mrs. McGinness' healthy longevity, I quickly found her an inspiration far beyond her years. She remained flexible, ever mindful of the past and its place in the present, her wisdom grounded in making the best decisions in the toughest times.

"The hymn said, 'Work 'til Jesus comes then we'll be gathered home.'" She laughed modestly. "As long as Jesus lets me live, I'm willing to take it. Then I'll be ready to go."

I wasn't ready to let Mrs. McGinness go and I missed seeing her during my father's last months. I was alarmed by a TV report of a fire in her house on Christmas Eve. Her phone was disconnected, but I was told she was safe and had moved to a neighbor's under a nurse's care.

After my father died, I visited Mrs. McGinness for a final interview. I found her fragile and subdued in a wheelchair by the window looking to her house down the street. "I wish I could go home," she said. "I'm sorry your father died."

I clicked off the camera. Rebecca McGinness gave me her hand and I held tight. With her own days diminishing, what did she now want to say? How did she want to be remembered?

"Just remember me as one woman who enjoyed life and gave it back to people ... to youngsters," she said. Then, Rebecca Fuller McGinness, still teaching, still making time count, her voice trembling, suddenly summoned strength she no longer had and sang what she believed: "Do something for somebody every day; do something for somebody all along the way." I held on.

A week later Mrs. McGinness was driven to the hospital, where she died peacefully on March 28, 2000. Her obituary read 107; some said she was 108.

The First Baptist Church filled full for her funeral. Well-wishers — white and black, old and young — passed silently by the open coffin shrouded in flowers. She seemed to be sleeping, patiently receiving those paying their last respects, blessed by her friendship, guidance and good sense.

I sat in the balcony as the pews crowded below to her most fitting hymn, "How Firm a Foundation." Today, I still hear her singing, "Do something for somebody every day; do something for somebody all along the way."

PASSIONATE PURPOSE

Twenty years from now you will be more
disappointed by the things that you didn't do than
by the ones you did do. So throw off the bowlines.
Sail away from the safe harbor. Catch the winds in
your sails. Explore. Dream. Discover. —Mark Twain

As my mentors fended off grief and loss with renewed creativity and direction, they heeded the observation of philosopher and psychologist G. H. Lewes: "The only cure for grief is action." These older people gradually distanced themselves from their pain; they persisted by incorporating their life losses into imaginative outlets that furthered their interests, often in invigorating and unforeseen ways.

While aging, they still anticipated discovery. They maintained their identities, consciously or unconsciously, moving forward and meeting new challenges.

Former *Washington Post* publisher Katharine Graham reasoned, "No one can avoid aging, but aging productively is something else."

When entertainer Eartha Kitt was asked the secret to her longevity—to say nothing of her still sexy voltage at 81—she said, "First you have to *want* to keep at it. Then you decide how best you will do it."

The late behavioral psychologist B.F. Skinner agreed: "Old age is a problem to be solved. A good time to think about old age is when you're young because you can then do much to improve your chances that you will enjoy it when it comes. Visiting a foreign country, prepare yourself before you go."

In *Why Survive? Being Old in America*, Dr. Robert Butler also pushed for planning. "We still must confront the fundamental existential questions concerning the purpose and meaning of life in old age. 'What are we to do in our old age? How should we conduct ourselves? How can we continue to be contributive and productive?'"

Dr. Butler, also founder of the Department of Geriatrics and Adult Development at the Mount Sinai Medical Center in New York, concluded in his longevity research that "Those individuals who had something to get up for in the morning — goals in life — lived longer and better than those who did not have any specific purposes or goals."

Howard S. Friedman and Leslie R. Martin confirmed such findings in *The Longevity Project*: "Striving to accomplish your goals, setting new aims when milestones are reached, and staying engaged and productive are exactly what those heading to a long life tend to do. The long-lived didn't shy away from hard work; the exact opposite seemed true."

Longevity researcher Margery Silver also documented that centenarians still setting and achieving goals fared best in their later years. "We found that the centenarians' common theme was having a purpose, whether through lifelong causes, religion or their families. Whatever they chose, it was important to have a feeling of contributing," said Silver, then retired as Assistant Professor in Psychology at Harvard Medical School.

"People also benefited from staying involved, being active and creative. A number of centenarians wrote their biographies; this is creative on two levels — the writing process and looking at their lives to make a cohesive story."

Dr. Silver's research found that formal education per se was not required for retaining intellectual skills in old age; it was important to challenge oneself mentally, learn new things and take risks. "People who take calculated risks, not necessarily without fear — show a willingness to proceed with things that are right for them. They have a basic belief that they can make things turn out well or deal with what comes. It's important to take the chance even if it may be very difficult. They're not afraid to be themselves. They are more authentic. You can't avoid the possibilities of what will happen so they ask, 'Why not go out there and enjoy your life?'"

Our friend Francis Harrison Fife at 95 trooped ahead as a self-effacing, on-the-scene political activist. The Charlottesville native and retired banker was moved to outrage in the 1960s by urban renewal plans that displaced African Americans from their Vinegar Hill neighborhood. He ran for City Council as an independent Democrat and lost, but ran again and was elected Mayor in 1972. During his eight years on Council, Fife worked with other councilors to get more African Americans and women elected.

Fife's fellow councilor and second wife, Nancy O'Brien, served as mayor from 1976 to 1978. Together, they kept working for fair housing as well as organizing and supporting local, state and national Democratic candidates. What kept Fife still involved in politics?

"Republicans!" Francis jested. "I felt there was always need for our society to change. A need for civil rights and for people to be treated as well as they should. We needed to encourage that (behavior) and better the community."

"Attitude towards aging is important," added Dr. Butler. "There are even data to suggest that happiness is kind of genetic. There may be a kind of fundamental character that is indelible, but there are also a lot of opportunities in aging to reinvent, to put out a second, third or fourth edition of the newspaper."

When she died at age 122 in 1997, Jeanne Calment of Arles, France, was considered "the world's oldest person." According to the Associated Press, Mrs. Calment "took up fencing at 88, and still rode a bike at 100. She liked her port wine, olive oil, her chocolate and her cigarettes, and she released a rap CD at 121." Calment's CD, "Time's Mistress," played her reminiscences to a score of rap and popular tunes.

In *Stay Young: 10 Proven Steps to Ultimate Health*, Dr. Mark Anderson and co-authors Dr. Walter and Judith Gaman cautioned readers to cultivate optimism because thinking negatively releases cortisol and other hormones that can cause aging, whereas positive thoughts create serotonin which helps increase sleep quality — a must to longevity.

"Yes, science suggests that it helps to have an optimistic point of view," said broadcast journalist Barbara Walters in an AARP interview. "It is the ability to accept loss. It is the ability to move on…. It would be lovely to feel that the older you got, the wiser you got. But I don't think that's necessarily so. It can make you very angry, very bitter. You can look back on your life and say, 'I've accomplished nothing.' Or you can say, 'I'm alive, and I'm well, and I'm going to try to do something.'"

So if a positive attitude is imperative to living long and well, when exactly should we face the facts and start setting new and productive goals? How old is old anyway? Some pundits and cartoonist even proclaim, "Seventy is the new 50." Good news for Baby Boomers.

When 102-year-old Mae Bishop, a former housekeeper at New York's Delmonico Hotel was asked her age, she replied, "Just past the 72nd anniversary of my 30th birthday."

Bernard Baruch, adviser to Presidents Wilson and Truman, once said, "To me, old age is always 15 years older than I am."

I'm with Baruch. After the death of my father, I felt officially elevated to senior status, an honor I preferred to postpone. Age in my family was always a bit of an anomaly. The fact that my mother was a year older than my father was seen as scandalous by her in-laws. She joked that she was "21 plus" and kept her driver's license where only she could find it.

I, too, was reluctant to volunteer my age, fearing the truth would somehow separate me from writing opportunities and younger friendships. Where was the ghost of that girl who'd tripped down the aisle in taffeta and lace, who'd once worn bikinis and eaten double bacon cheeseburgers? Where was the young reporter who arrived at work at 7 a.m. and later hoisted a child in each arm?

Who was this pale, gray-haired woman yawning back at me in the mirror? The one now invisible in shops that sold lingerie or stiletto heels? The same lady who was handed Medicare forms and senior movie tickets before being asked. The woman who was willing to accept an occasional seat on the bus, but winced when called "dear" or "honey" by a young doctor, nurse or dental hygienist.

To quote actress Debbie Reynolds, "I look in the mirror and everything has moved. Where did my body go?"

Jokes or reality, most of us push away from age, fearing our decline and finality. Old age means preparing for death.

Robert Fulghum, author of *All I Really Need to Know I Learned in Kindergarten*, wrote an essay in which he vowed to keep dancing, particularly the tango, as long as he could; then he'd be content to "pass on because there wasn't another dance left in me."

Attracted to Fulghum's sentiment, I wrote him for more thoughts on aging well. His reply: "[M]y attitude toward notions like 'aging,' 'retirement,' 'senior citizen' and 'old,' … those words are not in my active vocabulary and are absent from my thinking. I'm in my 79th year. My body is not exempt from the numbers, of course. But I am not old, don't do old, think old, act old, dress old, feel old, or live old. And I avoid old people. Thanks to resilient genes, I'm in good health and good shape, despite the onslaught of my often reckless lifestyle and habits.

"My life insurance agent had me take a life-expectancy test and it seems that I'm good to 93 plus years. My bucket list is long enough to not be checked off until well beyond that. If you asked me how old I was, if I didn't know or did not look in the mirror, I would say, without hesitation. I think about what I want to do with my life the same way as I always have — not as a way to accommodate or fulfill my remaining years."

Fulghum wrote in *Handbook for the Soul*, "The older I get, the more I realize the importance of exercising the various dimensions of my body, soul and heart. Taken together, these aspects give me a sense of wholeness. I want to be a whole human being rather than one who limps on one leg because I don't know how to use all my parts. Intellectual, emotional, and physical activity are not separate entities. Rather, they are dimensions of the same human being."

Dr. Butler, speaking from the Mount Sinai Medical Center, described "a new healthy old age which is more vigorous and robust" than old age as we typically think of it. People who stay healthy well into their eighties and beyond benefit from an improved diet, exercise, medication and a youthful outlook. "Old age begins when your health declines. From a practical point of view and from an individual's perception, when you begin to lose function is when you really begin to feel 'age;' when you have problems with mobility, vision and cognitive function. As long as you've got your health, you've got everything."

Dr. Ian Maclean Smith, Emeritus Professor in the Department of Internal Medicine University of Iowa Hospitals and Clinics, saw many older patients consciously *choose* active aging. "Such vital, active elderly people led me to conclude that disuse, not aging, is the cause of disability in the elderly. With this in mind, we can concentrate on prevention and the right frame of mind. I read in the medical literature that optimists live longer than pessimists. I'm sure this is true.

"It's been said that old age is the season of loss, but much of the loss is due to disuse. By active exercise and use of our faculties, the health record of the old-old can often be improved. Moreover, prevention of many of the disabilities of old age has not received enough critical research, and we must encourage more effort in this area with special emphasis on Alzheimer's disease."

The numbers of those working past the age of 65 also has reached new heights, and retirement is often postponed as life work goes on. Self-employment and entrepreneurship give us new opportunities for reinvention.

Syndicated columnist Ellen Goodman at 68 found that increasing numbers of Baby Boomers were still working, "more interested in renewal than retirement." Rather than competing with younger generation, they could be "mentors in the changing business of aging."

Golden Girls TV star Bea Arthur at 86 remarked, "People retire from jobs they don't like. Actors don't retire.... Don't miss the chance to sing."

"We are the lucky people who go on playing all of our lives. We think of work as play," said actor Gregory Peck in his daughter's documentary, *A Conversation with Gregory Peck.*

During the 2016 Virginia Film Festival, I scrambled for a front row seat to see on-stage interviews with actresses Shirley MacLaine and Liv Ullmann. Still provocative, funny and in charge, MacLaine at 82 had "four projects in the works." Topping the list was "The Last Word," a comedy-drama in which MacLaine played a retired businesswoman hell-bent to write her obituary as she wants her life to have been.

All in black accented with a gold silk vest, chains and necklaces, MacLaine was not above onstage flirtation. She wondered aloud why she'd never been hit on by her directors or leading men. In 2014, she starred with Christopher Plummer in *Elsa and Fred*, a romance that asked, "When does friendship end and love begin?"

Academy Award winner Shirley MacLaine still practiced her disciplined work ethic, rebuked an America that had become too materialistic, and held to her "metaphysical" doctrines.

"I believe in the laws of karma," said the author of *Out on a Limb*. "Energy returns to its source. What you put out, you will get back. You also have to be yourself. If you're really authentic, everything works. My philosophy is that your point of view, if authentic, leads to spirituality.

"Life itself is show biz. You're the actor, the director, the producer, set and costume designer, the financer of your own life. You are the star of your own production."

Liv Ullmann took questions after a screening of *Liv and Ingmar*, a documentary of her life with fabled director Ingmar Bergman. She had acted in over 40 films and numerous plays as well as directed and written scripts and memoirs. At 78, she was ethereal, honest and humorous, disarming and deeply serious. Her Nordic blue eyes shone unclouded and curls complimented a face free of makeup. "I'm not close to young anymore. And I'd prefer to be a storyteller rather than impersonate others," said Ullmann. She wanted to write, and maintain work with the Women's Refugee Commission which she co-founded in 1989 to protect women and children displaced by conflict and crisis.

Shifting from an admired acting career to introspection and service, Ullmann brought the audience into her quest. She spoke as if we were together in someone's living room. "We are all participants. What is life asking of *us*?

"I have been meeting friends in a discussion club for 25 years. We talk, listen and comment. One of the members recently said he had cancer and was going to die. He said, 'This is my last journey; it will be exciting.' He wrote down the dates of the next meetings. He did not come in November."

She peered into the dimmed theater. "Maybe there is a beautiful, exciting journey there. I want to use my life to see what direction awaits for my last travels. What is life asking from *me* now?"

Our later years can be a time of entrenchment or a time of

restoration and possibility. In 2013, endurance swimmer Diana Nyad at 64 made her fifth attempt at swimming 103 miles from Havana, Cuba, to Key West. A lifelong dream begun in 1978 was on record as Nyad swam ashore, the first person to make the marathon swim without a shark cage. She had three messages for reporters: "'One is we should never ever give up. Two is you are never too old to chase your dreams. Three is it looks like a solitary sport, but it's a team.'"

Two years earlier, Nyad was stopped halfway to her destination due to hazardous currents and jellyfish stings. Still, when I heard her speak in Key West, she hoped that her "quest might inspire others her age to begin energizing their lives with exercise.... People my age must try to live vital, energetic lives. We're still young. We're not our mothers' generation at 60." Her advice for those over 60: "Live a life with no regrets and no worries about what you are going to do with your time. Fill it with passion. Be your best self."

At 74, Althea Gibson finally made it onto the Wheaties box, her champion's profile long overdue. The first African American to win Wimbledon, the U.S. Open and the French Open had been energized over the last 30 years as "an ambassador of sports" to young New Jersey athletes. In 1998, she co-founded The Althea Gibson Foundation to introduce golf and tennis programs to further their opportunities.

Frank Finger, retired UVa psychology professor and former wrestling and cross-country coach, at 65, won the 200, 400 and 800 meter National Championships races. At 76, he held the world record for hurdles in the 75 to 79 age group. "I don't really feel old," said Finger, modest, smart, supple and strong. "I guess people think I am because of my age, but I don't ever feel it unless I am injured. I guess as long as I can keep my muscles intact, I'll keep running." Frank lived to 87, yet another role model for running and running and running the distance.

Most of us aren't super athletes or blessed with purpose that reaches the passionate, but hopefully we have a reserve of curiosity, and plentiful fuel to keep us contributing and pursuing our interests, hobbies and dreams. "I could not, at any age, be content to take my place by the fireside and simply look on," said Eleanor Roosevelt. "Life was meant to be lived. Curiosity must be kept alive. One must never, for whatever reason, turn his back on life."

Foregoing the fireside, it was time to start planning the next decades, to mind psychologist B. F. Skinner's warning to prepare for a fulfilling later life without regret.

As Sadie Delany, famous for *Having Our Say: The Delany Sisters' First 100 Years,* reminded me: "Life is short. It's up to you to make it sweet."

Before her last bon mot, I saw Julia Child whipping up a final chocolate soufflé. I loved her zest for all things culinary and copied her example as a flip-it-off-the-floor-and-into-the-pot kind of cook. I also believed in her liberal use of butter, sugar and cream.

I rooted for Julia, chest-high in fishing waders, studiously taking instruction from a Norwegian salmon guide on a PBS special. She zipped her line over and over into the rolling river with no results. When finally dismissed to the grill for preparation of the guide's catch, Julia thanked him profusely. She sloshed ashore declaring, "A merciful end to the sporting day!" An angler after my own heart.

She turned down an interview request, wishing me "success," as she moved from Cambridge, Massachusetts, back to her childhood domain of San Francisco. In 2000, she said in *Esquire,* "I don't believe in heaven. I think when we die we just go back to the great ball of energy that makes up the universe."

I'd continue my journey with Child's apt dictum taped to the refrigerator: "Life itself is the proper binge."

I would be fortunate to meet role models who'd consciously chosen productive paths, men and women who had few regrets and considered successful aging lucky as well as an achievement and a privilege. Many, like Eartha Kitt, astutely understood what made them happy and how to keep at it. They wrote poetry, joined political causes and collaborated in creative endeavors. They set new goals or furthered their life's work; they overcame barriers; they tried the unexpected or cultivated fresh opportunities in established careers. They put force to their ambitions. They realized dreams they hadn't conceived earlier. They spoke out, worked out and kept entertaining in style.

They agreed not to waste years wondering what might have been. Stretch your skills and venture on to the undiscovered. Focus on what's still to be and fulfill your purpose with passion.

PHOTO BY PAUL CHILD, SCHLESINGER LIBRARY, RADCLIFFE INSTITUTE, HARVARD UNIVERSITY

Julia Child, Chef/Author

PHOTO BY ELIZABETH HOWARD

Richard Wilbur, Poet

When one thing won't work, there's something
else I can pick up or turn to.
I just like just fooling around with words.

12

Using Variety and Play To Expand Creativity

POET RICHARD WILBUR, A NEIGHBOR on our first Key West visit, once joked that the Wilburs lived long and well and then one day they just keeled over. When I'd last seen Dick he was still defying gravity biking past the graveyard, gingerly missing two strutting roosters. By then, the former Poet Laureate and two-time winner of the Pulitzer Prize, had outlived his friends on Windsor Lane — poet John Ciardi and writers John Hersey and Ralph Ellison.

At 80, Dick remained lofty as a royal palm, still concentrating on what was to be. I found him busy repotting plants on his deck hidden in tropical greenery. Hummingbirds hovered over the red and orange hibiscus. The French doors opened to the balmy air. Dick's wife, Charlee, rested upstairs, her knees now stiffened with arthritis.

Richard Purdy Wilbur was born in New York City on March 1, 1921. His father, a commercial artist and portrait painter, died at 79, and his mother, a hardy descendant of journalists, died in her late 80s.

"My father did look very boyish until the cigarettes got him. He was destined to be older because my family on both sides has an awful lot of long drawn-out aging and dying," said Dick.

"My mother was a woman of great nervous energy. She came from a long line of other such nervous people. Mother never walked anywhere; she always trotted. My parents had a lot of energy and they had a good time. They also had extraordinary innocence and, no doubt, that helps. They could make a game out of a snowstorm. They didn't have a lot of dreads or bad expectations in life. Their innocence was helpful to them on many counts."

Dick inherited his parents' exuberance as well as their love of play if not innocence. For now, work awaited on Wilbur's desk under the window, his yellow pad and pens neatly aligned next to the manual typewriter.

"I'm happy that I've always written different things. When one thing won't work, there's something else I can pick up or turn to. I like just fooling around with words. Word play," said Dick. "Crossword puzzles. I don't write poems all the time. You write the ones that have to be written. I better get going (writing more poems)." Wilbur had published eight volumes of poetry, his last, *Collected Poems: 1943–2004. Anterooms: New Poems and Translations* was published in 2010.

Cordial, urbane, prudent and patrician, Dick also wrote essays, verse dramas, translations and lyrics, including ones for Leonard Bernstein's *Candide.*

"Actually there's something to be said for having variety and diversity. And having something that you do well and truly enjoy doing. Something which gives pleasure to other people. I think that can contribute to longevity."

His new satisfaction was anagrams, word play he'd begun in childhood and perfected with his Key West writer friends. "This week, I'm pleased to have found 'ermine' contained in 'undermine,' to have found 'ape,' hidden within 'trapeze,' and 'pig' within 'spigot.'" Dick's recent finds were designed for more playful books and drawings dedicated to his three grandchildren. He and Charlee had three sons and a daughter.

His talent for pen and ink illustrations had once made Wilbur consider becoming a newspaper cartoonist. His amusing drawings and poems were now paired in *Opposites, More Opposites and A Few Differences*, a slim volume sparked by another Wilbur family game — who would be first to find the perfect antonym:

What is the opposite of string?
It's gnirts, which doesn't mean a thing.
and
What is the opposite of nuts?
It's soup! Let's have no ifs or buts.
In any suitable repast
The soup comes first, the nuts come last.
Or that is what sane folks advise
You're nuts if you think otherwise.

"Even though my children are all grown up, humor allows me to commune with their former selves. It's nice to keep the child part of yourself going," said the former English professor at Harvard, Wellesley, Wesleyan and Smith colleges.

Wilbur's wry humor and his ability to identify and describe his fears undoubtedly lessened his apprehensions. "I'm sure being verbal and writing poems about things is always very fortifying. If you can name what it is that scares you, it gives you a certain control over it. There's nothing worse than a nameless dread.

"When G. K. Chesterton spoke of 'the descent in death,' he was probably happily defusing the idea of mortality.... I suppose it's a matter of temperament and some kind of childish trust in things, but I don't feel any dread of death so don't write gothic poems about the subject. I think the dark subjects that I may deal in are inherently upbeat."

As a World War II staff sergeant, Dick had survived combat in France and Italy and knew something of death. "One advantage of getting older is that you have been through it before; though it doesn't do very much good, you can tell yourself that you will come out of it, that you will write again, and therefore you can stay somewhat this side of despair."

Did he consciously write poems about death? Did such poems dissipate despair?

"I guess anybody past 80 better have some consciousness of those things. I'm sure that [mortality] got into poems in which I had no intention to project any sense of my own age and coming dissolution. For example, 'Zea' is primarily a poem about corn. You drive past a cornfield in fall, and if they haven't cut it all down you see one crazy little leaf that's still going. A friend read it at funeral and made me aware of having borne one's fruit, done one's work, feeling a kind of relief and lightness as a consequence, gradually becoming ready to be whatever that little leaf stands for. Other poems also have that sense of things coming to a close."

If sensing *things coming to a close*, did Dick then link the roles of poetry and religion?

"'Poetry and religion are sisters but not twin sisters,'" Dick quoted his friend and mentor, Robert Frost. "I don't think I'd want the distinctions between poetry and religion to be erased. Much of the time poetry is not making any affirmations even though the whole flavor of any poem is likely to be positive and upbeat. It just can't help being. One job of any artist is to see how fair the creation is.

"The task of poetry is to rescue us from inarticulateness, giving us words which are adequate to the world and to our hearts. If you are a serious poet, it's a task in which you try to use all of the words for experience — to do justice both to the good and to the bad, the dark and the light. When you say dreadful things and say them very well, there's a kind of high morale in that. It's fortifying. Poetry can help people whose main business is not words to find words for what they feel and be liberated. I hope I will be visited by some poems again soon."

Until then, Dick characterized himself as a slow and patient worker. As someone committed to order, Wilbur upheld the forms of traditional poetry while advocating for creativity within prescribed meters and norms. "I think it's very important to keep taking risks in the arts. You have to be surprised by what you do or you really won't see any reason to go on with it.

"I think one thing that almost all artists consciously do is celebrate the world. In that sense, a poem is a high moment of control and understanding, of finding the right words for things. Every writer wants to record transcendent moments as well as to record absolutely daily and everyday awareness. Words are a large part of the pleasure for any writer who wants to get it right. I hope not to find my vocabulary diminishing and my memory failing. That could be a bother."

The 2003 Key West Literary Seminar, "The Beautiful Changes," honored Wilbur's command of words. His poem's title extolled beauty's power to amaze and transform.

> ...Your hands hold roses always in a way that said
> They are not only yours; the beautiful changes
> In such kind ways,
> Wishing ever to sunder
> Things and things' selves for a second finding, to lose
> For a moment all that it touches back to wonder.

Wilbur's reading brought us to our feet. "It happens that I like performing poetry..." he said in an 1999 *Atlantic* interview. "Initially

I had hysterical sore throats and muttered at my audiences, but I have gotten to be, within my limits, a showman, and I do enjoy that. I also enjoy being able to do something with the important feelings of my life. I think that to be inarticulate can be a great suffering, and I'm glad that my loves, and my other feelings, have sometimes found their way into poems that fully express them."

The performer added a postscript. "If what you do is regarded as having social value, then you have the backing of other people; I think that also can contribute to longevity. Unless for health reasons you're somehow taken out of the action, you have impetus; if you don't lose your eyesight or find that your feeling for words is impaired, you have an ongoing life. You have something that need not stop. I know people start dying when boredom overtakes them, and they don't have that sense of being needed. I wouldn't really know who I was unless I was writing on some front or other."

Wilbur's writing won him the 2006 Ruth Lilly Poetry Prize, awarded to a living US poet whose "lifetime accomplishments warrant extraordinary recognition." The $100,000 prize is considered "among the most prestigious awards that can be won by an American poet."

Dick, still ebullient at 88, was asked if he was an optimist by nature. "If an optimist is somebody who thinks everything will come out all right, I'm not," he said. "But, if it's optimistic to think that the world is fundamentally a great wonder and a great order, yes, I subscribe to those things." At 92, he was teaching at Amherst College.

The morning we met, Dick rose to check his herbs flowering in the cool sun. He anticipated digging in his garden at home in Cummington, Massachusetts. "I want to get the seeds in for an early planting. I still enjoy tramping in the woods and love to use a shovel."

And Dick still moved with certain grace, a gentleman whose formality, refinement and emotional honesty became him. "After my hip operation it took me quite a while to be unconscious of walking and walking rather trippingly," he said. "I've always liked — although I'm not a particularly good dancer — the feeling of good footwork. I've always loved a certain amount of rock climbing and jumping from rock to rock.... My confidence, my pleasure in locomotion has now come back."

PHOTO BY ELIZABETH HOWARD

Gordon Parks, Photographer

One has to take risks, experiment with possibilities....

13

Choosing the Right Weapon

"THIS WAY!" GORDON PARKS SHUFFLED SLOWLY, waving me onto the 18th floor of United Nations Plaza, suited in white sneakers, chinos, a sapphire blue warm-up jacket, and his baseball cap cocked backwards. He raised his "breakfast smoothie" in a Princeton beer stein.

Cozy and casual and maybe not how I'd imagined photojournalist, poet, novelist, filmmaker, composer, fashion and portrait photographer Gordon Parks. His most famous photograph, "American Gothic, Washington, D.C.," posed a black cleaning woman at attention with mop and broom before the American flag in the halls of government. I'd hoped somehow our paths would cross since seeing his 1977 retrospective "Half Past Autumn: The Art of Gordon Parks" at Washington's Corcoran Gallery.

On a clear afternoon in June 2003, I was keyed up, pleased to finally meet Parks at his New York apartment — thanks to his business manager, right hand, trusted ally and photographer Johanna Fiore. She'd shot many portraits of Parks including the book cover of *Half Past Autumn*. Johanna let me know on arrival that Parks, now 90, was up for a visit but that my time would be limited.

Parks spoke close to a whisper, a rich blend of sugar and salt. I moved closer to share his airborne view of the East River and the U.N. gardens below. Books, like dominoes, rimmed the floor and crowded the shelves: *The World of Allah, Allure, Lovers, The Great Jazz Day, Land of the Free, A True Likeness.* Mirrored panels reflected paintings by Dufy and Chagall, as well as Matisse bronze dancers and Parks' photographs — a street orphan, and doves blurred in flight. "Both were shot in South America. I had the camera pointed towards the dove. It malfunctioned, double-exposed. The dove flew away and the second exposure was where the dove had been standing against the wall. See the wall?" He waited. "As far as I'm concerned, my most beguiling photographs were taken by accident."

Life magazine's 2003 commemorative issue, *100 Photographs That Changed the World*, lay unopened. It included many of Parks' captivating and less than accidental photographs, the most famous, "American Gothic" and "Flavio," a tubercular boy "already old," balancing on one leg on his bed in the slums of Rio de Janeiro. "Flavio" was also chosen for *Life: 75 Years* in which Parks was described as a photographer who "shot wide and then bore in."

Parks was hired in 1948 as *Life's* first African American photographer. His ability to *bore in* drew immediate attention with a photo essay on Harlem gang wars featuring Red Jackson, a rough, young leader. During his next 20 years at *Life*, Parks' powerful images documented urban crime and the Civil Rights movement. He exposed hardship on the faces of Maine migrant farmers, grease plant workers, waterfront stevedores, welfare mothers and their children. He captured dramas of the famous — Ingrid Bergman scandalizing in Stromboli; Eldridge Cleaver exiled in Algiers; Malcolm X and Muhammad Ali, raising their fists in protest.

"My camera was my choice of weapons against racism and poverty. I could have easily picked up a knife or gun like many of my childhood friends did. I felt I could somehow subdue these evils by doing something beautiful that people would recognize me by and make a whole different life for myself. It's proved to be so."

Gordon Roger Alexander Buchanan Parks was born on November 30, 1912, the son of a dirt farmer in Fort Scott, Kansas. "I'm my father's 15th child, my mother's tenth. I was the youngest of all the family."

Photographs of Gordon's parents in Victorian dress were coupled in black enamel frames between a vase of dried roses. "We lived in a two-bedroom, clapboard house. The girls all slept in one room, the boys in another. I went to segregated schools and all that sort of the thing … the hardships that went along with racism and discrimination in small-town Kansas."

The words of Gordon's white school counselor still stung. "Mrs. McClintock was an advisor for the black kids. She used to tell us — and I think she was being honest with us — we shouldn't waste our parents' money going to college because we were all going to wind up as porters and waiters. That hurt some of the kids very badly. I didn't do what she advised, which was just finish high school and let that suffice. I decided to let her advice skip over my head." He smiled, his lips turned down.

Instead, young Gordon took the challenge of his upstanding Methodist mother, Sarah. "My mother was the type who wouldn't allow me to come home with any excuses for not being successful because I was black or harassed. She said, 'If a white boy can do it, you can do it and you'd better or don't come home.'" Gordon was only 15 when his mother died in her late fifties.

"Before my mother died, she'd asked my father to get me outta Fort Scott. Get me to St. Paul, Minnesota, where my sister lived with the gentleman she'd married. And that's what he did. A couple of hours after she was buried, my father took me to Minnesota. My sister's husband didn't like kids. We didn't get along very well. They eventually kicked me out in the snow at 35 degrees below zero just before Christmas."

Parks reevaluated his abrupt eviction. "I was on my own. All of my brothers and sisters were scattered out there in the world somewhere. That's when I think I realized that survival came from working hard. Whatever you want in the world somehow or another comes to you through hard work."

Gordon had not finished high school and scraped to find profitable work. He began as a day laborer. He played piano in a brothel, joined a semi-pro basketball team and waited tables in the club car of the North Coast Limited. "Those early days," he said, "I worked to endure, not yet knowing my purpose. A lot of things chose me instead of me choosing them. Like music. I started playing the piano when I was nine years old. Later on, I picked up photography by accident; music and writing by accident. All that came through happenstance. They all fit together. Photography wasn't something that I was just driving for at the beginning. Photography, music and writing were something that would give me a hot dog the next day. That was it."

Parks inherently knew when to grab an opportunity. At age 25, Parks saw a distressing photograph of migrant workers that prompted him to take his own pictures and to buy his first camera — a Voightlander Brilliant — for $7.50 at a Seattle pawnshop. He started shooting.

Parks' first paid photography was for a women's clothing store in St. Paul. Marva Louis, wife of heavyweight boxing champion Joe Louis, spotted his fashion photos and advised Parks to advance his career in Chicago. Soon he was shooting portraits of Chicago's white society women and taking photos of poor black people in the South Side.

In 1941, work shown in the South Side Exhibition earned Parks a photography fellowship with the Farm Security Administration, a Depression-era government agency in Washington, D.C. F.S.A. boss Roy Stryker urged his first black photographer to aim his camera boldly against bigotry. Parks — along with photographers Walker Evans and Dorothea Lange — were assigned to document and educate viewers about poverty and discrimination, especially in the rural South. Parks shot with conscience and compassion. His FSA iconic image, "American Gothic," gained fame for its duality of victim and survivor.

While quiet-spoken, Parks was never the victim. In 1944, fed up with discrimination in Washington, he moved to Harlem. He took his varied portfolio to *Harper's Bazaar*. "'It's beautiful but we've got a problem,'" said the editor, 'This organization is owned by Hearst and they don't hire black people to even sweep the floor.' So I said, '*You've* got a problem; I don't have a problem.' I walked out. Edward Steichen sent me over to see Alexander Lieberman (editorial director) at *Vogue* and they said, 'We're going to give you a chance.' And they did. So it depends upon individuals in charge."

Vogue sent Parks to Paris. Dior, Galanos and Balenciaga were among the haute couture designers appreciative of his flair for fluid, artistic scenarios, "moving with the models at slow speed" as they strolled the Seine, Montmartre and the Rue de La Paix.

"No black photographers ever worked for *Vogue*, before or since." Parks remained dismayed. "I took my family with me to Paris for a couple of years. If I had good enough material, I could walk in any place and show it and expect to be accepted. I didn't let my blackness bother me.

"If you're going to live among human beings, which we're placed here to do by God on this planet, you give yourself to people who you want respect from. You don't spend your time hating people because they're not worth it. You rid yourself of them and go do what you have to do. Be with people you can learn to love no matter who they are, no matter what color they are. That's the way I've survived." Parks' eyes like black onyx — the gemstone to sharpen wits and ward off negative thinking — fixed on what mattered most.

"My brother Leroy died young. He used to call me Pedro. He passed some words to me before he died: 'Pedro, you can't whip the world with your fists, you have to do it with your heart.'

"Even though I may have been surrounded by racism when I was a kid growing up, I could still find beauty in nature around me. I'd go in my father's cornfield and hear June bugs and think they were a symphony orchestra. I'd never heard of a symphony, but they were my first symphony. June bugs buzzing in the cornfield. When you live around wonderful people like I did in my family, you saw beautiful things."

Sitting peacefully beside Parks, I heard a healing harmony as gulls and terns dipped and dove by his window. He watched the tides roll on the East River remembering his 1952 arrival in Paris, "seduced" by its beauty and kindred artists, writers and musicians. "I met (Alberto) Giacometti in Paris. We used to go and have flageolets and veal livers on the Left Bank. We had a great friendship going. His English wasn't the best and my French wasn't the best. We got along." A Giacometti nude statue — shadow thin and stripped to its elemental core — stood dusty on the windowsill.

In Paris, Parks also met composers Maurice Ravel and Erik Satie and began writing his own musical compositions. His first "Concerto for Piano and Orchestra" was performed in Venice in July 1952 with the celebrated African American conductor Dean Dixon.

Although Parks' photography career and musical interests flourished in Paris, his 28 year marriage to Sally Avis ended. With downcast gaze he said their split was caused by "too much time apart." Parks first married at 21 and then again at 50 to Elizabeth Campbell. Their 11-year marriage ended in 1973.

This charming suitor married a third time to Genevieve Young, his editor for *The Learning Tree*. His racially charged, autobiographical, coming-of-age story was set in 1920s Kansas. Parks adapted his 1964 novel to film, the first Hollywood studio movie to be written and directed by an African American. He later launched the successful detective "blaxploitation" series, *Shaft*. Its "Don't Misunderstand" score lay on the blond Bechstein grand piano, a gift from Genevieve whose photo clustered with others in their silver frames.

Gordon confided that although they were "amicably divorced,"

Genevieve had modeled for *A Star for Noon: An Homage to Women in Images, Poetry and Music* — his nude studies in devotion to the female form. "I wanted to do something different, and get away from documentary work for awhile." He laughed. "There's nothing wrong with beautiful women. I think they're God's gift to earth."

Parks set his sensuous images against his own nature backdrops accompanied by his poems and musical compositions. Not deterred by age, Parks found new ways to cross-pollinate his talents. "I was recently working at photography and I'd just finished a novel — *The Sun Stalker* based on the life of famous English painter, J.M.W. Turner — when I realized that what Turner was saying to me was, 'If nature has not provided you with a backdrop for what you're doing, create it yourself.'"

Seeking music for his book's companion CD, Parks took to the piano. "The conductor said, 'Why don't you play this particular piece? You have more feeling than the ordinary pianist since you composed it.'" He smiled, remembering.

"I said, 'I don't know.' I practiced it for about an hour and recorded with the orchestra. It all came together.... I listened to my favorite composers, Rachmaninoff, Satie, Debussy, while reading and automatically something of my own popped up into the picture."

Parks also composed *Tree Symphony* and composed and choreographed *Martin*, a ballet honoring Martin Luther King, Jr. He'd performed with the National Symphony at the Kennedy Center in Washington and was collaborating on a composition with cellist Yoyo Ma. "When I have nothing to do, I feel lost. When things die down at the computer or typewriter, I go to the piano and compose."

If he were to shoot more photographs, what would they be?

"It's difficult to say. Pictures have to come to you. Providence sort of plans for you to see a particular thing and there it is looking at you in the face. I'd probably photograph the homeless; photograph the evils in the world *and* the good things about the world that I see."

Parks still looked for the dark and the light and listened for the buzz of those June bugs. "One has to take risks; experiment with possibilities. It might be risky but gives you some excitement; risk keeps your pulse regulated."

At only 52, Parks published *A Poet and His Camera*. His poem, "Old Age," ran beside the photograph of an elderly woman sitting in a medieval doorway, her head lowered and hands clasped.

Old Age
Snow covers the autumn leaf.
Time has granted me full cycle. I know
The wintry anguish of hunger, sickness —
                              family loss.
And more than once, man's ignobleness scraped
                              my heart, but
I don't cut easily to raw edges of things now.
I look back, without sadness, without nostalgia.
The full passion of living struck the balance.
This season, eternal, inevitable, signals
The coming of yet another. The end is not the end,
                              but
The whole purpose of the beginning. So,
These leaves mix with earth to nourish others.
                    And when snow is gone
They become the shade of another spring.
copyright & courtesy The Gordon Parks Foundation

Three decades later Parks told a reporter: " I have a constant feeling that I must not fail. I feel at 85 that I am just ready to start. There's another horizon out there, one more horizon that you have to make for yourself and let other people discover it. *'Half Past Autumn'* has arrived.... If you live a decent, honorable life, you'll die decently, honorably. I hope to at least, anyway."

Parks celebrated his 90th birthday with 90 African Americans photographers gathered on Harlem's 126th Street near where he once lived. He was photographed stepping from a black limousine as friends sang "Happy Birthday."

Beside his birthday photo on the grand piano were those of his four children. Parks' eldest son, Gordon, Jr., front and center, wore a flight suit. He'd also been a photographer and filmmaker; he died in a plane crash in 1981 at age 44.

"Depression drops over you," said the steadfast soldier. "You have to be careful that it doesn't take advantage of you. You don't want to wake up in the morning or go to sleep with it. You have to work at it. You have to do things that will make depression disappear for hours at a time because it creeps back in on you.

"I've never had to realize I was 90 before. It suddenly dawned upon me that 90 means you've been around quite a while.

"Some days, you wake up and feel like 21, some days you wake up and feel like 121. You choose the smaller number. You know, age slips up on you. When I was 87, I wouldn't have thought seriously about becoming 90. The new book I'm doing is based on another party, one people gave me across the way, on my 89th birthday. I came home and couldn't sleep. In my dream, I kept seeing the big number 90 pop up into the darkness. I thought 'what is this?'

"I guess I'd had too many red wines. Out of that, I started the book that's now about 500 double spaced pages. My working title is *The Hungry Table Cloth*. The tablecloth is for learning — vast, wide and hungry. All the things that I've attempted to do."

And choosing to feel younger, Parks held to his creativity and family affections. "I'm not saying these are the happiest moments in your life, certainly, but I'm fortunate to have five great-grandchildren, five grandchildren, a wonderful son and daughter, wonderful relatives and three ex-wives who still love me." Parks cuddled his grinning grandson in a photograph signed, "We love you, Pepe."

More photographs evidenced Parks' constant devotions — Qubilah-Bahiyah Shabazz, his godchild and Malcolm X's daughter; actress Dina Merrill, socialite designer Gloria Vanderbilt arm in arm with Gordon in tuxedo and bow tie in gala surroundings.

I'd often spotted Parks with many a lady in the *New York Times'* "Evening Hours," snapshots at spiffy art, theater and opera openings. "I gather women play an important role in your life?"

"Rather." He was fast to flirt.

I was ready to step out on the town with this reputed "Renaissance man."

"People spin the word Renaissance on me. I don't feel it. I've done a lot of things. I suppose that qualifies me, but I don't claim the word myself. I daresay I haven't learned how to spell it."

"Claim it anyway."

"Mind if I smoke? I smoke one a day."

"Take two."

Parks lit a Marlboro. "I got a lot of exercise. Tennis. Skiing." He conceded to high blood pressure and injuries to his Achilles tendons. "I don't sleep on pillows. But the main thing is you go on and work. I just want to do what I've been doing only better."

Parks stayed frisky and prepared to play. This contented but competitive man with the sleepy voice had known anger, shame and fury. He'd grown wise and patient shaped by shrewd decisions, decency and a deep respect for those he photographed and rightly trusted him to show their lives without sentimentality. He'd shown us the faces of despair, longing and hope.

I hoped Gordon Parks' school counselor had seen her former student's work exhibited around the world, and heard he'd received many honorary doctorates, his 50th recently from Princeton. He couldn't resist the irony. "I'd like to have handed Mrs. McClintock my degrees. I realized I've come quite a distance."

Johanna, friend and protector, returned. "Ten more minutes," she warned.

Parks whispered, "It's OK."

"May I quickly take your picture?" I couldn't believe I'd asked.

"I don't look presentable." Parks straightened his Princeton baseball cap. "Tell me where to sit."

"How about at the piano?"

Parks stepped to the piano bench, a still cool contender in front of the gold leaf and red lacquer screen on which Chinese women danced in flowing kimonos. His nails neat, his long fingers caressed the keys. His tender touch played smooth and mellow. I shot twice and prayed I had Gordon Parks in focus.

"The light's better by the window," he said. I fumbled with my Pentax, wanting Parks' coaching, wanting to do him right. He stepped into the natural light, allowing me a full, candid shot, unblinking; he was back at work teaching his not so young student how to see.

My time was up. Johanna, his defender and watchdog, plucked the Marlboro from Parks' lips. "What can you do?" she asked. He rolled his eyes and we all laughed together.

Weeks later, I received a special delivery in the mail — Parks' print of *Ingrid Bergman at Stromboli, 1949*. His handsome photograph hangs in my hall, a gift beyond measure and constant reminder of Gordon Parks' generosity on that June day high above the river.

Gordon Parks died at home in New York City on March 7, 2006. He was 93.

PHOTO BY KONSTANTIN

Edward Koch, Former New York Mayor

*I believe you should still be relevant
and live your life to the max.*

14

Staying Relevant

IN HIS BOISTEROUS MEMOIR, *I'm Not Done Yet! Keeping at It, Remaining Relevant and Having the Time of My Life,* former New York Mayor Edward Irving Koch ordered readers to "Stay relevant and live life to the max!" No small order from a man who'd survived a stroke, heart attack and quadruple bypass surgery.

I'd seen Koch working the crowds at city street fairs and gallery openings and was once dwarfed at his side in a too-tight elevator. When we actually met, Koch — a swell in starched blue shirt and striped suspenders — was reading the *New York Times* in his law office within dancing distance of Radio City Music Hall. He didn't look up from behind his desk or rush to finish the *Times*, showing me PDQ how to remain relevant.

"So what's your question?" Koch demanded. Maybe not the Dalai Lama, but role models come in sundry guises, right? We clicked on our tape recorders in unison.

"I've read that many people who live to 100 do so by staying involved. You've said it's important to remain relevant. How have you done it?'"

Koch jumped in. "I have no desire to live to 100. None at all. My father lived to 87. That seems like a good age. I'm prepared to go tomorrow if God wants me to join him. The reason: I've enjoyed my life. Done what I wanted to do."

And was still doing. At 77, pugnacious Koch, besides practicing law, tweeted, wrote movie and restaurant reviews, columns and books — four of them Manhattan mysteries, 13 others on the world according to Koch, including *Mayor* (1984) to *Buzz: How to Create It and Win With It* (2007). He'd taught, lectured and presided as judge on TV's *The People's Court*. He'd hosted a radio talk show, endorsed products and co-starred with Minnie the Elephant in a commercial welcoming visitors of all political parties to New York. This lifelong Democrat endorsed Hillary Clinton for Senator in 2000 and also stumped for three ranking Republicans: New York mayors Rudy Giuliani in 1993, Michael Bloomberg in 2001, and President George W. Bush in 2004.

No slouch when it came to the spotlight, Koch also played himself in walk-on screen roles including *The Muppets Take Manhattan* and *Sex and the City*. The 2013 documentary *Koch* examined his political career, the good, the bad and the belligerent. He was censored for racial slurs and party scandals and commended for housing redevelopment and bringing the city back from the fiscal brink.

Koch ran as "a liberal with sanity" when elected to New York's City Council in 1966. He served nine years as a Democratic Congressman from Greenwich Village prior to election as mayor in 1977. The city's 105th mayor remained contentiously in charge until December 1989. During his term, Koch dealt with drugs and rising crime, restored parks and added thousands of affordable apartments for low and moderate income residents. In 1982, he ran for governor and lost. He left the mayor's office in 1990 at the age of 66, making it clear that he had no plans to move to the country and raise chickens.

Koch closed in on 80, resolute, pushing his platform and venting sharp political views on anti-semitism, racism, terrorism, Israeli and US relations, and overdue trade with Cuba.

"I send my letters and think they have impact. I think what I do best is educate. I like to think I enlighten people with the facts. I'm doing everything I want to do and taking on the bullies of the world; no fisticuffs. There are opportunities to join in the good fight, to help people in their needs. Sometimes the reason for their plight is that there's someone standing between them and justice."

In 2010, the *New York Times* reported Koch putting his political bluster to New York Uprising, a group "to shame — and oust — [Albany] lawmakers he labeled, 'enemies of reform.'"

Born in the Bronx on December 12, 1924, the second of three children credited his Jewish immigrant parents for his work ethic and activism. His father was a furrier and partner in a shop that closed in the Depression. His mother ran a hatcheck concession. "My mother constantly worked to make her condition in life better. When she was young, she had come over from Poland; she had an accent; she couldn't write English. After she had her third child, she hired a tutor to teach her to read and write English and to lose her accent. And she did. That's something that stuck with me all my life.

"My father had two jobs all his life. A hard-working man. I'm hard working," said Koch, in case I hadn't noticed. At age nine, he too checked coats and hats in a Newark dancehall. Later, he clerked in a deli and attended Newark's South Side High School where he was president of the debating society. He worked as a shoe salesman when attending Manhattan's City College. "While it's always better to have an income from your work, if that's not doable, then be a volunteer. I believe it's exceedingly important not to retire." I got his gist.

"My advice is to young people — if you don't like your job, get out of it. Don't wait until your obligations are so great that you can't get out of it. Do it now. I believe you should still be relevant and live your life to the max. Provide your energy with the outlet of doing as much good as you can before God takes you."

Not rushing the finale, Koch ticked off his close calls — hospitalizations for pneumonia, an enlarged prostate, heart attack, angioplasty and stroke. In 2009, he underwent quadruple bypass surgery and replacement of his aortic valve. "Stroke is the scariest thing imaginable as you're lying there in the hospital bed," he said to dramatic effect. "I remember discussing in my head my fate with God. I happen to be a believer in God. I said, 'Take me whenever you want to. I have no fear of death. But if you're gonna take me ultimately, don't take me in salami tactics, a little at a time. It's all at once or not at all.'"

Koch's reasoning worked for me. He'd worn a pacemaker ever since he collapsed with an irregular heartbeat in 1991, and now walked, watched his diet and worked out daily with a personal trainer. "I don't like exercise but I do it. I'd like to lose weight. I avoid cheese and bagels, and I'm the best tunafish (salad) maker in America — chopped onion, mayonnaise, balsamic vinegar, salt and pepper. That's it." He smacked his hands eager to eat.

The peppery, plugged in press personality explained that he woke early to join the hubbub. "I get up at 5:30; I don't go to bed before midnight. I don't need much sleep. I take a catnap for 10 minutes. I wake up refreshed." In 2011, Koch wrote *Eddie Shapes Up*, a semi autobiographical children's book that he claimed was intended "to help children understand the importance of a healthy diet and exercise through their lives."

Maybe those catnaps were the secret. Along with a combative, contradictory ego and urgent engagement in all things Manhattan. His fierce love of the city and a chance to chat up its citizens kept Koch riding the buses and subways and going to the streets to exchange political and personal perspectives.

As a bachelor, Koch refused to address his private life and sexuality. In 1989, he co-authored *His Eminence and Hizzoner: A Candid*

Exchange: Mayor Edward Koch and John Cardinal O'Connor. The Cardinal fought city and state legislation ensuring homosexuals' civil rights, including legislation supported by Koch as Mayor, which prohibited discrimination in employment, housing, and public accommodations.

"I happen to believe that there's nothing wrong with homosexuality," said Koch. "It's whatever God made you. It happens that I'm a heterosexual."

Working into a second wind, Koch suddenly rose to his full height, bidding me an abrupt farewell. Class dismissed. Interview over.

I punted for more time, asking the brash pol to identify his Who's Who of photographs and memorabilia. He delivered rapid-fire facts with his none too subtle subtext: stay in the good fight; speak out, make a difference while you can.

"This is me conducting the New York Housing Authority orchestra. That's the Dutch Ambassador giving me a medal; Jacques Chirac giving me the Legion of Honor. That's the President of Columbia when he was mayor of Bogota giving me a medal. The Ambassador of Sweden giving me a medal. President Mitterrand of France gave me the next level of the Legion of Honor. That's a medal given to me by Sadat, President of Egypt." Koch, a World War II draftee, earned a Victory medal and European-African-Middle Eastern Campaign Medal with two campaign stars.

He was on a roll. "That's City Hall with President Carter. Gracie Mansion with Ronald Reagan. The White House with George (Walker) Bush. Hillary after her Senate win. I was quite important in her election."

I scribbled, Koch in the lead, his chutzpah showing. "That's when the Pope came, 1980, '82. I met him at the airport. Mother Teresa came to City Hall. She sent me two letters. She said, 'Give me your AIDS prisoners and I'll take them.' And she opened up a hospice which I very much appreciated. It had 14 beds for AIDS patients. Here's a parchment sheet to me by the City Council of Jerusalem designating me as a guardian of Jerusalem."

Koch pivoted and shook his head. "That's a picture I'll never get out of my mind — an Israeli soldier being thrown out of an Arab-Palestinian police station and killed.

"And that's the cover of my book with Cardinal [John] O'Connor and a letter from him to me, sort of his last goodbye. That's it!"

Off went our tape recorders and relevant he remained.

Edward I. Koch died in New York City on February 1, 2013. He was 88.

PHOTO BY ELIZABETH HOWARD

Helen Thomas, White House Journalist

*I used to write about things as they are; now
I write about things as I want them to be.*

15

Asking and Answering the Tough Questions

TALK ABOUT REMAINING RELEVANT. Journalist Helen Thomas covered the administrations of Presidents Kennedy to Obama always asking the tough questions. Thomas was a United Press International correspondent for over 57 years and a columnist for Hearst Newspapers from 2001 to 2010. The seventh of nine children of Lebanese immigrants, and a fervent believer in democracy, remained a prickly presence at White House press conferences, a pioneering newswoman notable for her directness, pluck and endurance.

At age 88, Thomas still sat in the front row where she was called on promptly by President Obama at his first press conference: "All right, Helen. This is my inaugural moment here. I'm really excited," said the President to laughter from the White House Press Corps. Thomas quickly punched back: "Are the Pakistanis offering safe havens to terrorists? Are there countries in the Middle East that have nuclear weapons?"

Obama declined "to speculate" on Thomas' questions.

On Thomas' and Obama's mutual birthday — August 4, 2009 — the President sang her "Happy Birthday," and presented Helen a kiss and a cupcake with a single lighted candle for her 89th birthday.

Less than a year later, on June 3, 2010, Thomas interviewed Rabbi David Nesenoff on the White House grounds. He asked, "Any comments on Israel?" Helen didn't hold back. "Tell them [Israel] to get the hell out of Palestine."

Thomas' bluntness caused instant repercussions. The next day she posted an apology on her website: "I deeply regret my comments I made last week regarding the Israelis and the Palestinians. They do not reflect my heartfelt belief that peace will come to the Middle East only when all parties recognize the need for mutual respect and tolerance. May that day come soon."

In three days, Hearst Newspapers issued its own statement: "Helen Thomas announced Monday that she is retiring, effective immediately. Her decision came after her controversial opinion about Israel and the Palestinians were captured on videotape and widely disseminated on the internet."

The White House Correspondents' Association, over which Thomas had once presided as its first female president, called her statements "indefensible."

If Thomas' uncensored comments caused controversy and unceremoniously ended her illustrious career, she will also be remembered as "The First Lady of the Press," the ground-breaking, popular reporter who asked Ronald Reagan why he opposed civil rights legislation, George H. W. Bush why he "really" went to war in Kuwait, and Bill Clinton the nature of his relationship with intern Monica Lewinsky. Her urgent questions required answers in *Watchdogs of Democracy, The Waning Washington Press Corps and How It Has Failed the Public.* "The press," she wrote, "is the only institution that can ask the administration questions. If we don't, who will?"

I remembered Thomas' two-fisted alarm against the Bush administration 26 days before September 11th. "I think we are letting our leaders get away with too much," she said speaking at the University of Virginia's Miller Center for Public Policy. She later signed copies of her book, *Thanks for the Memories, Mr. President.* "I used to write about things as they are; now I write about things as I want them to be," said Thomas. She wore a cherry-red dress with fingernails to match, two watches, ropes of pearls and a heart locket; her cropped hair was the color of licorice, her shoes kicked off under the table.

"For over 50 years, I censored myself. Well, now it's go for broke. I have an opinion on everything that moves. I'm focusing on racism in this country; foreign policy, the issues of the day. I give them a hard time. What else are Presidents for?"

Like Cronkite and Koch, Thomas voiced her own opinions later in life, using her influential platform to speak truth to power. When we talked by phone soon after 9/11, Thomas remained uncensored, her sentiments and single-mindedness never clearer. "Since September 11th, we've had a rude awakening that we are no longer invincible, protected by two oceans. We may never be the same again, but I think we should fight to keep our Bill of Rights intact. We must not forego our basic individuality and liberty. I believe we are big enough and sophisticated enough to rise to the occasion without ceasing to be a democratic nation. I think the leaders now understand this is a global village and we're all in it together. I believe that the US will prevail in this struggle. As the saying goes, 'My country may she ever be right, but my country right or wrong.'"

Thomas' relentless criticisms of the Iraq war led President Bush not to take her pointed questions for three years. She kept on, however, putting her disapproval on the record in syndicated columns, among them, "War is Hell," "Bush Recalls No Mistakes in Presidency," "Where Are All the Leaders of Faith," "Obama Learns Limits of Bipartisan Overtures."

Hellbent to write things as she "wants them to be," Thomas owned to being "a lifelong liberal," committed to patriotism and democracy probably delivered in her DNA. Helen Amelia Thomas was born in Winchester, Kentucky, on August 4, 1920. Her Lebanese parents arrived in 1903 at Ellis Island where her father's surname was anglicized from Antonious to Thomas. Her parents did not read or write; her father worked his way to Kentucky selling miscellany from a loaded wagon. The family moved to Detroit when Helen was four.

"We were always so happy that our father didn't miss the boat," she said. "We really felt very lucky to be born in this country. We took everything very seriously in terms of the Constitution, the American heroes. The whole impetus was to be a good citizen, make our best effort, and know that the opportunities were there. All of us were so impressed with how much courage it takes for any immigrant coming to this country — being penniless, not knowing the language, venturing forth into the unknown. And embracing the values and the wonderful principles of democracy.

"The struggle for equality has always been there for me from the day I was born. Growing up in a mixed neighborhood in Detroit, I felt if you weren't blonde and blue eyed, you weren't American. If you came from the Mediterranean area, you were a 'foreigner.' My parents were deeply religious; we went to Greek Orthodox services every Sunday. My parents gave me a strong sense of right and wrong, and all the guilt that comes if I didn't do the right thing.

"My father gave us morality by osmosis, a desire to be a better person. He's why I am still fighting against discrimination and for civil rights and the people's right to know. He was not a man to upset the status quo. His children did that. My father had a grocery store. Every day, he carried groceries on his back to the neighborhood. My mother raised nine children in the Depression and she was there when we came home from school. She was the rock, our security and lifeline. My parents knew there were more mountains to climb."

And Thomas, nearing 90 with pen and pick-ax in hand, still climbed more mountains. She started her ascent during World War

II as copy girl at the *Washington Daily News* after graduating from what is now Wayne State University. She was soon promoted to cub reporter. She joined United Press as a radio writer in 1943 and stayed on their roster for the next 57 years. She proceeded from social news to reporting on the end of the war, President Truman, and Brown v. Board of Education to her well read column, "Backstairs at the White House." Assigned to the White House in 1960, Thomas made history covering nine administrations — JFK's assassination and Johnson's Great Society; Nixon from China to Watergate; the collapse of the Berlin Wall and the Soviet Union; Reagan's Star Wars; Bush's Gulf War; Clinton's impeachment; George Bush under siege; and Obama's ascendancy as the country's first African-American president.

Thomas earned many firsts for women reporters — serving as UPI's bureau chief and as president of the National Press Club, the White House Correspondents' Association and the Gridiron Club. In 1972, she was the only female print reporter to accompany Nixon to China. She published six books, one for children. In *The Great White House Breakout*, "First Child, Sam" leads a comic chase through Washington while his mother, the first woman President, is on duty at home.

Her most memorable hour?

"I remember I was at the White House in the press office. We were all watching the moon landing on television and I jumped 10 feet high! It was exhilarating!"

Thomas received a Lifetime Award from the White House Correspondents Association in 1998 along with plaudits from President Clinton: "For all of us at the White House, Helen is a rock, the embodiment of fearless integrity for her insistence on holding government accountable."

She was a journalist who remained fearless and unintimidated when the years could have easily silenced her passion. President Ford supposedly said that Helen Thomas practiced "a fine blend of journalism and acupuncture."

In her autobiography, *Front Row at the White House*, Thomas quoted her own hero. "Lincoln said, 'Let the people know the facts and the country will be safe.' I've always believed that the people can handle the truth, no matter how unpalatable it may sometimes be. As a White House reporter, I saw many presidents wrestle with the truth. I tried to report it."

"As for the presidency," she said into the phone, "I hope in our search, or need for heroes now, that we do not pump up personalities who are running the country. I don't think this should be a one-man show. I would prefer collective security and flying under the United Nations banner."

In 2000 First Amendment defender Thomas resigned on principle from UPI after the wire service became allied with the Unification Church of the Reverend Sun Myung Moon.

The first woman to open and close a White House press conference temporarily gave up her front row seat and her ceremonial bidding, "Thank you, Mr. President." She happily regained both, newly invigorated as a columnist for Hearst, writing on national affairs and the White House. "Who," she asked in my ear, "doesn't want to be front row center and ask the questions?"

And Thomas kept showing up first each morning at the White House. She was often the last to leave. "Whenever I meet a young person who wants to go into journalism, I say, 'Go for it. What profession gives you an education every day?' You have to keep learning. You have to keep reading. You are part of the world. You can participate by informing people, by giving them the right impetus."

Being part of the world, participating and informing hopefully helped to lessen Helen's losses. "A lot of wonderful people with the same ambition as I have, have died," said Thomas, widowed in 1982 from AP White House reporter, Douglas Cornell. She and Cornell, a widower 14 years her senior, married when she was 51. They had no children and were together seven years. Cornell developed Alzheimer's, and Helen and one of her sisters, cared for him until his death. Her tone warmed. "I was lucky to be born into a big family, and the enduring love of my brothers and sisters continues to sustain us. Those of us who are left remain close to one another and to many children who have followed."

Helen didn't advance to old age without joy or a fight. "I don't exercise. I do a lot of walking in my work. I watched Clinton and Bush jog. Spectator sport. Eat, drink wine and be merry!" She advised. "It's the best way to live. "I think it's important to live as long as you can be on your feet, as long as you can do things. You also have to have the energy, the enthusiasm, the passion. You have to really *want* to be there. You have to *want* to put in incredible hours, accept very low pay. But there is no job — in my opinion — that is more rewarding than journalism."

Thomas' dedication to her trade made her a role model for many aspiring journalists. ABC News' reporter Sam Donaldson acknowledged Thomas as his teacher: "Helen taught me a valuable lesson: 'Never stop working.'"

While avoiding retirement, might Thomas have been wiser to box up her dignity, notes and tape recorder sooner and head for her place in the history books? She thrived on breaking news but not on becoming the story herself. It was painful to think of her reading the papers sequestered in comfortable confinement, bridling for yet another White House press conference.

And, Thomas — seven months after stepping down from her Hearst post — began writing a political affairs column for the *News Press*, a free weekly across the Potomac in Falls Church, Virginia. Her uncensored columns ran for a year and covered everything from Social Security reform and the capital gains tax to Obama's State of the Union address. Her editor said Thomas' reporting stayed "sharp as a tack" even as her health failed.

I liked to think that Helen Thomas, fearless and proud, didn't put down her pen. She was still living her own philosophy. "I think courage begets courage…. Life — to coin a cliché — is a gift," she told me. "My philosophy is to try to live each day and make the world better if you can. Especially if you have luck and good opportunities in your profession. There's no shortcut to the truth. Presidents should live up to their promises. And a journalist's job is to keep their feet to the fire."

Helen Thomas died at home in Washington, D.C., on July 19, 2013. She was 92.

COURTESY OF *THE REPUBLICAN* BY MARK M. MURRAY

Hal Holbrook, Actor

*"(Mark Twain's work) was like an invitation
to me to say something about my country."*

16

Voicing Your Convictions

FIRST I SAW THE BLOOM OF WHITE HAIR. Then the thatch of eyebrows and full mustache. The just pressed white linen suit. The gold pocket watch. The halo of cigar smoke, and then the dry, sardonic voice tuned up once more to keep all feet to the fire, reminding us with shrewdness and satire of our country's ills — legislative, religious and moral. Hal Holbrook paced from podium to leather-top desk on Charlottesville's Paramount stage in the fall of 2014, his 2,298th performance as writer, sage and social critic Mark Twain.

I remembered Holbrook as Twain when he acted the role in Charlottesville in 1961 when I was a reporter for the local paper. He was then only 36, and now approaching 90 with minimal makeup, Holbrook still held his sold-out audience with finely timed, dramatic recitations culled from Twain's irreverent and ironic writings as topical today as at the turn of the century.

Holbrook had outlived his inspiring role model, Samuel Langhorne Clemens, by 15 years. He still owned his solo act of 60 years; he knew every pause, every intentional laugh. He jousted with targeted political pokes and observations. However practiced, the material was strenuous and barbed and Holbrook met the challenge.

In July 2015, Holbrook phoned from his Los Angeles home, willing to disclose the behind-the-scenes drama that had shaped his character and compelling career. I learned that Holbrook's long life had been a quest for acceptance and approval, for fairness and tolerance. He'd found fame and his unlikely platform in depicting Mark Twain. And still looked forward to his next curtain call.

Hal was only two when his parents disappeared out the door. Years later, he and his two younger sisters were told that their mother had packed her bags to become a New York chorus girl. She subsequently moved to Hollywood, never to be seen again. Their father pursued her, and refused his father to go into the family's prosperous shoe business. In retaliation, Hal's grandfather placed his son in an insane asylum.

Weathering family turmoil, Hal and his sisters were raised in the 1930s by their paternal grandparents. Hal's grandfather became his "hero" despite stern discipline and the decision to send seven year old Hal to a New England boarding school where the headmaster routinely beat the boys.

"I didn't have a family, I never knew what family meant. We had no mother, no father. My grandfather took three little babies — one, two and three years old — to South Weymouth, Massachusetts, and raised us. Grandpa was strict. You arrived with your hair combed at six-thirty for breakfast; you did not speak until you were spoken to. But my grandfather was the most important person in our lives. I was brought up to respect my elders and Grandfather took these three little children when nobody wanted us. Nobody. That never really occurred to me much until lately; nobody wanted us."

Hal was 12 when his grandfather died. He and his sisters were then sent to live with their grandmother, a woman "mostly interested in her clothes, shoes and makeup." On the children's arrival, she announced,

"I've loved this little boy since he was a baby. But I do not like girls." His grandmother's cruel declaration "crippled the girls' lives." Hal felt "used" by his grandmother and was glad to leave her Cleveland mansion to attend the Culver Military Academy in Indiana.

Hal became a distance track runner at Culver, and halfheartedly took a drama class to fulfill his hours to graduate. "It was the first time in my life people were listening to me. I think that did it. At Culver I got into the stage stuff and really loved it. I found myself a kind of home with those people."

More footlights and kindred connections awaited. "I hadn't been at (Denison) college more than a couple of days and I was lonely, scared and nervous. Ed Wright, head of the drama department, invited me to his house with a lot of his students.

"For the first time in my life, I suddenly began to feel I was part of a family. I had people who were friends. Ed Wright was an inspiration — his dedication and devotion to the theater, being an actor. It was a serious and fun thing for him. It was a way of life.

"What Ed Wright taught me by example never left me and formed my beliefs as an actor. Ed taught us to go out on the stage and enjoy being there. Ed taught us to do it FOR an audience, not to say 'look at me.' And to have a good time acting for them. And that's what we did." Hal especially loved disguises, some taking three hours to make up for a walk-on part.

Before graduation, Hal also served three years in the Army during World War II. He was stationed in Newfoundland where he met his first wife, Ruby, "a natural-born star." Together they returned to Denison and developed a two-person show impersonating historical characters, Queen Elizabeth and Hamlet among them. Ed Wright suggested they add an interview sketch with Mark Twain. "I didn't know anything about Mark Twain. I couldn't understand why in the world the audience was laughing. I thought it was corny as hell," said Holbrook.

But Hal trusted Ed Wright's judgment and he and Ruby toured their new act for four years on the Southwest school assembly circuit. Twain's comic interview was the audience winner. The Holbrooks traveled coast to coast before moving to Manhattan with their first child. Once mothering full-time, Ruby could no longer tour.

Hal sought professional direction from the son of Twain's lecture manager. "He was very, very tough. He just looked at me and said: 'Why don't you do a solo?' I said, 'A solo? What do you mean?' He said, 'Mark Twain.'

"'You mean go out on the stage *alone?*'

"'I think you can get bookings.' That's all he said. He didn't smile. I walked out onto 45th Street and thought, 'Oh my god, oh my god. How can I do this? I don't know anything about this guy, Mark Twain.'

"I had to earn a living and we had nobody. No family. No money, 200 dollars in the bank. Period. Nobody *at all* to bank us. I was desperate. When you're looking at cement streets and cars going by in a huge city and you're nobody, you can be pretty goddamn scared, I can tell you that."

If distraught, Hal kept walking uptown to Lexington and 59th Street to the old Argosy bookstore. "Where's Mark Twain?" he asked, not having read any of Twain's books.

Hal started with *Tom Sawyer;* it raised his spirits. Next was professor Philip Foner's *Mark Twain: Social Critic.* "Foner's book is still a revelation to me every time I open it. Foner condensed quotations from Mark Twain's work, the social commentary that described what was happening to our government, the distortions that politicians made and are still making of what we call America; the wars, the encouragement of racism," said Holbrook.

"In 1956 the riots at Central High School in Little Rock ignited the beginning of what would be called the Civil Rights revolution. Ruby and I had played there. It was a revolution as much as any we've had since 1776. It affected my whole view of Mark Twain. In *Huckleberry Finn*, I saw Twain was writing about our racism as clear as any bell that ever sounded.

"Avoiding the truth is a game we play from birth to death. That includes me and everybody else. But Mark Twain spoke the truth about who we are and to miss it, we have to pretend he's writing about someone else."

And so at Twain's prodding, Holbrook tackled his own prejudices and sense of injustice and created his tour de force act, *Mark Twain Tonight!* "Finding Twain was a strange connection. Like an invitation to say something about my country if I dared, because our country is in trouble.

"I have the kind of personality that responds to challenge. If I feel something needs to be said, I'll make trouble. I think we should make people think by giving them the facts; we should go out and make trouble instead of shutting up."

Thanks to Twain, Holbrook kept making trouble. On the Paramount stage, Holbrook meshed his consciousness with Twain's on topics from racism to religion, all delivered with perfectly aimed paradox, parody and scorn:

"Congress, that benevolent old national asylum for the helpless. The only distinctly native criminal class in America."

"It's the best government money can buy."

"It does seem a shame that Noah and his party did not miss the boat."

"I wonder if God invented man because he was disappointed in the monkey."

"Man. The only animal that has the True Religion. He loves his neighbor as himself and cuts his throat if his theology isn't straight."

"What a hell of a heaven it will be when all those hypocrites assemble there...."

Twain's insights felt especially contemporary to Hal given recent racial and political conflicts. "After this terrible, terrible shooting at the church in Charleston, I took out 'The Silent Lie.' In the 1960s when lynchings and black church burnings were going on down South and demonstrations were hot, I developed 'The Silent Lie' of slavery. I performed it all through the South. I was at the University of Mississippi in Oxford in 1962, when the riots were ending and the army troops were still there. Reporters were in the motel from the *New York Times* and the *Washington Post.*

"Everything had been cancelled. The football game cancelled, a big deal at Ole Miss. I realized I was the guinea pig. I'd been speaking Twain's thoughts about slavery and racism throughout the South. We'd had a bomb threat in Georgia. I bet on the audience at Old Miss and they took it.

"'The Silent Lie' makes clear and unequivocal how deeply racism is embedded in our country. The boy who shot those people in church proved it once and for all. This is a racist country and we don't want to admit it. I haven't said the word 'racist' in the show before. It's time." He readied for conflict.

"The lie of silence has protected racism for decades and we are all guilty of it, myself included. We're not willing to stand up and defend the ideals that Abraham Lincoln laid in front of us in the Gettysburg Address and got shot to death for it. We hide out in science and more often than not in the church. Silence has been our enemy since before the 1960s; it is our enemy now."

Holbrook checked his reins. "You can become overheated and it doesn't do anybody any good. Mark Twain did not shout. He got hold of an idea and shook it until common sense rose up for air, so I have to sit down and be calm. Calmness is not my game, but my dear Tennessee wife, Dixie Carter, exerted that influence on me. It was more profound than anybody's in my whole life. I can hear her voice over my shoulder." Hal dipped seamlessly into Dixie's Southern lilt.

"'Now Hal, darlin', everybody's not bad. You have to remember there are good people.' She kind of slowed me down. She still does."

If slowed to a jog, Holbrook vented his views and researched Twain's ever-current material. He'd performed *Mark Twain Tonight!* in 50 states, as well as across Europe and in India. He'd won a Tony on Broadway and an Emmy nomination in 1967 for his 90-minute CBS Twain special viewed by 30 million people.

A 2014 documentary, *Holbrook/Twain: An American Odyssey*, showed the veteran actor in character as well as backstage preparing for his strenuous role with daily exercises — stomach crunches to leg lifts.

Besides *Twain*, Holbrook's extended career included film, television and stage. He debuted in Sidney Lumet's 1966 film *The Group*. He played "Deep Throat" in *All the President's Men*, and won Emmys for TV roles as *The Senator* and the 16th President in *Sandberg's Lincoln in 1976*.

As Holbrook identified with Twain, he also found his concerned voice in portraying *Sandberg's Lincoln*. "I was deeply, deeply emotionally and intellectually committed to performing Abraham Lincoln," said Hal who withstood 49 days of four-hour makeup sessions to become his character.

"What Lincoln had to say was tremendously important to me. I flew to Springfield and drove up to New Salem to retrace his earlier life. The park had closed, dusk was falling. A light snow was stinging into my face. You could almost feel in the edge of that evening Abe Lincoln's presence there.

"I was reading Billy Herndon's biography of Lincoln. What Herndon had to say about Lincoln — the way Lincoln talked, the way he walked, the way he stood speaking on the stump with his feet close together and straight ahead, gesturing with his long arms — everything was as near to Lincoln as you're going to get. In Gentryville people still had the accent they'd been born and brought up with for generations.

"I found the cabin where Lincoln was supposed to have been born. I took a piece that was hanging loose. You're not supposed to touch it, but I did. I kept it for years and years, and last year after working as Preston Blair in Stephen Spielberg's *Lincoln*, I sent my piece of Lincoln's cabin to Stephen as a way of thanking him for the wonderful, dedicated work he did for that film."

Twain and Lincoln have lasted as Holbrook's inspirational icons even as he sought more rigorous roles. In 2007, he earned Academy Award and Screen Actors Guild nominations playing a retired army veteran in *Into the Wild* directed by Sean Penn. At 82, he was the oldest actor to have been nominated for the Oscar's best supporting actor.

"An actor always carries in his gut this little voice that says, 'Did I do that OK? Are they going to think it's OK?' With Sean, the first day I did a scene, I turned around and looked at him and figured he was going to do it again. He just stuck his thumb up. I realized that whatever I did was going to be OK. I stopped worrying about acting. I just did it."

In *Water for Elephants* in 2010, Holbrook played an old man whose wife had recently died. "I did that movie only a month or two after Dixie passed away. Years of torture with goddamn cancer. She tried so hard to beat it. Three years. Her Beverly Hills doctors refused to test her for cancer until it was too late." Dixie died at 70. She and Hal married in 1984 and had been a couple for 30 years.

"She was so courageous. Wonderful, thoughtful toward everybody. Dixie worried about everybody else while she had this horrible thing attacking her. Most of all, Dixie was *kind*. She tried to make other people feel good." And succeeded.

"The film was a very, very powerful experience. I had to talk about my wife who was gone played by Reese Witherspoon. I loved talking with Reese because Southern girls, they understand *men* in ways that other people don't. They understand how to *treat* a man. That's what Dixie did. She just made you feel good about yourself."

Hal drew out a deep breath. "I have made so many mistakes in my life. As a father I was a mess. My idea was that a father was supposed to work, become successful and pay the bills. Work all the time. That's what my grandfather did. I tried my best, but hell, I was on the road most of my life."

Hal fathered a son and daughter with his first wife, Ruby, and a daughter with his second wife, actress Carol Eve Rossen. In the documentary *Holbrook/Twain: An American Odyssey*, his children spoke with honesty and affection of their often absent father.

"But Dixie *forgave* me for being who I was, encouraged me and told me what a wonderful man I was. She made me start to think I was OK. It's really wonderful to meet someone like that, they can change your whole life."

Hal's mood cheered, perhaps in sight of Dixie's special touches in the home they'd found and remodeled together. "I like to say I love our house because Dixie and I bought this house up on top of the Santa Monica mountain ridge and made it our own. I can see the San Gabriel Mountains across the valley. Trees and mountains all around. I love the look of it."

Dixie, the quick-quip interior designer Julia Sugarbaker on the sitcom *Designing Women*, also plied her talents off screen. "She took this house that needed a lot of work and transformed it into a beautiful place. She had unbelievably good taste. The paintings, walls, coverings, colors, the rugs, everything." Dixie chose pinks, pale blues and hints of yellow to enrich rooms furnished with family heirlooms.

Hal and Dixie added rooms for her parents. "My dear, wonderful, mother-in-law was one of the greatest people I ever met in my whole life. She was an angel. She was a believer. And she loved me. Just loved me, that's all. And I never forgot it."

Since Dixie's death, Hal had lived alone with the help of Juan, his resident housekeeper, who had shopped, cooked and overseen the house and grounds for the past 25 years. Hal also looked forward to the daily arrival of his assistant of 30 years, Joyce Cohen. "They are as much family close by as I have now," he said. "You could never ask for better friends in your whole life."

Hal chuckled. "They don't allow me to drive anymore but I sneak out on 'em. When Joyce was gone to Las Vegas and Juan was off, I got in my car and sneaked out. Didn't hit anything, not one garbage can."

Hal now awaited a new arrival. "Tomorrow, a whole new chapter—I don't want to say in my life—in *our* life, begins. My grandson William is driving across the United States with his father to live with us. He's a good boy. He's going to live here until he finds jobs and his own place to live." Hal, as the grandfather, would have his chance at beneficence. "Maybe it will be wonderful. Let's wait and see."

While not implying he was lonely, Holbrook—after resting three months from his last national tour—was raring to return. "Being home was OK for a month or so, but it's driving me crazy," he said. "I'm tired of swimming. The only thing I have left is to go out and do my show, get out there and say something and do something! Get on the damn road and wear yourself out and see if you can still make it. Forget the 90 years old and all that crap and keep going.

"I don't know anything about life except to keep trying, keep working. It's all I ever did. It's all I know about, get up and start *moving* again. And when I can't move, it's really like being in prison. It's difficult for me. The threat of death is looming over my head all the time. I don't even want to *talk* about it; I don't *like* it; I don't look forward to it and all that sort of thing."

Holbrook shared Twain's aversion to aging. "If I had been helping the Almighty when he created man, I would have had him begin at the other end, and start human beings with old age," so wrote Twain. "How much better to start old and have all the bitterness and blindness of age in the beginning!"

Twain avoided bitterness adding: "Let us so live that when we come to die even the undertaker will be sorry."

"But," proposed Holbrook, "what Twain really thought was much deeper: 'Like soap bubbles we are blown upon the world, we float buoyantly … then vanish with a little puff,' and "What shows and shadows we all are, without our clothes and our pedestals. We're not suns, as we pretend to be, but merely candles. And anyone can come along and blow us out.'"

Hal pronounced he wasn't "a dusty Christian," and praised Dixie's religious beliefs even as he second-guessed his own. "My wife was a Christian, through and through, not a person who went 'round preaching and criticizing people. She lived her belief in the goodness of people. I respect that. Most people do not.

"My religion is lying in bed before getting up in the morning and asking questions and trying hard to believe in the kind of godliness that Dixie Carter saw in people. It's very tough. I'm facing the human race."

So Harold Rowe Holbrook, a thoughtful, brooding, restless and impatient man of conscience, aired his angst and as yet unanswered questions. "I worry about Heaven. I worry about God. I worry about where is Heaven. What is it? I try to believe in a God even though I pick up the paper in the morning and my belief is shot down. Shattered by what we're doing to each other, the superficiality and ignorance of governments, the lying that cripples the human race."

I wondered if out his window, Hal now traced clouds shadowing the distant San Gabriel Mountains. "I think of Dixie so much of the time and I say, where *is* she? She's in heaven. I know she's in heaven. Where is heaven? Why do I hear her talking to me right over my shoulder? Next to me? Is that heaven? Is it all around us? Is it here in this room? Everywhere?" Waiting, he said ever so quietly, "Maybe it is …."

PHOTO BY ELIZABETH HOWARD

Holmes Brown, Public Relations Innovator

I've always thought when I wake up in the morning, 'What can I do today that will not only be fun but useful to someone besides myself?

17

Celebrating 100 and Beyond

NOT RUSHING HEAVEN, HOLMES BROWN at 100 seemed a merry man. No matter that he was widowed, and recently had a serious fall and moved from his spacious home to two rooms in assisted living at Westminster Canterbury in Charlottesville. Brown, a retired, reputed public relations executive, kept to a productive routine that reached well beyond his limited space. He rose at six, read the *New York Times* and *Financial Times of London* and then put his mind to his "current passion."

"I've always thought when I wake up in the morning, 'What can I do today that will not only be fun but useful to someone besides myself? I might not come up with anything but if you have that attitude in the morning, it's not a selfish one. If you wait until later in the day, you say 'Hey I gotta think about myself.' I try to do a little sculpting first thing in the morning…. I also try to get the damn newspapers read." He laughed. "I don't feel different being 100." He and Hartwell Priest.

Brown wore khaki shorts, shirt and black down vest. He pushed his walker away, hosting from a club chair by the window; late fall leaves were turning gold and red. We'd met at his 100th birthday when a former neighbor threw a street party in his honor. A birthday balloon bobbed above us.

Although now reduced in living space, Brown was surrounded by reassuring, chosen belongings — a family oriental rug, an African American's painting of Detroit dockworkers, a still ticking, pillar and scroll clock. He'd turned the cluttered, tidy rooms into a handsome retreat with no hints of a medical institution. His sculptures — clay busts of his wife, his twin brother, three sons, his father and mother — dotted the leather topped tables and breakfront shelves. His mother's sculpture wore a gold paper birthday crown.

At his party, stocky Brown sported the crown, bow tie and a tweed jacket. He delivered his puckish advice on longevity: "Chase women and don't catch them."

Friends and family clapped, knowing that chasing his high school sweetheart Mary Ellen Lynch, was Holmes' prize catch. He and Mary Ellen were married in 1938, a union of 67 years. His wife, partner, advisor and friend, died in 2005 from complications due to Parkinson's.

"She was five feet two, eyes of blue. Lovely," said Holmes, wistful without schmaltz. "Her death was a terrible shock. Still is." He addressed Mary Ellen's miniature form on the shelf. "When I had a very, very tough problem, I'd talk it over with her and we'd decide what to do. I don't know if that kind of talking happens much anymore."

While Holmes still approached his day as an astute public relations man, he did so straightforwardly with credit to his wife and upbringing. He and Mary Ellen considered themselves "Rockefeller Republicans" reared from modest and inclusive Midwestern backgrounds. Holmes was born an identical twin in 1914 in Prescott, Kansas, and moved with his parents to Ames, Iowa. "I was raised in a town in the middle West that was all white except we had two black families, two Mexican families and one Jewish family. Supposedly, I would have had an awful lot of bias, but my father (a chemistry professor at Iowa State) was a real honest-to-goodness liberal in the finest sense. He believed anybody who needed help should get it from public or private sources. You wouldn't think a scientist would be that active. "When we traveled anywhere — Chicago, New York, San Francisco — we'd always go through the slum areas so that we'd see that a lot of people weren't being treated right and realize that we were living in an exceptional class in Ames. My father wanted to be sure that we grew up honest liberals helping others. He was the most honest person I knew. If I was ever not in business, I'd like to have been a history professor because of him.

"My father taught until he was 70 years old. He worked very hard and loved his students. He died running up the stairs to hold a lecture. He played tennis and beat me when he was 50 years old," said Brown.

Guided by his father's basic integrity, Holmes and Mary Ellen and their three sons, ventured from Iowa to the North, East and South, their ties as dependable as their home state's grains and livestock. Brown relied on Mary Ellen's counsel as he was promoted in advertising and public relations at General Electric, Martin Marietta, the Ford Motor Company, American Locomotive and American Airlines.

Brown claimed his success grew from his natural facility to focus quickly on selling points to promote corporate America. "I found out I had a real talent, an ability to write business letters. I used that knack off and on throughout my life. Still do."

At General Electric's industrial center in Schenectady, New York, Brown's ability surfaced in direct mail to utility representatives across the country, extolling the need to buy GE mechanisms. When he moved to the Ford Motor Company in Detroit, Brown worked with Ford's Vice President Robert McNamara in creating an attention-getter "safety car" to compete with top-ranked Chevrolet.

"We still got clobbered, but I figured out that we sold 200,000 more cars than we would have if we hadn't made the safety car. That got me quite a reputation in the public relations business."

Brown, amused at his business renown, soon put his talents to more humane use. When Ford's Bob McNamara became Secretary of Defense in the Kennedy-Johnson administration, Brown was named Director of Public Affairs by Democrat Sargent Shriver, director of the Office of Economic Opportunity. Their goal was to launch an educational program for disadvantaged children before the first grade. "Sarge and I went to Congress to get some startup money. Going up in his limo, Sarge said, 'You know we better name this program before we get to the Hill because I think if it has a name it sounds solid.' He suggested all kinds of sports advantage expressions. I said, 'Sarge, you're not following the right sport.' I was a track man and what we wanted was a *head start*. He said, 'You just named the program.' Damn if I know whether I'd done it or not."

Afterwards Brown wrote a letter sent to 100,000 educators, asking them to test the pilot program across the US. Receiving record replies, six weeks later they had some 10,000 centers with a half million children signed up. The next year, Head Start expanded into a full year program. Brown helped design the Head Start flag which now hung over his desk. Beside it, his successful solicitation letter began: *Poverty starts early!*

If Brown crossed party lines to work with Sargent Shriver, he made President Nixon's extended Enemies List for supporting George McGovern for President and marching with other businessmen protesting the Vietnam war when he was vice president of public relations at the Continental Can Company. His fellow protesters included Senator Edward Kennedy, activists Bella Abzug and Black Panther Hughie Newton, journalist Pete Hamill, and actors Gregory Peck and Carol Channing.

Brown's often bipartisan approach seemed inevitable, given his fair-minded upbringing and subsequent exposure to discrimination, especially when he and Mary Ellen moved into an Italian neighborhood in Schenectady. "The Italian people were treated miserably," he said, "They were treated as badly in Schenectady as black people were in Virginia. There was a lot of prejudice almost anywhere you went. But I didn't really get active in civil rights until after the war."

In 1950, Holmes and Mary Ellen moved to Colonial Williamsburg for him to head their public relations. As a tennis enthusiast, he sought the best, and usually younger, players. "I found the best tennis player was a black guy. We couldn't play on any of the public courts.

"I went to meet with William and Mary's President and I asked him would it be possible for me to play tennis on his courts. He said, 'The College has rules about black players playing on our courts.' I said, 'What do I do about that?' He said, 'Go play on them.'" Holmes laughed. "So I did." He also quietly convinced the whites-only Williamsburg Inn to integrate after assisting a black army captain and his wife to register.

And now Brown got up each morning looking forward to working with an African American fund-raiser to underwrite college scholarships for 32 qualified African American high school graduates out of some 100,000 annual applicants. Another 100 students were recommended to US colleges across the country.

"When a young black person has four years paid for, he or she can pick any university in the world. None have picked any overseas yet. I want to figure out how to make it attractive for 10 percent of them to go overseas and then increase it over the years." Brown was back in business. "These graduate are so successful, they'd be wonderful to get into the global economy either with companies here or there."

Brown put his persuasive powers in writing again. "My friend called last week and said, 'One of your letters really worked. We raised $80,000.' I forgot to ask him which letter it was." His Santa Claus twinkle lit up. "The more I think about it, the more remarkable this program seems. It's my current passion and I want to get it done."

A practical realist with plans to pursue, Holmes Brown kept bettering lives without sentiment or self-promotion. He preferred to solve problems rather than brood on the past.

"Many times people I admired those I'd be competing with. "They'd be people my own age. I admired Ralph Nicholson (Senior Assistant Postmaster General under Kennedy and Johnson) for his skill and the way he conducted himself. He was a former World War II Marine Corps major, a New York advertising executive and later a vice president of Public Broadcasting. He rebelled against his very privileged upbringing and lived a very useful life. He was a very good man. He would be a role model for how I'd conduct my whole life. He did things to make the world a better place.

"Others are here on my 'athletic row.'" Brown identified his sculptures of tennis star Bill Tilden, down the shelf from busts of FDR, President Obama and Hillary Clinton.

And always admired most was Mary Ellen. "I need to get downstairs to my studio to finish a new one." Holmes kept his eyes on her likeness. "They lift my spirits. I'm sure she's here. She guides me still...."

Holmes Brown died at Westminster Canterbury in Charlottesville on February 6, 2015. He was 100.

PHOTOGRAPH COURTESY OF THE ESTATE OF ELEANOR LAMBERT

Eleanor Lambert, Fashion Publicist

Fashion is a passion. I'll always love
clothes and I'll never retire.
At my age it would be ludicrous!

18

Staying Stylish to a Purpose

THERE WAS FASHION PUBLICIST ELEANOR LAMBERT on the pages of *Harper's Bazaar* wearing a silk paisley turban and robin's egg blue tunic, her neck draped in garnet and pearl medallions. "The Empress of Seventh Avenue" reigned in charge between her son, poet and art critic Bill Berkson, and grandson, Moses Berkson, a photographer and filmmaker. Father and son smiled politely while the 97-year-old founder of Fashion Week and *The International Best Dressed List* confronted the camera. "Fashion is a passion," said Lambert. "I'll always love clothes and I'll never retire. At my age it would be ludicrous!"

Eleanor Lambert, a force in raising the profile of American fashion and designers, was still on the job when we met in 2003. Her Asian housekeeper ushered me into Lambert's bedroom overlooking Central Park.

Miss Lambert, as she was addressed professionally, was pillowed on her regally draped bed with no makeup and wisps of fine hair flying. She wore a trim taupe pantsuit, otherwise unadorned, diminutive beneath the high ceiling and the lofty mirror reflecting her upturned profile. Cecil Beaton's "Ascot" sketch for *My Fair*

Lady hung on walls papered in faded mattress ticking and above the nightstand's freshly cut roses. I felt a trespasser until realizing Lambert's bedroom and office were one and the same. She was prepared for work — books and fashion magazines piled by the bed; her phone and papers waiting on the Queen Anne desk.

In the 1930s she established Eleanor Lambert Inc., the first New York public relations firm specializing in fashion designer clientele. Lambert's stellar clients came to include both American and French designers — Adrian, Bill Blass, Pierre Cardin, Halston, Anne Klein, Calvin Klein, Mollie Parnis, Norman Norell, Oscar de la Renta, Yves St. Laurent and Valentino among her promotional triumphs.

"Let's go into the library," directed this still formidable lady, unsteady in her patent-leather Belgian flats. "Apparently, my health is all right except I limp because of my bad knees. I don't like the idea of using a stick. But I have to. I'm not limber exactly, but I want to be able to move my legs and not feel crippled. I do stretching leg exercises in the shower and in bed. I was a swimmer." She volunteered to having macular degeneration and taking many medications and vitamins as well as live-cell therapy treatments from a German clinic.

Lambert reached for my arm and her black lacquered cane, stepping cautiously into the foyer. "That's a Beaton of me. And [Isamu] Noguchi carved this head in the '30s when he needed money." Stems of white orchids shaded the sculpture and sketch. Beaton's photograph showed an innocently seductive, bare-shouldered young woman resting on feathered pillows.

She tightened her grip, her Chinese red nails one shade bolder than the library's felt-covered walls. Sprays of tulips and lilies in crystal vases matched the chintz and flanked bookcases brimming with glossy titles: *Chanel, The Grand Canal, Landmarks of New York.* Silk-scarved tables displayed porcelain pill boxes — a camel, poodle and King Charles spaniel — along with photos of socialite and fashion icons Queen Sirikit of Thailand, Lambert's pick for the 1960 *Best*

Dressed List, and Gloria Guinness, contributing editor to *Harper's Bazaar* from 1963 to 1971. Guinness was named to *The International Best Dressed List* Hall of Fame in 1964.

Lambert's luxury surroundings and influential career likely surprised even Eleanor who was born in Crawfordsville, Indiana, on August 10, 1903, the youngest of five. Her parents divorced when she was three months old. Her father left for New York to become an advance man for Broadway road shows and the Ringling Brothers Circus.

Eleanor grew up wanting to be a sculptor. She wrote shopping columns for the *Indianapolis Star* and the *Fort Wayne Journal Gazette* to pay for classes at John Herron Art Institute in Indianapolis. She eloped with fellow student Willis Connor. They both enrolled at the Art Institute of Chicago, but when their sculpting skills didn't score top marks, they hopped the train to New York. It was 1925 and Eleanor was 22 years old. She and Connor would later divorce.

After moving to Manhattan, Eleanor only saw her father twice. "I got busy earning a living for my mother and me. I supported her for a long time," said Lambert. Her first jobs — low paying shifts for a fashion newsletter and a book publicist wanting more clients — garnered attention for her innate talent in art and fashion publicity.

She knew how to snag catchy celebrity stories. One night Lambert scouted at the fabled Algonquin Hotel. She joined writer Dorothy Parker and a boozy crowd of actors on a jaunt to a Bowery tattoo parlor where she took the evening's dare. Eleanor raised her trouser cuff to uncover a blue star ankle tattoo.

At ease with young, talented artists, Lambert began publicizing their work directly instead of through their more famous galleries. This career decision singled Lambert out as the first artist's publicist. Cecil Beaton, John Curry, Noguchi, Jackson Pollack and Grandma Moses numbered among her clients. Salvador Dali paid Lambert with a painting, "Eleanor Above The Clouds," which started her own art collection.

Lambert's singular promotion of new artists led to approaching the Metropolitan Museum on their behalf. When met with resistance, she thought big. She became one of MoMA's founders and the fledgling Whitney Museum's first press director.

"I only drifted into the fashion world," said Lambert. "I've always loved fashion; I've always loved clothes. Adele Simpson tracked me down for publicity saying American designers don't get much press. 'I'm an artist, too. I make clothes.' That intrigued me."

So Eleanor Lambert turned to Seventh Avenue and staked her claim as fashion's star publicist for decades. Lilly Dache, Valentina and Hattie Carnegie signed up early.

Convinced that fashion design was its own art, Lambert pushed the Metropolitan Museum's creation of the Costume Institute in 1937. In 1939, Lambert produced the first annual March of Dimes spectacular fashion shows starring Broadway and Hollywood's best. Later even Marilyn Monroe sashayed the runway. New York socialites clamored for Waldorf Astoria Hotel seats and wrote checks totaling into the millions.

To Lambert's frustration, fashion magazines favored French over American designers. Then in 1940, France was invaded and fashion houses closed. Lambert seized her chance. She renamed the French best-dressed list as *The International Best Dressed List* and publicized top of the line, coutured women worldwide. In 1942, she dreamed up the first Fashion Week and brought reporters from across the country to New York to cover fashion. Lambert next initiated the influential Coty Fashion Critics Awards for Design Excellence to further American fashion and designers during World War II. "The Oscars of fashion" lasted for 41 years.

Eleanor Lambert, the Midwestern outsider who impacted the greater fashion world, was soon sought by up-and-coming European designers for her publicity talents. She simultaneously promoted Christian Dior's "New Look" in Paris and New York.

After the war, Lambert, working with the Departments of State and Commerce, traveled the US and around the globe with American designer trade events and fashion shows while avoiding France, the couture capitol. She rightiy sensed a turn to post-war, more informal apparel.

In 1962, she founded the Council of Fashion Designers of America to bring competing designers together to air their concerns and further their brands.

Jackie Kennedy asked Lambert's advice, and she proposed that the new First Lady buy Halston instead of Givenchy. Halston's pillbox hat will be forever remembered at Kennedy's inauguration. Mrs. Kennedy, with Lambert's assistance, initiated the National Council on the Arts. President Johnson appointed her officially to the Council in 1965.

Her finger ever on the fashion pulse, Lambert promoted her protégés — Blass, de la Renta, Anne Klein, and Stephen Burrows — at a joint French-American fashion show at no less than the Palace of Versailles. It would be headlined in *Harper's Bazaar* as "Versailles: 1973: How One Show Changed American History." American designers outshone lavish competing French designers Givenchy, Pierre Cardin, Marc Bohan for Christian Dior, Emanuel Ungaro and Yves Saint Laurent.

"It was a turning point in the history of fashion, one in which American designers took center stage and the easy-going, relaxed informal style of the 'American Look' was being embraced and copied by fashion designers all over the world," wrote John Tiffany in *Eleanor Lambert: Still Here*.

Tiffany, having worked for Eleanor Lambert in 1995, described his mentor as "one of the most powerful people in the fashion industry.... She raised the visibility of American fashion design as well as the entire industry. Eleanor Lambert was truly a modern genius. She was a rebel and revolutionary (dressed like an Empress) who could spot talent. She was inclusive and farsighted, the first to use black models back in the 1940s! She put American fashion on the map and changed how it was viewed and embraced worldwide."

For 40 years, Lambert reported global trends in the *World of Fashion*, and wrote "SHE," a fashion column syndicated in 60 newspapers. In his biography, *Genuine Authentic: The Real Life of Ralph Lauren*, Michael Gross wrote, "Eleanor Lambert is the memory of the American fashion business. She's the stations of the cross."

If Lambert was about memory and devotion, passion still propelled this stylish doyenne of very advanced age. Style was the champagne that kept its fizz. She carried on against the odds in an era when couture seemed outdated or only fit for the few. "I still have a business, and I'm doing *The Best Dressed List*," she said with a pinch of pique. "The ballots are already out. On the Tuesday before Easter, I have the final meeting, this year at home. When that's finished, I'll spend Wednesday writing the release and on Thursday, I'll distribute it to the newspapers on my list. We get *The List* out for Easter weekend."

The phone rang loudly. Lambert conferred with her assistant from her office on 58th Street. She drummed her fingers on the receiver. "I keep my office and staff going. Now my secretary of many years has decided she only wants to work four and half days a week. You don't get many new accounts, but you keep the ones you have. I find I can be quietly at home and continue to work."

She smoothed wrinkles from her tunic, opting for the understated styles of Geoffrey Beane and Bill Blass. "I'm very conscious of still wanting to look well. I believe old people should wear uniforms. I just wear pantsuits. It's better than changing dresses all the time. An old woman in fashion just doesn't look right. You won't see me in a tight skirt!

"Some people who are old will continue to buy big party dresses and go to big parties. Maybe Brooke Astor wants to and she's a year older than I am. I don't have any particular style; I like turbans; my hair is too fine and too hard to keep. You can add to your own way of dressing with jewelry that you like, real or not. It's important in aging to stay neat and well dressed. Style and taste are important. It makes me feel ready for anything."

In a 1993 interview Lambert recalled her first party dress. "It was yellow and it had black velvet ribbons on the sleeve. I looked like Chicken Little in it, and I thought I was the cat's meow."

Lambert approved of Paris cum New York fashion doyenne Pauline Trigere who, at 92, challenged a *People* reporter, "If you're dressed up, why should you have an ordinary black cane? Discover your own style." Trigere wore elegant jumpsuits with sexy necklines and splashy jewelry. She'd developed "Gold Violin," accessories for stylish seniors that included Bukhara woven purses, ostrich leather pill boxes and brass-tipped canes in her signature red.

Lambert tapped her own lacquer cane, dazzle firing from a David Webb diamond and enamel ring. She'd adjusted her style and business, and still made her deadline and bottom line, an accomplishment of over 70 years.

As declining health and vision made the larger world less accessible, Lambert, like Parks, found pleasure in beauty at hand. For 23 years, she and her second husband, Seymour Berkson, a journalist and publisher of the *New York Journal,* collected treasures from their travels — translucent Irish Delft, Imari plates and Turkish rugs. A cobalt blue Chien L'Ung porcelain screen hung in the dining room where Lambert had hosted reporters covering Fashion Week, her innovation still on couture calendars. Here, too, Lambert had served her "designer meat loaf" and billi bi, a cream of mussels French soup, when entertaining such guests as Ambassador Clare Booth Luce and the Duchess of Windsor.

After her husband's death at age 53 in 1959, Lambert sought positive ways to grieve and to honor his memory. "(My son) Bill was only

19 when my husband died. I sold our house in the country. I wanted the money to go to something my son and I could do together. I said, 'It will be our memory.' We decided to buy pictures. We had the biggest fights." She laughed. "But it worked out. That's a Larry Zox.

"Come see the Alex Katz in the living room." Lambert accepted my hand. "That's the Katz my son bought. It's a road on Long Island. I love the perspective." If a solace for loss, the oversized Pop Art landscape added a contemporary, edgy element to the otherwise formal, pale gold decor. Past its minimalist lines and grays and greens, the morning mist rose over the New York reservoir and the park's bare trees.

I asked Eleanor Lambert if I could take her picture under the painting that she and her son had bought together.

"Oh dear," she said and then agreed. "OK. You can if you want." Her chin up, Eleanor Lambert posed under Katz's disappearing drive. She wore no adornments, her hair threading, eyes dim, frailty turned to fortitude.

"Keep on living until you die," commanded Lambert on the horizon of 100. "Be thankful for what you've had and accept what you haven't got. I'm just glad I've got my marbles. Don't give up. More than anything else, if you can keep going in some way, that's a gift from heaven.

"If your life has been with entertainment, like the stage, or fashion, you're just always interested. You do continue to have an interest in what goes on. I'm perfectly interested." Maybe even passionate.

And Eleanor Lambert Berkson, sticking stubbornly to her professional routine, outfitted with smarts, style and passions, refused to pack up her party clothes. I saw her photographed stepping out for causes. She wore red and a feathered mask at "Save Venice Inc.'s" annual fundraiser at Cipriani 42nd Street. She was among "the hipper fashionistas and their myriad exponents of all ages, stripes and attitudes" at City Opera's Thrift Shop benefit, a night of dinner and dancing to Peter Duchin's Orchestra in the Skylight Ballroom. Eleanor Lambert arrived on the arm of her grandson Moses, then making a film about his grandmother. He wore a tuxedo and she her stylish, silk turban.

Eleanor Lambert died at home in New York on October 7, 2003. She was 100.

PHOTO BY SEAWELL

Bobby Short, Cabaret Singer

*The great reward is that the music
makes people so happy....
It lifts you up a thousand degrees.*

19

Entertaining to an Uptown Beat

AT 77, CABARET SINGER BOBBY SHORT kept raising the bar. He hit the ivories for his 35th season at the Cafe Carlyle, promising diners a heady mix of up and downtown beats and high-voltage renditions of Cole Porter classics from *The Great American Songbook*. Tuxedoed at the keyboard, he rewarded listeners with glitz, glamour and New York nostalgia — "Manhattan," "Autumn in New York," "New York, New York... it's a helluva town."

When not performing at the Carlyle, Short was still occasionally "putting on the Ritz" on the road. He'd played from Paris to the Pacific, Carnegie Hall and the White House for Presidents Nixon, Reagan and Carter, and drawn encores from Pearl Bailey and the Duke and Duchess of Windsor. On the 100th anniversary of Cole Porter's birth, Porter's family presented Short with their first "You're The Top" award.

Introduced by his friend Jean Bach, Short greeted me with a strong handshake at his apartment nine floors up, three blocks from Sutton Place and a cross-town taxi to the Carlyle. His foyer opened onto a zebra rug, a Peruvian portrait of Saint Catherine, and a 19th-century Moroccan palace statue at full salute. All was as laid out in *Architectural Digest*—globe-trotting pizzazz from the get-go: African carvings, brass, glass and a grand Bechstein black lacquer piano. To say nothing of original, contemporary art work — Olga Sacharoff's *Adam and Eve in the Garden of Eden,* Bill Traylor's crayon and gouache *Black Cow,* and a minimalist screen-print by sculptor and painter Richard Serra.

"Chili," Short's 14-year-old Dalmatian, pranced us to the den, a tony mix of taupe, brown and black that matched her owner's black rugby shirt and sleek, tan jeans. Short's cordial, gentlemanly ease fit right down to bare feet in Gucci loafers. "Chili" was named for World War II "pinup girl" Chili Williams, fabled for her black and white polka-dot bikinis.

Short's offstage elegance affirmed an appealing dash and defiance to his years. I thought of still stylish Eleanor Lambert, her wardrobe bolstering self-esteem and her prevailing presence at the party. My father — a man who usually took pride in his appearance — ignored stains and wrinkled suits immediately after my mother's death. He wore the same shirts and jackets for days and sometimes didn't shave. When he cut his hair, sent his suits to the cleaners, bought a new blazer and snuck peeks in the mirror, I knew he was on the way to recovery. Vanity can be a good thing.

"I dress comfortably, but I hope I have a sense of propriety about it. I believe in good tailoring; I think clothes should fit us all." Short crossed his ankles and recalled the day he traded knickers for his first long trousers. "The older you grow, the more attention must be paid to your appearance. You must dress as well as you possibly can and be squeaky clean. And I think one should get a firm grip on what one's possibilities are and stay within the parameters."

While style and decorum aren't panaceas for aging, Short's decision to dress well and defer to the bounds of aging, underscored his natural poise and sense of correctness learned from his mother.

Bobby was the ninth of 10 children and only saw his father twice a year when he came home from the coal mines of Kentucky. "My father left before my fourth birthday. I never knew my father, and he died when I was 12. My mother was a housekeeper forced to work during the last years of his life to make enough money to raise us, so I grew up greatly under my mother's influence."

Short said his mother's impact meant being disciplined, minding your manners and doing the right thing. Her authority ruled during childhood recitals at the Second Baptist Church, local saloons and roadhouses, his vaudeville debut at 12 and onward to adulthood in New York and Harlem's Apollo Theater.

"I had two years out on the road. In vaudeville, many of the people I met were uneducated, harsh, crass; many would never have measured up to my mother's standards of good behavior or civility," he said. "And then of course, something else sets in. Your sense of self and pride in what you're doing. It's a built-in kind of discipline. You don't want to see yourself looking foolish, unable to do your job. If you're lucky, that takes over."

Short's own timeless tempo took over and his classic repertoire still delighted. He defined his expressive, jazzy and sometimes plaintive baritone as a blend of blues, Broadway, nightclubs and movie idols Maurice Chevalier, Mabel Mercer, Fred Astaire and Bessie Smith. "All of them contributed to whatever style I have today. In this show business, we have to find a niche to make ourselves commercially successful," said the singer once described as "an ebullient jazz cutup."

"I think I would have taken whatever was handed to me. And being an everyday performer was never handed to me. I realized suddenly that a certain kind of person with a certain kind of sensibility was going to accept what I had to offer. And with that, came glamour, high society, fashion, Cole Porter sophistication. Then the final cap, of course, the Hotel Carlyle (since 1968). That adds up to quite a lot of glamour." His eyes popped in wonder. Such acceptance — and approval — were likely no surprise to his friend Gloria Vanderbilt who smiled from a heart-shaped frame in Short's powder room.

A natural sophisticate, Short's contemporary arrangements paid homage to the past and classic renditions of his celebrated role models. "I think I'm kind of a minor historian, a link to the past — Duke Ellington, Count Basie," he said. "They also dressed up; so I dress up. I put on a dinner jacket. The performers back in those days were always dressed, even in the radio studio. Women in fox furs, mink coats. Often the conductor was wearing a tuxedo in the studio. You got dressed in traveling outfits to go on a plane.

"The elements of glamour are so elusive; glamour itself is elusive. I think it's a wonderful quality that we don't have enough of these days. It's not about clothes. There's mystery involved in it. It's a certain aloofness, a certain unattainability or inaccessibility, I suppose. A certain kind of mystery. Coupled of course, with all the things that go with that — a certain look and attitude."

I spied many one of a kind pieces with a certain look and attitude. A monogrammed Cartier silver ice bucket. A birdcage modeled after the Carlyle Hotel. Haute couture sketches, and signed photographs of Claudette Colbert, Tallulah Bankhead and Billie Holiday. Cole Porter's autograph hung beside tribal masks, sculpted giraffes and statuettes. Neatly fanned, oversized books spanned history, art and travel; *The Riviera* featured Short's swish summer haven in Mougins.

"I'm interested in art and have a minor collection of African art and contemporary pieces. History and culture fascinate me. Human behavior fascinates me. You've got to be curious." Short echoed Eleanor Lambert, Walter Cronkite and Ed Koch. "You've got to have a sense of wonder, and ask what's around the corner. That's why I first went to France. I've just come back from China, Burma and Bali. I also like to eat well. I like to go to museums, the opera. Interest, that's what keeps you alive."

And lit up. "I sat around yearning to act. Finally Carroll O'Connor gave me a chance in *The Heat of the Night*. I had a very good time doing that movie because it was a challenge. I've done commercials and even been a clown in the Barnum and Bailey Circus. Trying all of those things has been icing on the cake."

As Bobby Short embraced many interests, he also gave back. March 2, 2001 was proclaimed "Bobby Short Day" in Danville, Illinois, his birthplace on September 15, 1925. The Danville Community Public School Foundation endowed a liberal arts student's annual scholarship in his name. In 2002, the Arts Commission of New York and the Museum of the City of New York awarded Short their annual Most Distinguished Citizen award for his leadership in creating a Duke Ellington memorial.

Jazz aficionado Jean Bach congratulated Short's community involvement on the CD notes of *Thirty Years at the Cafe Carlyle:* "He continues to find every new challenge stimulating. One recent stunning victory is the installation of the Duke Ellington monument in Central Park, thus culminating nearly two decades of real work on Bobby's part, steering the project through tricky political shoals, supervising the fine tuning ... and raising the seven-figure amount of money needed to float such an ambitious undertaking."

Ed Koch, a dignitary of the day, added, "Without Bobby's stick-to-itiveness, the project would never have gotten off the ground."

Short's "stick-to-itiveness" ruled out retirement. "I don't see any sense in retirement. I don't understand it," he said. "Unless you're a very talented person — in the art of living, that is — retirement is a very bad idea. What do you do if you retire? How do you construct your day? It is an anathema. At least it's better to retire in the city. In the country, there's nothing you can do. What do you do at night?"

For Short, nightfall still meant performing, even if at a protective pace. "I have a bad back; steps are completely crazy for me. And stress is so damaging. Understand what stresses you out and do everything in your power to avoid it," he warned. "My mother said, 'Look after yourself. Take care of Bobby.' If you don't feel like doing something — and you absolutely don't have to do it — don't do it. The world is not going to come to an end because you didn't go to a dinner party. You must have the presence of mind to protect yourself and the power to say, 'I just can't do it. I'm sorry, I can't have you for the weekend or whatever.' At 77, I really think doing two shows a night at the Carlyle five nights a week is quite enough!"

Short had learned his limits and listened to his body. "I walk in New York and swim in France. I think it's very important to get physical exercise, but you've got to find what suits your stamina and your body. My body is my instrument and I have to look after it. When I'm performing, I have no alcohol and I try to eat only a mid-day meal. By the time I do my first show, I'm free to sing; I can breathe. And there's nothing like a little nap every day. It's marvelous!"

This perennial performer was not one to disappoint. "I'm lucky because I've chosen to work in a profession that pleases me. The great reward is that the music makes people so happy. Some nights your feet hurt or you are bone tired, and I think, 'I'd pay money not to do this.' But you do it, and the audience is responsive. It lifts you up a thousand degrees. It's very, very moving. And not many people experience that. It's like a miracle. My plate never seems to be empty," said Bobby Short, the giver and receiver.

In a few hours, Short would don his tuxedo and taxi to the Carlyle. He'd tickle the keys and again deliver the magic, lifting all of us sitting in the dark with his unfailing, up tempo touch. "New York, New York'... It's a helluva town."

Bobby Short died in New York on March 20, 2005. He was 80.

Bobby Short with his friends Jean Bach and society columnist Liz Smith

PHOTO BY ELIZABETH HOWARD

Captain Tony Tarracino, Barkeep

My advice is to laugh, smile. Help out.
Let every heartbeat count.

20

Playing The Game For All You're Worth

CAPTAIN TONY'S SALOON HAD ITS OWN Key West cachet. To say nothing of its owner, Captain Tony Tarracino. The gun-running shrimp boat skipper. The cheeky, bantam barkeep. The former mayor headlined as "intrinsic to Key West history as pirates and palm trees." Captain Tony's 88 years was the stuff of B-movies and Black Jack stakes. He was still in the game, playing for all he was worth.

Tony arrived on the arm of his daughter Coral, a bartender at Rum Runners on Duval Street. She helped him up the cottage steps to the wicker sofa and promised to return at noon. He wore a just-pressed shirt and khakis, his white hair and beard spritzed from the shower. Craggy and slight, he'd recently recovered from pneumonia and a heart attack. He coughed asking, "Do you mind if I smoke?"

"Whatever you like. How about tea or coffee?"

"No, thanks." Tony lit and inhaled a Lucky. "Nice legs," he said. "I thought you'd be older."

I laughed. "I'm getting there!"

Tony's brass and bravado were catching. He launched into his life story as if it was brand new. He was born August 10, 1916, in

Elizabeth, New Jersey, the third of four sons to Italian immigrants who'd sailed from Naples in steerage for 25 dollars. His parents didn't read or write, his father dug ditches; his mother scrubbed her floors and children with Oxadol soap, and bought their shoes at the Salvation Army. Tony served as an altar boy and performed in puppet shows with his family at the Catholic church. "Theater," he said, "was everything to us."

And, I bet, still was. Along with a lifetime appetite for risk, adventure and notoriety. I took my seat front row center. "I quit school after the eighth grade and grew up fast on the mean streets. I was always a gambler. I played dice in the alley since I was five years old; that's how I made dimes and nickels."

Tony swaggered that as a teenager he'd outsmarted the mobster bookies from whom he learned his trade. Then one day at the track, his chits came due. "When I went to get my money, two big gorillas — hoods in Chesterfield overcoats — picked me up and put me in a limousine and drove me to the big city dump. They beat the hell out of me. Broken jaw. Ribs. They left me for dead on a pile of junk. One guy said, 'Shall I knock him off?' The other said, 'Naw, the bulldozers will come in the morning.' I played dead. I lay in the swamp for two days and finally snuck home."

Tony pumped his fists in full action character. "I had to get out of Elizabeth. I only had 15 dollars. I hitched a ride south on a milk truck. All I knew of Florida was Hialeah, the racetrack. But the next day, I woke up in Key West and I never left. Key West is my utopia." Gotta love this guy.

Tony cruised into "the wide open Conch Republic" in July 1947, his sea legs then limited to crossings on the Staten Island ferry. Unfazed, he ventured into shrimping, and for two decades captained the "Greyhound" charter. "I caught more fish on my boat than you can fathom to guess," he said. "I made Key West the sport-fishing capitol of the world."

Key West was the ideal backwater for Tony's daredevil talents and sagas. He had me at the stage whisper, his hush-hush cameos in murky plots triggered to kill Papa Doc in Haiti and Castro in Cuba, gunrunning for the CIA and shooting live ammo in the Everglades. His split second, double-crossed escapes became the stuff of myth and movies, Tony's capers reenacted by actor Stuart Whitman in the 1978 B movie, *Cuba Crossing*.

Actor or hero, Tony Tarracino, surviving scrapes and the bad guys, held to his sassy stock and trade. After too many close calls, Tony opted for a safer role behind the bar. In 1962, he bought Ernest Hemingway's original Sloppy Joe's Bar and renamed it Captain Tony's Saloon. Here, Tony had befriended writers Hemingway, Tennessee Williams and Truman Capote. Singer Jimmy Buffet wrote "Last Mango in Paris" in gratitude to the mentor who gave him an early break.

Buffet also managed Tony's 1989 campaign, when at 73, he ran for Key West's mayor. Undaunted by defeat, Tony was elected on his third try. "I want it on record," he declared, that during his two-year term, he protested against over-development and fought to protect the rights of artists and vendors working the Mallory Square sunset crowds.

That same year Tony sold his bar but didn't deal out. Instead, he hosted guests aboard the gambling boat, Sea Krug. "I still like the hum of the engine, the sound of slot machines," said a man claiming to have won and lost millions.

"I was always a gambler. I was always in the action. I made my whole life gambling and women. Any woman is living dangerous; they're the biggest risk, but worth it." Tony wagered on. "I married three women, lived with three others and fathered 13 children." Tony and his 58-year-old wife, Marty, had been married for 34 years.

Tony coughed and continued after a brief intermission. "Risk meant my life. And every risk paid off. I never had a plan; everything just happened. Life is very temporary. You're not even a mosquito on a mouse's testicle. I made my life (about) people."

And the philosophical, surviving Tarracino son still counted on lady luck. "Aging hasn't affected me. I never had a chance to grow old mentally. I think local doctors think I'm sort of something that shouldn't be. I should have died a long time ago. I smoked three packs of Lucky Strikes for about 50 years. In 1995 I had a heart attack and I quit smoking for about a week. I smoked two packs with a filter; that is like using a condom. I didn't think I could live without smoking.

"I was always a Scotch man too, but to hell with it, I gave it up. I never did drugs. Maybe a joint at a party to make others feel better. I never go to bed without my three coffees. I still go to sleep about two a.m. And I'm up by eight. I take a heart pill and a blood thinner. My wife said, 'Take vitamin C.' I'll die when I'm ready and not before.

"My advice," said Tony, boxing to the bell, "Laugh, smile. Help out. Let every heartbeat count. Treat others like you want to be treated. But if someone is going to screw you, beat them to the punch. I worried I would get old, sour and crabby. It never happened. I still love life. Like an old barber chair, crank it up and use your body every day."

Tony was going to cheat the deck in any way possible. His down and not so dirty advice was worth attention. If more fiction than fact, defiance provided Tony his familiar script with an ending we both applauded.

He hesitated at a knock on the door. Coral had returned at noon. Tony grinned. "We're just getting started."

"Let's talk more. When can I come by Captain Tony's?"

"Seven to 10 Tuesday, Thursday and Friday. I'll be there," Tony promised with a high-five.

"I'll see you on Tuesday."

It was dark inside Captain Tony's — a brew of beer, smoke and good times on Greene Street. Low beams were thumbtacked with business cards, tie-dyed shirts, shark jaws, and fire helmets. Bras and banners proclaimed "Key West or Bust," or "Off-limits: US Government Property." "Elect Captain Tony T. Mayor" campaign posters were draped behind the pool table and bandstand. "Peachie" played Buffet's "watchin' the sun bake"…"Margaritaville."

Tony waved from his official barstool. Other stools were labeled Dustin Hoffman, Sean Connery, Peter Fonda and Bob Dylan. "They always steal my stool." A photo of Tony and Walter Cronkite snapped them chatting elbow to elbow at the bar.

Tony lit another Lucky. Ringed by regulars and tourists, Tony maintained top billing. Entertainer, myth maker with moxie, crowd-pleaser out to trump the competition and reminisce into the steamy night, his spicy tales only to become more so. There on stage, I whiffed Tony's tonic, the fortifying brio behind the bravado that made "every heartbeat count."

A young saloon visitor touched her cheek to his. She smiled for a camera close-up. "In the hour I've been here, I've had my picture taken 27 times," Tony teased, not about to tame his appetite and raunchy bluster. "She's going to have my last baby. Honey, take an hour. Take your time!"

★

Captain Tony Tarracino died in Key West on November 1, 2008. He was 92.

PHOTO BY ELIZABETH HOWARD

Laurent deBrunhoff, Author of Babar series

Now more and more I work with Phyllis
about the story; I do like it a lot.

21

Collaborating For the Fun of It

DOWN A LESS BAWDY KEY WEST LANE, I discovered smartly attired elephants, wild tigers and rhinos. I'd first glimpsed Babar the elephant while turning those big, bright pages with my father. Scenes of exotic foreign ports and elephants with bull's eyes on their behinds made me leery of the jungle but raring to grow up and visit St. Tropez and the bazaars of Morocco.

According to the calendar, Babar, King of the Elephants, should have celebrated his 75th birthday in 2006. Remarkably — despite the responsibilities of four children and a sizable kingdom — Babar had stayed his youthful, royal self — spry, kindly, formal and frisky. And as time allowed, Babar still cavorted with his creator Laurent deBrunhoff.

I found deBrunhoff on South Street penciling new sketches on his drawing board. At 81, the author of some 37 *Babar* books now collaborated with his wife, Phyllis Rose, a writer and former English professor at Wesleyan University. "The text comes after everything is done. When we — or Phyllis — has an idea, we talk about it. I start composing the book with some sketch — pencil first, watercolor on top — just a study, very loose. Sometimes it's easy, sometimes it takes longer. So to have her suggesting ideas and doing the text, I do like it a lot....

"From the beginning I have always been more an artist than a writer. Now more and more, I work with Phyllis about the story and she actually writes the final text," said Laurent, a Parisienne *homme du monde* with both French and American citizenship. He and Phyllis, 64, met in Paris in 1985. They came to Key West in 1989 and spend half the year in Florida and half in New York.

Laurent and Phyllis first joined talents to write *Babar's Rescue*, the story of a camping trip gone awry. Phyllis subsequently contributed to *Babar's Museum, Babar's World Travels* and *Babar Comes to America* and together would produce *Babar's U.S.A.*, a family safari from Hollywood to Graceland to New York and Key West.

Their most recent collaboration came by chance. A yoga practitioner for 30 years, deBrunhoff asked Phyllis to join his morning exercises. "I was doing some little sketch for her of positions to help her start yoga, and Phyllis said, 'Why don't you do that with elephants?' Since it was a wonderful idea, immediately I started doing the positions in an elephant's body which is not very easy but amusing."

In *Yoga for Elephants*, the ageless pachyderm stood on his head in the Place de la Concorde and loosened into the Lotus position in Times Square traffic. "Yoga's wonderful for stretch, it's wonderful for balance; it's helping your muscles, your stomach and your back," said Laurent, still limber and lean, and perhaps the model for a trio of toy Babars in "Yoga" tee shirts.

Phyllis danced barefoot in and out of the studio and up the stairs: "Call if you need me." Her large photographs edged the studio floor. One of nearby Fort Zachary Taylor incorporated watercolor sketches of Babar sunning himself on the rocks.

Laurent and I settled in the living room flooded with June-in-January sun. Lazy breezes swelled the gauzy curtains. "Vinny,"

(Vincenza) the vigilant Yorkshire terrier, staked out the shade as deBrunhoff remembered Babar's birth and his parents' own collaboration. "Babar was a bedtime story that my mother (Cecile deBrunhoff) told us about a little elephant whose mother was killed by a hunter and Babar running away to the city, and getting dressed like a human being. She was not the kind of mother who every night tells a bedtime story. It was a special occasion. I was six, my brothers Mathieu, five and Thierry, a baby.

"My father [Jean deBrunhoff] was very amused when my mother told him the story. He was a painter, and in 1931 he started to make some drawings for us, and he did the whole book. He gave Babar his name because in the story of my mother, it was 'bebe elephant.'"

In 1937, when Laurent was only 12, his father died of tuberculosis at age 37. "When my father died, I was young, very young. It was a tragedy, certainly at that time. He disappeared. To see him sick at the very end of his life was very hard.... It's something you just bear." He shrugged.

At the time of his death, Laurent's father had written seven Babar books and established his memorable characters as a breakthrough in children's picture books. Then too young to consider writing his father's stories, Laurent studied art and painting at Academie de La Grande Chaumiere in Paris. "I started to do figurative painting ... after I switched to abstract because I was fascinated by this (kind of) painting." Above Laurent hung two of his watercolor abstracts — feathered blue and rust red strokes — inspired by sea, sky, the cliffs and rocks of the American West.

If memories of being an abstract painter had long faded, Laurent recalled his 20th birthday in 1946, the day his uncle Michel deBrunhoff, editor of Paris Vogue, asked him to resume writing his father's sought-after stories.

"So," I began, "you decided that you wanted ...."

"Babar to live again." deBrunhoff finished my sentence,

confirming his early decision to further his father's vision. "And that's why I tried to make a book in the same style as my father. I didn't say to myself, 'All my life I will draw elephants.' But I never suffered doing the same kind of art as my father. After a couple of books, I was so involved that it was exactly as if Babar was my own creation. Everybody was happy to see Babar again; that's why I went on and on. And I've done that for 60 years."

Over 70 years, in fact, deBrunhoff created more than 50 whimsical works of immortal elephants for new generations of readers. In 2002, he announced the birth of Isabelle, Babar's late in life, plucky daughter in *Babar's Little Girl Makes a Friend*. The arrival of brave-hearted Isabelle also marked significant changes in Laurent's life. "I didn't dare touch this family created by my father by making something different…. Except when I came to America in '85 to live with Phyllis, I said to myself, 'Well, something happened in my life, maybe to Babar also.' And that's how there was another kid born."

Phyllis' memoir, *A Year of Reading Proust: A Memoir in Real Time*, traced their romance back to the mid 1980s when she was a divorcee living in Paris and researching a biography of singer Josephine Baker. Referring to Laurent only as "L," Phyllis wrote, "He dug me out of the sand and brought me to life."

"At that time," said Laurent, "I was still married so it was not easy for a few years, but now we are very happy and have been happy together for 20 years." And their happiness showed. Beyond their literary partnership, Laurent and Phyllis also swam, snorkeled, gardened and biked Key West's byways together. "I love gardening — taking care of the plants, cutting whatever has to be cut, pruning cleaning," he said. "Phyllis is the designer, she has the ideas for planting. She's also the cook and I am the help. Preparing the vegetables, peeling. I can do some cooking if it's necessary … roast chicken. We are always both at the same time in the kitchen. We like to travel together, too."

Phyllis' memoir described their mutual passion for the West and its "sublime" terrain. Laurent, she wrote, "found a landscape that matched his soul.... Here, he said, 'I am not a religious person, but I keep thinking of God.'"

So do deBrunhoff and King Babar possess similar souls and beliefs?

"When you're talking of peace, certainly that's me. The peace that has not changed for me from the first *Babar* book.... You could say there's a message in Babar, which is to understand each other and be happy with others and never hate anybody who is different from you. But it is not because I wanted this message to be in the book, it's just because when I create a story, that's me.

"That doesn't mean that I can't feel some difficulty or conflict, but this is not my life. When the peace is disturbed, it is not the important part of my life.... But I must say there's no tragedy in my life. I'm very lucky." His calm was catching.

And no matter how dire Babar's scrapes, he still seemed sure to end in a world of deBrunhoff's benevolent design. "There's no suspicion or hatred," he agreed. "With the rhino there are some problems sometime, but Babar always gets to a nice ending. This kind of atmosphere of family love, fun all the time... this is certainly appealing for kids and parents." And for a writer wanting happy endings.

Through the years, Babar has stayed suspended in time, his monarch birthright intact. The upper-crust characters are models of family correctness with a certain Gallic gentility, chic and esprit. Babar still wears spats, vest, and morning coat; Celeste hardly ever appears without her crown, and Arthur has yet to outgrow his beret or sailor suit. Together, the family ice skates, skis, plays tennis and flies in hot air balloons; they play the piano and violin; they vacation on cruise liners and beaches in the shade of palms and casinos. Only lately has deBrunhoff's herd been introduced to computers, television and spaceships. They've retained their innocence and dapper Babar's idyllic rule in "Celesteville," a realm likely named for Laurent's intrepid mother who lived to be 99.

Some critics have read deBrunhoff's depictions of sveltely outfitted elephants in elitist city surroundings as metaphor for French colonialism. Would they also fault their lucky longevity? When might these privileged urbanites age, especially the little Old Lady and Cornelius, the learned, eldest elephant?

"She's not aging at all," said Laurent to mutual laughter. "Nobody is aging. They are the same characters ... maybe it will happen some time. Cornelius is an old man but his mind is very good, he's intelligent. At first, the Old Lady was like the grandmother, but she became quickly a close friend of Babar and the whole family. The Old Lady actually looked much like my mother when my mother was young. Her silhouette was very slim like that."

deBrunhoff's sketches of Babar and brood awaited his final brush strokes. I wondered if they might trumpet forth with hints of extra years. Laurent smiled. "Maybe we will have Babar's children finally getting adult.... Flora getting married.... Arthur wearing long pants."

Celeste now wore glasses, Babar a slight frown. I was reassured that Cornelius and the little Old Lady looked much the same.

"Maybe," said Laurent, "Cornelius will be a little bent."

Maybe, but hardly enough to notice.

1963 PHOTO, ESTATE OF HELEN LEVITT,
COURTESY LAURENCE MILLER GALLERY, NEW YORK

Helen Levitt, Photographer

*What really excites me now is anything that
helps out animals. That excites me.*

22

Embracing a Cause

As Babar and family stayed still in time, a Helen Levitt photograph in our hallway seems to hold a moment of my New York childhood.

In the black and white photo, three children play on the stairs of a city brownstone. Maybe it was the little girl in the Halloween mask. She stood in the dark doorway, one step behind another girl and a boy, her socks rolled down and her hands poised on the wings of her mask. It reminded me of coming home to 17th Street after a Sunday trip to Central Park with my father to feed the monkeys, ducks and diving seals.

Levitt's photograph was included in the Museum of Modern Art's 1940 photography exhibit. MoMA was also the site of her first one-woman show in 1943, and her first color show in 1974.

Once called "the most celebrated and least known photographer of her time," Helen Levitt worked hard to take spontaneous photographs and never to be photographed herself. Levitt is praised for her penetrating and perceptive images of children and families in the city of the 1930s and '40s, many photos shot in Spanish Harlem and the Lower East Side. She had an uncanny eye for street theater, an ability to move in close on emotional scenarios and be unseen. She also attached a *winkelsucher* device to her camera which allowed her to turn it sideways and take pictures unnoticed.

The only image readily available of Levitt was taken on location during Ben Maddow's 1963 film, *An Affair of the Skin*. The romantic drama of a black woman photographer was mostly shot in natural light on the city streets. In Levitt's photo, she seemed to be between takes, alert to what others might miss.

I'd tried to interview Levitt with no luck. In her late 80s, she was said to still be brusque and tough-talking with no interest in discussing her work; she said her pictures should speak for themselves.

Levitt's significant career may have begun in boredom. She dropped out of her senior year at Brooklyn's Bensonhurst High in 1931 and started working for a commercial photographer in the Bronx. He taught this eager teenager to use a camera, develop and print photographs.

Levitt became an early disciple of documentary photographers Parisian Henri Cartier-Bresson and American realists Walker Evans and Ben Shahn. Her friendship with Evans began while helping him make prints for his 1938 text, *Photographing America*. With his tutelage, Levitt first published her photographs in 1939 in *Fortune* magazine. The Metropolitan Museum of Art and the San Francisco Museum of Modern Art held a joint retrospective exhibit of Levitt's work in 1991.

Still hoping to meet Levitt, I went to a 2002 opening at the Laurence Miller Gallery featuring her photographs of children's sidewalk graffiti and family street tableaux. The exhibition also aired *In the Street*, a 1940s black and white documentary in which Levitt worked as photographer and editor with writer James Agee and writer/cinematographer Janice Loeb. The 16-minute film animated the streets of Spanish Harlem as "a theater and battleground" for rough and tumble children and their combat-weary elders. Like the people in Levitt's still photos, adults watched the world from behind barred windows; aproned grandmothers swept their stoops and broke up street squabbles. Toddlers kissed, boxed and danced; kids in paper masks chased through abandoned lots and spraying hydrants.

I almost missed Helen Levitt among the gallery guests. She was the little wren of a woman in a brown skirt and jacket, circled by fans and sipping red wine from a plastic cup. I said I was sorry not to have been able to interview her. "Well," she countered, "I might as well talk to you. I've talked to everybody else."

The next morning, I arrived early on East 12th Street and climbed the five flights to Levitt's apartment. She waited at the top, accustomed at 88 to the steep ascent. A flyweight contender, she was decked out in black tights, a purple sweatshirt, red, blue and green silk scarf, navy socks and cross-stitched sandals.

I guessed that interviewing Levitt would be tricky but I'd see evidence of her half-century's work. Instead, Levitt's apartment showed none of her photos but presented an orderly mix of well-worn possessions — books and records, etchings of Roman ruins, a Bosch print, and a framed magazine clipping of a gorilla swinging her baby. Wide floorboards, Tudor beams, casement windows and skylight filtering winter sunshine evoked a London garret. A yellow tabby cat sprang onto the cluttered oak table, just missing a purple orchid in its pottery vase. "Binky, you're not allowed on the table, no!" She scolded. "He just loves the ladies."

Did Levitt mostly stay put with her curious cat or still venture out to photograph children and families on the streets?

"I'm not doing very much, just a tiny bit. I have a bad back (sciatica), and I can't walk very much." she said, frankly peeved. "In my kind of work, you have to walk around, but I work hard on my shows and inventory for my galleries. If I had the strength and energy to drive around, I'd go to a lot of farms and do the animals."

Surprisingly, it seemed that farm animals and related causes were far from incidental to Levitt and now took precedence in her later years. Her engaging photo, "New Hampshire 1985," caught an improbable trio of goat, lamb, and Shetland pony, jogging in tandem down a country lane. "My main interest these days is animal rights," she announced. "I have a whole slew of them I support. Send them money. Write letters to Congressmen. I don't go out and throw ketchup on fur coats." Levitt patted the piled letters espousing animal causes. I was glad she ignored the rabbit fur trimming my vintage parka.

"You know about the seals, don't you? Up in Northern Canada? They come with clubs and hit the baby seals and skin them alive in front of their mothers. They dye them black and then sell them as fur coats. Somebody from Savannah told me they build a platform like a blind and put food in front of it, and when the deer come up to eat the food, they shoot 'em. That's called hunting." Levitt shook her head. "What really excites me now is anything that helps out animals. That excites me."

I followed Helen past boxes of irreplaceable prints stored in her spartan bedroom overlooking rooftop water towers. One box was labeled "here and there," and another, "nothing good."

In the bathroom, a long-sleeved white nightgown dried on a line above the claw-footed tub. "I washed my prints in the bathtub," she said. "I borrowed an enlarger that used to sit on that table. I opened this up and put the trays here. See, I still have a developing tray. I put stuff over the window to make it dark, and it is fine." I imagined Levitt's photographs unveiling, one mysterious apparition after another.

Her valuable, iconic photographs, so painstakingly crafted, seemed decades from the digital age. Like Gordon Parks, she'd first shot with a Voightlander. Now that darkrooms were gone and digital cameras eliminated film, what equipment did she use?

"The Leica is all I ever used. I don't know from cameras. Besides, I hate them. I do what I have to do. Everybody wants to be an artist, and they figure it's easy to be a photographer. All you do is press a button." Levitt slipped a black and white print from its envelope, one of many sent by young photographers for her mentoring. "I just got this in the mail. This girl likes my work and sent me one of her pictures from school. She wants me to give her a critique."

A student print of a dog chasing vanishing taillights at night hung beside a Cartier-Bresson photograph of a man and his dog leaving a Paris bakery. His gift had been exchanged for hers of a little boy giggling in his carriage. In 2007, "*Helen Levitt: Un Art de l'accident poetique*," was shown at the Fondation Henri Cartier-Bresson in Paris, and in 2008 the Miller Gallery paired Levitt and Cartier-Bresson's photographs in a "Side by Side" exhibit.

Over tea and puff pastry cookies, Levitt signed *Crosstown*, the seventh of her eight collections. She was pleased by her work's recognition, but still preferred not to talk about photographs she felt needed no interpretation. In one, two older women laughed at something out of view up the block. "A girl saw this picture and called me up. She said, 'That's grandma.' She came over here and I gave her a print. Her father was in the hospital. She said she was going to give it to him to make him happy."

"What about these two men on the beach?" I asked. "Do you think the older man envies the young guy somersaulting in front of him?"

"No." She was certain. "He was just playing around on the beach. It made a nice picture, I thought. That's Coney Island. It isn't because he was old that I took the picture; it's just the juxtaposition of their bodies."

And now what did she think of growing older herself?

"It's mur-dah! Mur-dah! Look what happened to my thumb. Got cockeyed. Talk about arthritis. I did tennis, swimming and horseback riding all my life until I hurt my back. You can't do what you want to do. You're always going to the doctor. And now every part of you takes a different doctor. It keeps you busy. It's a real pain in the ass.

"But, I'm still able. It's modern medicine that keeps us going. There's nothing greater than modern medicine." Levitt held up her pill bottles — One-a-Day vitamins, glucosamine and chondroitin.

"Be healthy," warned the still unfiltered photographer. Her "feminist mother" had died at 90 and her father at 78, a Lithuanian Jewish immigrant and co-owner of a wholesale knit goods business. Helen was born in Bensonhurst on August 31, 1913, the youngest of three. "I still identify with my youth. I don't think of myself as old, naturally. One doesn't. I still give my seat on the bus to an old lady." Up went her eyebrows. "Now, they're giving them to me."

Like most of my mentors, Levitt resisted retirement. "If you're in the arts or an academic, why retire? Why give up that? It's interesting. If you stop doing it, it's boredom. Where are you going to look for fun? What are you going to do if you're not working?" Defend all creatures large and small.

Her forays were fewer but Levitt appeared content alone with her cat, causes and favorite possessions. "I like good books. I read a lot of fiction. I don't go out to anything anymore. Television, for the most part, is very boring. I have records I play, a jazz and a rock n' roll collection that I like very much. I listen to classical music too." She tweaked her hearing aid. "A nuisance, but I have to use it.

"I also play poker. I used to like to cook. I have a big box of wonderful recipes that I've never even tried. I collect them. But this damn bad back. It's hard to stand around and chop up things. I just cook what I have to for myself and that's it." Levitt's cubbyhole kitchen was barely big enough for a bottle of borscht.

"I lived with one guy — I guess I should consider that I was married to him — after all, we lived about 10 years together. That's when I cooked. But I like living alone now; it's fine as long as I have a good book. As long as I can use my eyes, I'm happy. All I need."

If Levitt had all she needed, energized by animal activism, she understood her legacy as a photographer who'd documented the circus of children's street life as none other. However private, she still received students, friends and even strangers.

Could I take her photograph? "I don't like to have my picture taken." Levitt handed me her photo in hard-hat taken during shooting of the 1963 *An Affair of the Skin.* Four decades later, she was still calling the shots.

I took a slow exposure in my mind, holding to Levitt's image as I circled back down the stairs. She watched until I reached the bottom step. We waved.

I walked a few blocks to our old brownstone on 17th Street. I raised my camera, sure I'd find a little girl still playing on the stairs.

Helen Levitt died at home in New York on March 29, 2009. She was 95.

PHOTO BY ELIZABETH HOWARD

Himan Brown, Radio Drama Producer

*The gods have given me the years to go
ahead and keep doing my passion.*

23

Leaving a Legacy

As a CHILD, I LOVED listening to the radio Saturday mornings as the steam engine chugged into New York's *Grand Central Station*, "the crossroads of a million private lives."

On Wednesday nights, I hid the radio under my pillow and scared myself silly tuned into *Inner Sanctum*. Sometimes I listened with my father.

In February 2001, I looked forward to meeting the 92-year-old former CBS producer who'd created these radio legends as well as *Dick Tracy, Terry and the Pirates, Adventures of the Thin Man* and *Mystery Theater*. Himan Brown opened the door with his eyes on his watch. Here was another man on a mission, this one not to be distracted by snowy views of Central Park or a floor-to-ceiling collection of priceless paintings.

Picasso's "Mother and Child" hung between the sealed windows with the steam radiator clanking to a boil. "It was painted during his 'Rose Period,' 1906," said Brown, impatient to start his own interview questions. "What did you *feel* when you listened to *Inner Sanctum*? What did you *feel* when a door creaked open and a voice said, 'Come in?'" I'd felt that spooky monsters had somehow escaped from the radio and were hiding under my bed.

"The magic word is imagination. On the radio, the audience meets you half way. *You* envision and identify with the characters. *You* create the scenery," said Brown from the director's chair. "Sure, on *Mystery Theater*, it was Boris Karloff, Peter Lorrie, Melvyn Douglas, Agnes Morehead or Claude Rains, but you listened and *became* Harry Truman or Emily Dickinson. This is a world that is all gone. There is nobody left from the '30s. I want to preserve the spoken word as it once existed. These dramas are timeless."

If Orson Welles' 1938 alien invasion drama, *The War of the Worlds*, lasted as a classic, Brown determined to find younger listeners for his own durable dramas. "The pleasure now comes from teaching students; finding new voices, new adherents to my spoken-word philosophy. Since I've been at this for some 70 years, I've made it kind of a holy cause. We don't know how to listen anymore. I want people to believe what I believe."

Faithful evangelist, Brown traced the origins of his conversion while coining his own book title. "I've gone from the crystal set to the internet. When I was a kid, radio became popular and I took a Quaker Oats box and wrapped copper wire around it. That gave me the beginnings of a radio set."

Although his childhood knack for radios might have destined Brown for the national airwaves, Chaim ("Hi") Brown was born in 1910 to Ukrainian Jewish parents in a tenement on New York's Lower East Side with no such ambitions.

"When I was born, there was 50 cents in the house. I couldn't speak English until I was five years old. The language in the house was Yiddish. There were four tenants on the floor with one bathroom.

"My father had a couple of (sewing) machines and a shop. The First World War was on. He was making nurses' uniforms. We went to sleep with the sun and got up with the sun. At 5:30 I helped my father sort out the work for the six or eight operators. I went to school at 8:30. I made the payroll; I went to the jobbers in Manhattan to get the buttons and the snaps and the trimmings. When I got through high school, my father wanted me to work with him. He didn't want me to go to college. I said, 'I will do what I have to for you, but I'm going to go to college.' I managed to do everything." He even learned the violin.

Sticking to a 24/7 work ethic, Hi assisted his father while earning BA and law degrees from Brooklyn College. Instead of practicing law, he satisfied his yen for drama and comedy doing standup on the Borscht Belt with Danny Kaye. Standup led to Brown's first radio role — the voice of Molly Goldberg's husband Jake on Gertrude Berg's live drama, *The Rise of the Goldbergs*, a family comedy set in the Bronx that aired in 1929.

By then, Brown knew radio drama was his stage. In the early '30s, he created the successful soap operas *Hilda Hope, M.D., Dr. Friendly* and *Joyce Jordan*, M.D. before launching *Dick Tracy* and *Inner Sanctum Mysteries*.

Brown was at the top of his career in the 1950s when radio began to be eclipsed by television. A shrewd adapter, he bought the largest television and movie stages in Manhattan and leased them to the networks and studios into the 1980s.

From 1974 to 1982, he revived the nightly *Radio Mystery Theater* for CBS. "I was *Mystery's* producer, director, check signer. I have always been a one-man operation. I risked making a career out of producing, but from the very minute I started, I was in pay dirt. And I was lucky. I can't point to anyone else who's had a more meaningful and productive career in communications," said Brown, proud to be a member of the Radio Hall of Fame and winner of the Peabody and American Broadcast Pioneer Awards.

This stubborn, savvy kid of the '20s updated and built on his experience. And he wasn't about to abandon what he knew best. He was currently producing *They Were Giants*, one-hour biographical performances before live audiences at Cooper Union's Great Hall. He'd directed actors Marion Seldes, Tony Roberts, Paul Hecht and Betsy Palmer in dramas about Abraham Lincoln, Walt Whitman, Thomas Mann, Emily Dickinson, Adlai Stevenson and Harry Truman. He planned to record the lives of famous American fashion designers and the great painters.

In 1946 Hi was the first to record stories of Holocaust survivors. He sponsored weekly Bible passages on the internet and a free telephone service, *Dial a Jewish Story*. Although protesting that he was not "religiously Jewish," Brown's bathroom walls were covered equally with Jewish charity and broadcasting awards. His munificence also profited the Metropolitan Museum, his reward, he claimed, in giving.

His own dizzying art collection began with purchases at a 1937 WPA auction. Big ticket paintings by Toulouse-Laurtec, Bonnard, Boudin, Utrillo, Sisley, Modigliani, Vlaminck, Copley and Degas adorned the dark, paneled entrance hall.

Wasn't that a Rouault "Christ" over the grand piano?

Brown itched to tell the backstory. "When my parents came, I couldn't say it was Christ; so I said, 'It's Abraham. He's got a tear in his eye because he's sorry for all the Jews.'"

Hi accepted his own sorrows without self-pity, even as he remembered the loss of his second wife, Shirley Goodman, founder of New York's Fashion Institute of Technology; she died of cancer in 1968. "I turned the apartment into a kind of hospital with a cook and nurse for her. You don't go and die among a lot of strangers and someone comes and visits you in one little room." He was still indignant.

"I got married a third time, but it was short-lived." Brown added that he only occasionally saw his son and daughter from his first marriage of 30 years but visited his granddaughters and their children in Connecticut.

The phone rang. Hi talked briefly to his brother in California, saying he was awaiting the arrival of his housekeeper. "She cooks like my mother used to cook." He smiled, looking forward to stuffed cabbage, knishes, gefilte fish. "The only thing that's wrong now is that I'm lonesome."

Given Hi's loneliness, was he glad to have lived so long?

He almost jumped out of his chair. "I think it's fabulous! My mother lived to 98. My father lived to be 92. What could be bad about it? The only thing is you have to be blessed physically. The deterioration, shall we say, has been minimal. The machinery wears out. Everyone in this business is now 35. I say I'm 'octogenarian.' That's enough."

Now pushing past 90, how did Hi find the courage to press on?

"I wouldn't use the word courage in relation to creativity," he corrected. "It takes courage to get up in the morning and go through a day with some of the aches and pains that come with 70 and 80. That takes fortitude, gritting your teeth. But, if you've got something purposeful, something meaningful, your day is filled. I'm very lucky. The word 'blessed' fits me. The Hebrew word is even more beautiful, 'gebentsht.'"

Hi checked that I was listening. "First thing is to get parents who live long. The only advice I can give is keep active, be involved. Have purpose in getting up in the morning that's beyond golf. The minute you retire, you've performed your funeral.

"The gods have given me the years to be able to go ahead and keep going. Audio drama is not only a passion, it's good for me emotionally to be able to use the experiences that I've been privileged to have because of the long years. These are dramatic years and I've had them in profusion. I wasn't cut short at 60 or 65. I haven't stopped."

His mission intact, Himan Brown knew the time without looking at his watch. "I've set these years aside so that I can keep the spoken word alive and let it flourish forever. I can bring it back to you."

Himan Brown died at home in New York on June 4, 2010. He was 99.

PHOTO BY NIC SILER

Dennis Weaver, Actor/Activist

Let's get together and save our environment.

24

Sharing Your Mission

DENNIS WEAVER of *Gunsmoke* fame strode on stage, part gunslinger, part *GQ* model. The Virginia Festival of the Book audience recognized the lanky strut and smoky drawl. They gave a big hand to Chester Good, Matt Dillon's deferential deputy as well as Sam McCloud, the laid-back TV marshal transplant to Manhattan and then to Washington as a senator fighting corporate polluters.

Taking his cue from McCloud, Weaver starred as an environmental activist while discussing his autobiography, *All the World's a Stage*. The 77-year old actor who debuted in 1950 in Broadway's *Come Back Little Sheba*, performed in more than 45 films, and served as president of the Screen Actors Guild, had turned his celebrity to critical, peaceful purpose, his intended mission made sweeter hand in hand with Gerry, his wife of 60 years.

The Weavers' mutual mission was no less than saving the planet. He spoke with urgency from the podium. "In 1992 the Union of Concerned Scientists came out with a very sobering statement that really propelled me forward. They basically said if we don't change how we treat the place where we live, we're headed for environmental suicide.

We will destroy life as we know it on the planet. Their statement was issued again in 1997 at the Kyoto Conference saying it's all the more important. So we listened to what they were saying."

Dennis and Gerry listened and put their later years to the cause that concerned them most. In 1993, they founded the educational, non-profit Institute of Ecolonomics to seek solutions needed to achieve a viable economy and environment. The Institute — based at the Weavers' home in Ridgway, Colorado — connected inventors, innovators and entrepreneurs to experts with market solutions and incentives, and promoted the use of alternate fuels including hydrogen and wind power.

After the Book Festival, Weaver called from Ridgeway to further our conversation. He described "Sunridge," his comfortable, energy-efficient home as "Earthship," one largely built from advanced eco-technologies and recycled materials including tires and aluminum cans. "It's packed earth covered in adobe to create a rugged Southwest look. It's very practical and economical. Gerry and I use solar power. We have no heating ducts, no air conditioning. We let nature do it for us. It's really quite beautiful. We look down at the flowered Pleasant Valley below the snowy San Juan mountains." Soon there would be mountain laurel, white and yellow daisies, purple morning glories and alpine blue forget-me-nots.

However unspoiled their setting, Dennis and Gerry often took to the road to lecture on the environment and support their community causes. "Our environment and our economy are totally connected," he said. "Both a healthy environment and economy are absolutely essential for human welfare, and if we fail in either one of them, we are going to suffer and suffer greatly." Weaver had last guest starred on *Touched by An Angel* as a scientist dying of cancer. He and a younger colleague attempted to perfect and deliver technology against global warming.

Weaver had since steered his Prius on the hydrogen-fueled "Drive for Life" from Los Angeles to Denver, and the "Drive to Survive" cross-country caravan from Los Angeles to Washington. He presented petitions to Congress and the United Nations calling for the use of efficient hydrogen fuel along with the end of foreign oil importation. He enlisted fellow actors Tom Hanks, Robin Williams and Ted Danson to join a hundred thousand other petition signers.

Besides his concern for the environment, Dennis also contributed to those less privileged in his community. He and actress Valerie Harper co-founded Love is Feeding Everyone, LIFE, a program to collect and distribute shelf-dated food from Los Angeles supermarkets. In 1986, he received the 1986 Presidential "End Hunger Award" from President Reagan.

Weaver became a role model as a volunteer at the Pacific Lodge Boys' Home. "With the boys," he said, "it was an inspirational kind of approach to give them self-esteem and charge them with possibilities and the potential that exists within them. It wasn't about my films, although that's what allowed me to have a podium."

Fame gave Weaver an audience, but his desire to better the world was likely sown in his family's response to the Depression and its dire environmental consequences to their farm life in Joplin, Missouri. "We had to give up the farm in the Dust Bowl period. When the wind picked up that defenseless topsoil and just blew it away, there was no way to grow the crops we were expecting to farm. We actually became semi-migrant workers. We went to Oregon and California, looking for work in various crops like strawberries, apricots and peaches.

"My mother was really the one who sort of took care of the farm and my dad remained at his job at the Empire District Electric Company that paid 60 dollars a month. Even in those days — when 60 dollars bought a lot more than it does now — it was not enough for a family of five. He tried to find ways to supplement his income.

"My mother was ready to jump at the chance to help somebody. That was one of the things about the Depression, somebody was always coming to the back door in those days wanting something.

There just weren't any jobs to be had. And although our cupboard was spare, a little sparse, it wasn't empty — she would give them something, some kind of a handout. But she would always ask them to do something to earn it. Rake the yard, chop the wood. Help build the cowshed. She said it was important that they keep their self-esteem."

If Weaver's mother was his role model for responding to need, he furthered his efforts with his life partner Gerry Stowell. In *All The World's a Stage*, he wrote that they met at a Joplin junior college sock hop in 1942. "When she was right smack dab in front of me, (my friend) Bobby gave Gerry a powerful whirl and her skirt twirled up, exposing the neatest pair of legs I'd ever seen. I got a glimpse of those red tights, and it was all over!

"She was the only one I danced with the rest of the night. That was the beginning of a grand partnership that has lasted over 50 years. She has truly blessed and enriched my life."

Weaver affectionately recalled their elopement in 1945 and subsequent move to New York where he enrolled in The Actors Studio. Between acting gigs, Dennis sold everything from tricycles and vacuum cleaners to women's lingerie to support Gerry and the first of their three sons.

After winning a Universal Studios contract in 1952, Dennis and Gerry hauled their tribe to Hollywood. His first film was *The Redhead from Wyoming*. His breakout role as an obsessive motel clerk in Orson Welles' 1958 *Touch of Evil* later spurred Steven Spielberg to cast Weaver as a driver defying a sinister, run-away trucker in the 1971 thriller, *Duel*.

Weaver's rugged good looks and resolute, informal appeal, ultimately led to starring roles in nine television series, most famously as Chester Goode in CBS' *Gunsmoke*. At six foot-three, he played an amusing sidekick with a limp, he said, to set himself apart from the lead, six foot-six James Arness. Weaver's characterization won him a 1957 Emmy for Best Supporting Actor.

He won two Emmy nominations as McCloud, the down-to-earth deputy on horseback fighting crime on the city streets. In 2005, he played a co-owner of Raintree Ranch on his last series, *Wildfire*.

Dennis and Gerry meanwhile performed their country Western spoof, *Calhoun*, and recorded duets, among them, "Me and My Friend Jesus" and "Make Love to Life."

In their late 70s, the Weavers were not only creative and devoted, they had found the right formula for aging well. "You have to be sensible, and you have to have balance. Balance in your physical activity. Balance in the food that you eat. Balance between work and rest. Don't overdue anything," Dennis urged.

"It all starts with the thoughts. You've got to be open to new ideas and thoughts. Don't let your mind become petrified. I'm not strict about anything. I think to be strict is very limiting. And you've gotta have interests. Gotta have goals. Gotta have something that holds your attention." Like saving the planet.

"Often older people move into a safety zone. The safety zone isn't always safe. There are things that you don't know that could be very interesting if you're willing to accept them. Try. Curiosity is very important."

Born June 4, 1924, Billy Dennis Weaver — the University of Oklahoma track fielder, 1948 Olympics trials competitor, and World War II Navy pilot — ignored his calendar years. "People ask me how old I am, and I say, 'I'm eternal.' I never say I'm this age and what, according to society, I'm now supposed to be." Meanwhile, Weaver kept to a strict exercise regimen of pushups, weight lifting, walking and working his property.

He'd switched to a mostly vegetarian diet due to the example of another *Gunsmoke* actor. "A 55-year-old lady who played one of the dance hall girls was a vegetarian and she was in there dancing with the 20-year-olds."

Weaver also practiced meditation. "Meditation," he said, "is very good for your health because it quiets the body down. It takes away stress: takes away a lot of stuff that we're dealing with today that is harmful to the physical form. When you get more interested in what's inside of you than what's outside of you, the outside begins to change for the better.

"You can go to that stillness through meditation. The Psalms say, 'Be still and know that I am God.' You can find a wonderful sense of comfort, a wonderful sense of peace, love. I call it the presence of God or the pull of God's sweet love, when your consciousness becomes saturated. It just naturally overflows in downward activity and everything is just a little bit better. Food tastes better and friends are friendlier and the car runs better. None of those things are actually true in a material way, but what changes is your attitude towards them. And attitude is the key.

"It's a tangible thing; it's a holy vibration; it's not something you've imagined, it's something that you experience. It enriches everything in outward consciousness because you are able to tap into that holy vibration, that stillness, that presence."

As a youth, Weaver accompanied his mother to various churches and as an adult attended Unity and Self-Realization churches.

Dennis and Gerry seemed to share an enviable sixth sense. I remembered Dennis looking to Gerry in the front row when stumped by an audience question at the Virginia Book Festival. She had the answer. They left the auditorium holding hands, Gerry in heels, barely holster-high to Dennis.

Dennis and Gerry met the press together after their daughter-in-law, Lynne Weaver, was killed by an elderly driver careening through the Santa Monica market. Lynne was a 47-year-old environmentalist, CEO of a nonprofit after-school program and mother of their granddaughter. "Our family's loss is the world's loss," he said. "Lynne was a universal spirit."

Tender and not so tough, Dennis Weaver rode ahead, he and

Gerry shunning the safety zone, still pursuing their passionate purpose. "She's half of what I am," Dennis said. "Everything that I'm involved in, she's involved in. She's extremely helpful. Gerry's just an incredible part of what I am. And we realize our oneness. My philosophy is that we are all connected; we are joined together; we share each other's pain and joy. When we realize that, we begin to behave differently."

Dennis ended *All the World's A Stage* at full gallop, asking us to share their urgent mission: "Let's get together and save our environment. Tomorrow's children await our answer. Tomorrow's world awaits our creation. Join me today for the sake of tomorrow."

Dennis Weaver died in Puerto Vallarta, Mexico, on February 24, 2006. He was 81.

FAITH. HOPE. LOVE.

Faith, hope, love. Of these three, the greatest is love.
First Corinthians 13:13

I FELT FORTUNATE TO STILL HAVE my husband with whom to share my hopes, dreams and concerns. Aside from Dennis and Gerry Weaver, few of my role models now had the support of their partners. Widowed or living alone, these men and women had to depend on their own resilience and self-sufficiency. Rather than feeling abandoned, they found courage and solace by cultivating new connections and friendships and enriching their lives through faith, hope and love.

John and I recently celebrated our 50th anniversary. Our son Jamie wrote us a tribute observing his parents' perhaps surprising, yet compatible, ongoing partnership, our differing interests and "irrefutable bond."

My father likes the country.
My mother likes the city.
My father likes quiet, rural landscapes.
My mother likes busy, urban landscapes.
My father finds peace in nature.
My mother has said on record that too much nature makes her nervous.

My father enjoys sports as participant and spectator.
My mother has no interest in either.
He likes fiction.
She likes non-fiction.
He reads the paper every day.
She reads from a stack at the end of the week.
He likes to get up early and greet the day.
She likes to rise early and ease into the day.
In many respects this was to be a story of two ships passing in the night — were it not for one thing they have always had in common. His cooking. He cooks for her and she cleans up. And they've enjoyed it — 365 days a year for a half century.

At 14, I fell for this impudent Yale freshman sporting a crew cut and a camel's hair coat with an upturned collar. Ten years later, my father asked why I wanted to marry John. I said, "He makes me laugh." His chocolate cheesecake clinched it.

We married in 1963 and moved to Episcopal High School where John taught English and was soon nicknamed "Johnny Weird," a moniker I considered a compliment. I sped off the confining campus and worked as an assistant to a radio correspondent in Washington, D.C. Jamie was born three years later. Shortly thereafter, we moved to New Jersey for John to teach at his alma mater, the Lawrenceville School.

Frustrated by the traditional teacher vs. student school model, John and a friend at nearby Blair Academy met over martinis at a country inn and hatched plans for their own school in which students would have more say and responsibility for their educations. They co-founded Tandem School in 1970 as a coed high school in Charlottesville. John was headmaster for 14 years. He taught English, raised funds, cleaned the bathrooms and made sure the kids obeyed the dress code: wear the clothes they left home in.

I returned to the local paper where I was dubbed "the death and disease editor." I later freelanced for magazines and taught journalism courses at the University of Virginia. I made documentaries about several inspiring older women including Hartwell Priest and Rebecca McGinness.

John, now retired from teaching and subsequent stints with the Nature Conservancy and the University of Virginia's Darden Business School, keeps cooking, planting his flowers and vegetables, tracking bird migrations, and fly fishing in streams that spawn paintings for gallery shows. He reads the *New York Times* and writes pointed letters on political incredulities. He rails against limbs that no longer allow him to play tennis, hunt, shovel snow or stack wood. He reads his best loved books — Ellis Peter's Brother Cadfael medieval mysteries and Patrick O'Brian's historical naval novels — and when finished, he reads them over again.

We still enjoy our travels, if not on far seas, then near by with no envy of those flying to foreign ports. We hold dear what once we took for granted. We appreciate our long history and unspoken radar for each other's opinions, feelings, tastes and physical challenges.

In their longevity studies, Robert Butler and Margery Silver both found that the people aging most productively had nurturing relationships or social ties. "Women do much better at aging. One reason they may live longer than men is they have a better support system, and in their relationships, they're more apt to be intimate and frank about their feelings than men are," said Dr. Butler.

The loss of several close friends makes those still in touch all the more precious. Suzanne, my college roommate, and I have become aging sisters of sorts. A widow, she doesn't have a television or computer but reads the classics and listens to NPR. We talk long distance, listen and value each other's perspective. Once we commiserated about bad boyfriends; now we chat about bad backs and bathtub safety.

I exchange frequent emails with Carol, a friend from first grade when my mother and I lived in Charlottesville while my father served in the Pacific. Carol and I were cast in *The Mother Goose Revue*, Carol as the Queen of Hearts and as I as Little Miss Muffet. We were maids of honor in each other's weddings, and have kept secrets since we were teens who snuck out for a moonlight ride with our late dates.

A survivor of multiple cancers, Carol became a family counselor and minister whose faith only strengthened over the years.

As friendships bring happiness and comfort in aging, so too can faith and spirituality. I watch faith at work in Carol as well our friend Jane Barnes, author of *Falling in Love with Joseph Smith: My Search for the Real Prophet*. Jane also co-wrote PBS specials on Pope John, the Mormons and confronting mortality. "I was naturally religious as a child," she said. "I found God in the fields and in the dark and perhaps because my parents were intriguing people, but remote, I felt God was mine.

"I couldn't believe it when I learned in Sunday school that He was with each of us equally all the time, that he wasn't mine really. Not exclusively. I was *mad!* God was chopped liver right there and then. Yet I kept experiencing His presence: in any sort of rushing water, in passionate conversations, in the presence of terror.

"Gradually, He's worn me down. The older I get, I see this is so not all about what is or isn't mine. I bow my head more often than I stamp my foot; I'm slowly but surely learning to ride His spirit as we go into the sunset."

Journeying into the gloaming, my faith feels far from certain. I hail from a family of mixed beliefs and am still searching my own devotional path. My father was descended from Episcopal ministers, and my mother from strict Presbyterians. I didn't go to Sunday school, and they only attended Sunday services late in their lives at a country Episcopal church. My father was elected a vestryman, and sang the hymns in a high tenor. His favorite was "Little Town of Bethlehem."

My mother kept her Bible by the bed and collected texts by theologians, psychic healers and clairvoyants. Both of my parents were thoughtful people who put their faith in love, kindness and generosity.

In elementary school, I attended Friends Seminary in New York City. Mornings began with Quaker silent Meetings and community service was implicit. Moving to Charlottesville, I went to St. Anne's School where daily services were held in the basement chapel, a forbidding sanctuary commanded by a stern headmistress. From the altar, she delivered brittle prayers, punishments and dismissals for student transgressions. Many tears were shed. Bible classes were epistles of Old Testament doom and gloom. The church felt a place of penalty and dread rather than a refuge for peace, mercy and hope.

At Sweet Briar College, although resistant to required chapel, I stood in line to register for classes on world religions and the study of faiths from particular perspectives. I chose to study life after death.

I was confirmed and married in a progressive Episcopal church where our children were also christened, but over the years, we seldom attended. Jamie doesn't go to church, and our daughter Virginia and her husband, Dave, go to Catholic mass.

I envy those who find refuge in their faith. I am still curious and search to define my beliefs and a kindred community. Howard S. Friedman and Leslie Martin reported in *The Longevity Project*: "Women who are religious tend to live longer than nonreligious women."

"Faith certainly makes a difference for some older people. Very much so," said Dr. Butler. "[But] the studies are a bit equivocal. It's hard to distinguish faith per se from the sense of a support system, a sense of congregation, having people who share at church or synagogue, a community. If you know people are praying for you and have faith in their prayers, it might actually help your immune system. If you know people care, that's part of community."

Pulitzer Prize-winning author Marilynne Robinson, in *AARP Magazine*, reasoned why people are more religious as they age: "You've seen the whole arc of life — babies baptized, people married, the old pass away. Religion articulates the beauty of it all. People have come to a place where their lives acquire the authority of meaning."

I saw my role models find meaning in their pursuits reinforced by definite convictions; religious, spiritual or secular. Some attended church or synagogues, others relied on humanist doctrines. Some mourned and felt bolstered by their beliefs as they grieved.

Actress Faity Tuttle's faith, practiced since childhood, provided refuge at the deaths of her husband and daughter. After her daughter's death, Hartwell Priest had a strong conviction that there is no death — that life goes on. When nearing death herself, Hartwell told her son Paul, "I'm not bothered about heaven, but I do want to meet God. What shall I say? 'Thank you from the depths of my heart.'" Paul saw his mother's art in spiritual terms: "I think God defined my mother's life. Art was a mode of expression, an activity through which she approached the spiritual."

At 90 when diagnosed with melanoma attacking his brain, Former President Jimmy Carter trusted his faith as "an adventure ahead." By his 91st birthday, he reported the life-threatening melanoma completely gone.

For couples like the Carters and the Weavers, faith only intensified their affections. Former First Lady Rosalynn Carter was raised as a Methodist, but for over 60 years has attended Maranatha Baptist Church in Plains, Georgia, with her husband, Jimmy. At 79, Rosalynn became a deacon of their church.

Like most people, I find death unfathomable, something to avoid as long as possible. "I think everyone is scared of dying, to an extent," said Dr. Alan Segal, author of *Life After Death: Afterlife in Western*

Religions, on NPR. "But the interesting thing is that death anxiety is lower among people who have significant religious beliefs. So if we look at the evangelical and fundamentalist part of our population, we see that they have, in fact, lower anxieties about death, as do the aged. The young people, who like to say that they don't believe an afterlife at all, actually have higher death anxiety than older people."

I warmed to atheist Diana Athill's hope in the universe's constant change and recreation as mentioned in *Somewhere Towards the End*. "It feels like a state of infinite possibility, stimulating and enjoyable — not exactly comforting, but acceptable because it is true."

At 93, evangelist Billy Graham wrote in *Nearing Home*, "We were not meant for this world alone. We were meant for Heaven, our final home…. God will prepare everything for your perfect happiness in Heaven, and if it takes my dog being there, I believe he'll be there."

How might Graham have answered Hal Holbrook's plea: "Where *is* heaven? … Is it all around us? Is it here in this room? Everywhere? Maybe it is…."

Bishop John Shelby Spong in *Eternal Life: A New Vision* focused on the present and "divinity as the depth of humanity." Death, he wrote, "is a step towards sharing the eternity and universal consciousness of God."

I remember my father's last months as a time Kunitz termed "the holiness of the heart's affections." My father talked of dying without fear. Speaking of my mother, he said, "I do not expect to see my wife with wings in some cloudy atmosphere."

Surely influenced by my father, I've come to believe in the spiritual here and now, feeling that our rewards and punishments are in the present. I'm comfortable with a degree of uncertainty — the source of creation, the nature of God and death remaining a mystery. I don't fear dying, just a long, debilitating illness.

"In studies of older people with infirmities," said Dr. Butler, "they were asked, 'If you had a choice now, would you like to have very high quality of life, but for a relatively brief time, or would you be prepared to be the way you are but have a longer life?' They tend to go for the latter. The tenacity with which we hold onto life is pretty powerful."

I know I can't change my inevitable ending, but I can change my attitude toward it. Age doesn't have to limit interest, and it feels less frightening when faced. If aging well feels uphill, being wise is an even steeper slope.

"We actually have to work hard to become wise. We must remain open to new experiences and actively seek new challenges — and that only becomes harder as the years go by," said Ursula Stundinger, Ph.D., Director of the Columbia University Aging Center and Robert N. Butler, Professor of Sociomedical Sciences, in the *New York Times*. "It is not enough to grow older to become wiser. In order for wisdom to emerge, many things need to come together. We need exposure to many difficult life situations."

"In the end," wrote Dr. Margaret Plews-Ogan, co-author of *Choosing Wisdom*, "wisdom implies integration of knowledge, experience, humility and compassion into a creative, good life — a life that makes the world a better place."

"The art of being wise is the art of knowing what to overlook," said philosopher and psychologist William James.

Or as Dr. Seuss prescribed: "Don't cry because it's over, smile because it happened."

Dr. Butler proposed that in one's later years, a "life review" to let go, or face and heal the hurts of childhood and adulthood is another natural, beneficial process to sum up and find meaning. "It is a time to take stock, to resolve conflicts, to look back and leave a positive legacy.

"For those who may feel they've wasted their life or that they did things they can't remedy, I think that's one of the sources of depression in old age," said Butler. "For a lot of people, however, who successfully resolve conflicts, it's terrific. They may reconcile with a brother they haven't talked to in 25 years; they forgive someone they thought was disloyal or hurt them. They may atone for acts that they felt responsible for or that they felt guilty about."

Author M.J. Ryan counseled that purposeful creativity also springs from gratitude, reviewing what we are now thankful for, what is still fruitful, pleasing and appreciated.

"Ask 'what do you like to do? What still matters to me? What environments bring out the best in me?' A willow bends but does not break. Focus on a positive future. The gift is in the challenge."

When better than now to forgive and make those overdue apologies. Get rid of guilt and regrets. Act on deep beliefs would be even better. Love without judgment is best of all. In aging, there's certainly a powerful desire to reconnect, redefine and hold fast to love. Parent and child. Grandparent and grandchild. Family. Friends. Lovers. Husband and wife.

Looking for new definitions of love for our later decades, I happened to receive an email in which professionals asked a group of four-to eight-year olds, "What does love mean?" The children gave their very grownup answers:

"When my grandmother got arthritis, she couldn't bend over and paint her toenails anymore. So my grandfather does it for her all the time, even when his hands got arthritis, too. That's love." Rebecca, age eight.

"Love is what makes you smile when you're tired." Terri, age four.

"When someone loves you, the way they say your name is different. You just know that your name is safe in their mouth." Billy, age four.

"When you love somebody, your eyelashes go up and down and little stars come out of you." Karen, age seven.

"Love is like a little old woman and a little old man who are still friends even after they know each other so well." Tommy, age six.

"You really shouldn't say 'I love you' unless you mean it. But if you mean it, you should say it a lot. People forget." Jessica, age eight.

Jimmy and Rosalyn Carter seemed in tuned with the kids. In *The Virtues of Aging*, President Carter wrote of Rosalynn: "We are still close after 52 years together. We seem to be bound together with ever increasing bonds as we've grown older and need each other more. When we are apart for just a day or so, I have the same hollow feeling of loneliness and unassuaged desire as when I was away at sea for a week or more during the first years of our marriage.

"There is no doubt that we now cherish each day more than when we were younger. Our primary purpose in our golden years is not just to stay alive as long as we can, but to savor every opportunity for pleasure, excitement, adventure and fulfillment."

His philosophy: "The simple things — our own happiness, peace, joy, satisfaction, and the exploration of love in all its forms — are the key to the virtues of life, at any age."

British playwright Sir Arthur Pinero added words I like to believe: "Those who love deeply never grow old. They may die of old age, but they die young."

Hoping to prove Pinero right, I next went seeking role models for faith, hope and love.

PHOTO BY MARK TURNER

President Jimmy Carter

PHOTO COURTESY THE ROSA AND RAYMOND PARKS INSTITUTE

Rosa McCauley Parks, Civil Rights Activist

My decision (to protest) is sustained by my faith in God and the teachings of my mother and grandfather.

25

Putting Faith In The Next Generation

"EACH PERSON MUST LIVE THEIR LIFE as a role model for others," said Rosa Parks.

Who, in fact, could be a better role model for an unflagging life of faith, love and hope than Rosa Parks? What gave "The Mother of the Civil Rights Movement" the character to defy the Montgomery bus driver on that cold evening in December 1955? How did she withstand the losses of her friend and leader, the Reverend Martin Luther King, Jr., her parents, her brother, and her husband of 45 years?

Rosa Parks wrote of unfailing family faith in her 1994 autobiography, *Quiet Strength: The Faith, the Hope and the Heart of a Woman Who Changed a Nation.* "I learned early to put my trust in God and not be afraid to seek Him as my strength. As a child, every day before supper and before we went to services on Sundays, my grandmother would read the Bible to me, and my grandfather would pray. We even had devotions before going to pick cotton in the fields. Prayer and the Bible became a part of my everyday thoughts and beliefs."

Rosa's grandparents were former slaves who raised her consciousness on inequality and the importance of activism. Her farmer grandfather stood guard, shotgun in hand, when Ku Klux Klan members marched toward his house.

The first child and only daughter of James and Leona McCauley, a carpenter and a teacher, Rosa dropped out of Booker T. Washington high school at 16 to care for her ailing grandmother and then her mother, whom, she wrote, "taught me self-respect. There's no law that said people have to suffer."

Parks described her mother in a *Rosa Parks Biography — Academy of Achievement* video. "She was a teacher in a little school and she believed in freedom and quality for people, and did not have the notion that we were supposed to live as we did, under legally imposed racial segregation. She didn't believe in it." Rosa spoke with graciousness, her voice leisurely and honeyed, strength in her core conviction.

At 19, Rosa married Raymond Parks, a barber and active member of the NAACP. Four years later, she earned her high school diploma and began working as a seamstress at the Montgomery Fair department store in Montgomery, Alabama. She also became the secretary to the president of Montgomery's NAACP.

I tried to visualize the late afternoon of December 1, 1955, when, after a long day's work at Montgomery Fair, 42-year-old Rosa Parks boarded the segregated bus for home. She was dressed properly in a suit and hat. She sat by the window behind the white passengers. When the driver ordered her to stand up and give her seat to a white man, Rosa refused. When he later stopped the bus and asked Mrs. Parks why she'd hadn't moved, she replied, "I don't think I should have to stand up." When the driver called the police, Rosa was arrested.

"Doing nothing was the doing," wrote poet Rita Dove in "Rosa."

Mrs. Parks, straightforward and undaunted, wrote in *Quiet Strength* that her refusal to move was not because she was tired, but because she was tired of giving in. "Since I have always been a strong believer in God, I knew that He was with me, and only He could get me through that next step."

While Rebecca McGinness and others had earlier defied similar orders to move from segregated seats, Parks' refusal to be intimidated made history. Rosa's action caused her arrest, a trial with a guilty verdict and fine for disorderly conduct. Her decision also rallied resistance that resulted in the 1995 Montgomery bus boycott led by the Reverend Martin Luther King, Jr. The boycott lasted 382 days and fortified national opposition to racial segregation. In June 1956, Alabama's segregation laws for public transit were declared unconstitutional. The city appealed, and on November 13, 1956, the Supreme Court upheld the lower court's ruling.

In 1955 when Mrs. Parks changed history, I was a student at St. Anne's School. Her act of defiance and the Civil Rights movement were never mentioned in or out of the classroom. When white public schools in Virginia closed rather than integrate in response to Massive Resistance in 1956, I was cocooned on Sweet Briar College's secluded campus with racial unrest far removed.

My parents never made racist references, but neither were they political activists. The only African Americans I knew and loved worked for my family. My grandmother's maid, Gladys Mayo, had cleaned and cooked for her since she was a teenager. Gladys called me "Miss Boopie" from the day I was born. Our housekeeper, Alberta Brown, taught me "the facts of life" as well as how to jitterbug and make pancakes. She fluffed my wedding veil and waved me off on my honeymoon.

My overdue consciousness was finally raised when my own young children started public school. The school John co-founded was coeducational and integrated. I interviewed African Americans as a local newspaper reporter and joined a white women/black women's discussion group. In filming my documentary on Mrs. McGinness, we became friends. She also taught me many lessons about her community, her heritage and its importance to the young. Rebecca and Rosa Parks, born 21 years apart, relied on indisputable faith in making choices of conviction that helped change their societies.

Rosa Parks' solid principles put her on the forefront of the civil rights movement as well as into the unsought limelight. Had she foreseen fame, its subsequent responsibility and harassment, death threats and the loss of her job and Raymond's? How wrenching it must have been for Rosa, Raymond and her mother to leave home to seek safety in Detroit in 1957. Had she felt foreign in her northern outpost, or finally fulfilled in her calling as secretary and receptionist to African-American US Representative John Conyers? She held the influential job for over 20 years.

After retirement, Parks kept to her mission. She stated in the *Rosa Parks Biography — Academy of Achievement* interview: "All of us should be free and equal and have equal opportunity and that's why I'm trying to…encourage and inspire young people to reach their highest potential."

A decade after Raymond's death, Rosa and her friend Elaine Eason Steele founded the Rosa and Raymond Parks Institute for Self-Development to help youths 11 to 18 achieve their highest potential. At 90, Mrs. Parks, like Rebecca McGinness, still gave her strength to students. She mentored teens in the Pathways to Freedom program which included an annual summer bus tour highlighting US history and the Civil Rights movement. "I urge children to have a spiritual awareness in their lives. If children work towards a positive goal in life, it will help them be successful when they become adults," she said in her *Academy of Achievement* interview.

"The advice I would give any young person is, first of all, to rid themselves of prejudice against other people and to be concerned about what they can do to help others. And of course, to get a good education, and take advantage of the opportunities that they have."

Students online asked Rosa Parks, "Have you ever faced something that you thought you couldn't stand up to?" She answered: "I can't think of anything. Usually, if I have to face something, I do so no matter what the consequences might be. I never had any desire to give up. I did not feel that giving up would be a way to become a free person. That's the way I still feel. By standing up to something, we still don't always effect change right away. Even when we are brave and have courage, change still doesn't come about for a long time."

Whether the challenge of civil rights or of age, Parks kept to her never-give-up credo. I wrote to Mrs. Parks hoping for a short conversation, a chance to ask what still stirred this indomitable lady.

The Institute's Director, Anita Peeks, told me that Mrs. Parks no longer gave in-person interviews but might answer a few written questions. I submitted 10 questions, and after many months, received answers to three:

What role does faith play in your life, now and as a civil rights activist?

"Refusing to give up my seat to a white male passenger on December 1, 1955 changed my life. My decision was sustained by my faith in God and the teachings of my mother and grandfather," wrote Mrs. Parks, a practitioner of both Christian prayers and Buddhist meditation.

What is your biggest reward working with young people at the Raymond Parks Institute?

"All the children I have been able to educate through Pathways to Freedom. I want all the children to know that knowledge is freedom. Each child is special to me and I want each one to learn as much as possible."

What has been most important to you in maintaining a long, productive life?

"Get a good education. Good health. Learn how to rest." Mrs. Parks coped with ulcers and bursitis. She used holistic and traditional medicine and ate a vegetarian diet.

And, as she became more delicate, I wanted to ask Rosa Parks how she wished to be remembered? Her autobiography had the answer: "I would like to be known as a person who is concerned about freedom and equality and justice for all people, a person who wanted to be free so other people would be also free ...."

Rosa Louise McCauley Parks, born February 4, 1913, in Tuskegee, Alabama, would get her wish. If a reluctant role model, she would be remembered as a woman of integrity who never lost faith in the struggle for equality. She was heroic yet humble; peaceful yet daring; vulnerable, reserved and unshakeable. She smiled freely.

While disappointed not to meet Mrs. Parks, I looked for clues to her endurance studying her historic photographs: Rosa Parks on the Montgomery bus, her hands folded, her sights far beyond the window; Rosa Parks proud with purpose when fingerprinted for civil disobedience; Rosa Parks, poised and deceptively small receiving the Presidential Medal of Freedom and Congressional Gold Medal from President Clinton. Rosa at 85 huddled in a crowd of young people with the Reverend Jesse Jackson at the 1998 "Save the Dream" rally. Her hat pulled down, her eyes bright and hopeful, she listened, alert and ready to march.

And, regal Rosa Parks crowned with silver braids, blew out her 90th birthday candles as friends, admirers and "The Three Mo Tenors" sang "For the Love of Rosa."

Rosa McCauley Parks died at home in Detroit on October 24, 2005. She was 92.

PHOTO BY BUTCH WING

PHOTO BY ADAM SLATE

Civil Rights Leader the Reverend Jesse Jackson

"When the walls come down, we all grow together."

26

Healing by Building Together

ON AUGUST 12, 2017 PROTESTORS and counter-demonstrators clashed in downtown Charlottesville at the Unite the Right rally. The rally was purportedly to protest the removal of historic statues of Generals Robert E. Lee and Stonewall Jackson. During the inflammatory confrontations, a young woman was killed and two state trooper pilots crashed in their helicopter. The crash exploded in our front yard, 30 feet from our front door.

We heard the helicopter's accelerated clatter and collision impact; we saw the instant fireball. We were afraid that our house would catch fire. John ran to the copter to see if the pilots had been thrown free and might be saved. It was too late.

We — and our house — were miraculously unharmed. We continue to be grateful — and confounded by the deaths and destruction we witnessed.

Two weeks later on August 27, the Reverend Jesse Jackson, recently diagnosed with Parkinson's, came to town to speak on "Healing and Rebuilding" at the Thomas Jefferson Memorial Unitarian Universalist Church. "We must stand together — black, white, brown, red and yellow — and fight for justice and equality for all," declared Jackson, an imposing prophetic presence from the pulpit.

He spoke in a rolling Southern tempo, his words rumbling low like an approaching storm. "I came to this bastion of liberalism in Charlottesville as this city and our nation are in mourning for those who died here, officers H.J. Cullen and Burke Bates, and Heather Heyer, killed when a car was used as a weapon against her. They were all victims of white supremacy.... Let us hold silence together, Love once again break our hearts open wide." We bowed our heads.

"Heather Heyer joins Rosa Parks and others (who fought injustice). She's in the lineage of those who gave, who paid the ultimate price for a more perfect union. Remember Heather and never forget her.... Her innocent death touched something deep within us.... She was a healer, a builder...." The choir sang "Love, Break Our Hearts."

The civil rights leader who called for healing, justice and political change knew of what he spoke, a struggle in which he'd forever been engaged. Jackson, now 76, rose to be a leader in the Southern Christian Leadership Conference (SCLC). In 1967, he was selected by the Rev. Martin Luther King as national director of Operation Breadbasket — SCLC's effort to boycott white businesses into hiring and buying goods and services from black business owners.

Jackson was with Dr. Martin Luther King Jr. when he was assassinated on April 4, 1968 in Memphis. A year later, *The New York Times* reported that Jackson was being viewed as King's successor by several black leaders and that Jackson was one of the few black activists who was preaching racial reconciliation.

In December 1971, Jackson, however, resigned from Operation Breadbasket over its leadership. In 1984, he started the National Rainbow Coalition. He combined the two organizations in 1996 as the non-profit Operation PUSH (People United to Save Humanity) to raise public awareness and pursue social justice, civil rights and political activism. He was a candidate for the Democratic presidential nomination in 1984 and 1988.

On this late summer Sunday morning, Jackson had taken a "red eye" flight from Los Angeles and driven directly from the airport to speak at the Unitarian church. He wore glasses, a navy pinstripe suit, a pale blue shirt and pink silk tie with a matching ascot in his breast pocket. An Operation Push button was pinned to his lapel.

Jackson entered to hoots, hollers and standing cheers. He was introduced as "an icon in the struggle for our mutual civil rights," a man who for "40 years has held a pivotal role for peace, kindness, equality and social justice. He's been called the conscience of the nation and the great unifier of the nation."

"I wanted to come to a church that was all inclusive. We're all God's children. Everybody matters. Put your hands together." We clapped and chorused back Jackson's message to prevail and carry on the struggle for equality.

The composed and commanding Baptist minister advocated that the statues come down along with the walls of racism and prejudice. "The statues are relics of the Civil war, sedition and slavery. Bringing them down is part of the healing process.

"Behind the walls are ignorance and fear, hatred and violence. We must adopt Christian values. When the walls come down, we will see each other differently. When the walls come down, we all grow together. We will all win. Tear down the wall!"

"Yes! Yes!" came the ready reply.

"Who benefits from the wall? Racism is learned behavior. Racism is 'fake news'.... We need a new direction. Fight for real news!" Jackson called to applause. "We must find common zone on all sides of town....

"I think it's important to reach out to the white community as well as the black community and the Latino community to show that Charlottesville is not just back and white."

He remembered his grandmother who took scraps of old family shirts, pants and rags and made a quilt. He urged his receptive audience to take our broken pieces and together build a better whole — support the Rainbow Coalition, conduct voter registration drives and focus on upcoming Virginia elections — "the centerpiece for a national frame of reference…. We can build coalitions together. We can choose the right side of history…. Don't let darkness overcome light…."

After the service in the pastor's study, Reverend Jackson answered questions from the press. I asked him who had shaped his thinking and been an influential role model. He said his father. Jackson was born Jesse Louis Burns, on October 8, 1941 in Greenville, South Carolina to Helen Burns, a 16-year-old high school student, and to Noah Louis Robinson, a 33-year-old married neighbor. Jesse was later adopted and given his name by his mother's husband, Charles Henry Jackson, a post office maintenance worker. Jesse said he thought of both men as his father.

"My father was in World War II to defeat the Germans and stop that genocide machine…. He had fewer rights when he got back than people he'd fought for. It was humiliating to him. I once asked my father about raking some leaves and cutting grass at a white person's house…. The guy came down the steps. He was dressed in an immaculate fashion. I said, 'Who is this guy? He talks funny…. He didn't talk like other Southerners. He was a German. I looked up and my father was crying. I asked him why.

"He said, 'Don't worry about my tears. You just go to school. Mama and I will handle this.' He was saying, this guy runs textile mills and I can't get jobs there. He endured the humiliation. He taught me dignity at all costs. Dignity is above dollars. Dignity at all costs. Some things are worth living and dying for. And learning to live together is a big piece of *learning* to live together. Hate is detrimental to the spirit. It's not good for the people."

Jackson said his father had been "bested" by Parkinson's disease, for which Jesse had recently been diagnosed.

And now what kept Jesse Jackson fighting, going on?

"Fear of going back. We need to go forward," he said. "If you don't fight, you will go backwards and I *fear* that. Fighting to go forward, I *hope* for that. So fear and hope. Fear and hope."

I thanked Reverend Jackson and shook his hand. His hand felt unusually firm and reassuring.

CHRIS RICHARDS PHOTO, BY PERMISSION OF THE
NORMAN VINCENT PEALE ARCHIVES, PAWLING, NY

Ruth Stafford Peale, *Guideposts* Editor

*We have to be positive; remember God is still over us all;
be ready to accept what comes; help as many as we can ....*

27

Thinking Positively

ON THE SUNDAY BEFORE SEPTEMBER 11, 2001, I joined a crowded congregation to celebrate Ruth Stafford Peale's 95th birthday at New York's Marble Collegiate Church. For 52 years, its members had been led by Mrs. Peale's late husband, the minister and motivational speaker, Dr. Norman Vincent Peale, author of the 1952 bestseller, *The Power of Positive Thinking*. Dr. Peale died at 95 on Christmas Eve 1993. His bronze statue — with arms outstretched — welcomed worshippers to the church on the corner of 29th Street and Fifth Avenue.

Mrs. Peale walked on her son's arm to the chancel encircled by lofty stained-glass windows. She wore a kelly green suit, a white orchid and sure as sunrise smile. Celebrants of all ages and races stood to sing "Faith of our fathers, holy faith, we will be true to thee till death."

Petite beside her children John, Elizabeth and Margaret, Mrs. Peale beamed during their testimonials to her exceptional marriage and ministry: "Our mother has a spirit of determination, self-reliance, grace, and understanding …. Peace and quiet are at her center. She's fun …. She opened us up to the wider world. We traveled to Kenya and to the Holy Land at Christmas.

"As a young bride, she shaped her life into a partnership that was unusual in the early 30s …. Dad was a cyclone, an innovator. She was a visionary. They were married for 63 years, a team in a worldwide ministry of love and honor. Their legacy was to serve others. She affirmed and encouraged others' gifts. And she gave us the gift of God in our lives."

The Reverend Dr. Arthur Caliandro praised Mrs. Peale's partnership in Dr. Peale's Reformed Church ministry from 1932 to 1984 and presented her with a commemorative plaque to be hung in the church vestibule. Then came a giant birthday cake and Mrs. Peale blew out the candles. "It's too beautiful to eat!" she joked. "Thank you. The Lord has certainly provided for me. I'm happy to still be here and am going to be here a long time. I hope you will come to my 100th!" Worshippers accepted with willing applause.

After the service, Mrs. Peale greeted family and guests in the pastor's rooms and handed out copies of her recent autobiography, *A Lifetime of Positive Thinking.* She reminded the invited guests, "You have to find what's necessary to bring happiness into your life; to have a purpose and keep a positive attitude."

She beguiled the photographer: "I'm 95 and expect to live at least to 100." If presuming can make it so, she would fulfill her expectations and the ministry begun with her husband. The author of *Adventures of Being a Wife* (1971) and *The Secrets of Staying in Love* (1984) was perfectly matched with the plain-spoken author of 46 books and father of the self-help movement. Ruth Peale assisted Dr. Peale in a weekly NBC radio broadcast, *The Art of Living.* From 1952 to 1968, the couple answered viewers' questions on the television program, *What's Your Trouble?* She accompanied Dr. Peale to the White House when he conducted a Sunday service for President Nixon and when he received the 1984 Presidential Medal of Freedom from President Reagan.

Dr. Peale initially desired to be a reporter but was persuaded by his mother to become a minister. In *The Ageless Spirit,* he underlined his successful thesis: "Thoughts reproduce themselves in kind, so if you deal in negative thoughts, you attract negative results. If you think positively, you tend to attract positive results. If you want to be a positive old person, positive people will come to you. The secret to overcoming loneliness is to learn how to be a positive and entertaining person."

A fast learner, Ruth Stafford Peale trusted her truth, and attributed her constructive philosophy to exemplar parents. Ruth Stafford was born in Fonda, Iowa in 1906, the second of three children of a Methodist minister who served small churches in Iowa and Detroit. "In our bringing up, my parents taught us a sense of purpose that stayed with me — always help and encourage others; it will lead to a deeper faith in almighty God. That has been very important in my life and career.

"My parents also gave me the feeling I could do anything I wanted to do. They helped and encouraged my brothers and me to do well in school. They complimented me on what I wanted to do. They said, 'Find a need and fill it.'

"My mother and father gave us a wonderful way to have a family, a model of marriage for me. It was a happy home. They sang duets in church and they had us sing in concerts along with them. They were a team."

Schooled in teamwork, Ruth and Norman co-founded the Peale Center for Christian Living in Pawling, New York. Mrs. Peale, now widowed for eight years, remained deeply committed to the Center's objectives. As CEO, she headed a staff of 360 that published *Guideposts*, one of five inter-faith magazines with combined circulations over four and a half million. She planned to publish several new youth magazines as well.

I phoned Mrs. Peale at the Peale Center in Pawling, "The Town of Positive Thinking." She'd just driven her 1983 navy blue Cadillac four miles to work, arriving at 7:45, on time for the day's meetings.

Since our meeting, a month had passed and New York had suffered the 9/11 attacks. On September 11th, I'd been alone in Jamie's apartment in Battery Park — two blocks west of the World Trade towers. Jamie was at our house in Virginia; John was marooned in the Salt Lake airport on his way home from Montana.

I woke to a blue-sky morning and looked forward to seeing friends for lunch. I opened Jamie's window to check the temperature and saw flames and white smoke billowing from the upper floors of the North Tower, One World Trade Center. *TODAY* show hosts Katie Couric and Matt Lauer, like all the morning broadcasters, assumed we were watching "a freak accident." I called home to report the news.

Jamie, steady in a crisis, hadn't seen the television and reasoned that all would soon be under control. "Stay there, Mom. You'll be OK." It was 8:46. Reporters rushed to sort out conflicting bulletins. I found my long lens and took shots of the burning Tower.

The fires spread. The sirens shrieked. News crews rushed to the scene. Panic crept into my stomach. Should I leave Jamie's apartment? Should I go to a friend's nearby building? I took the elevator to the lobby. Smoke blinded the entrance halls. Distressed residents patrolled back and forth, scared to leave. A woman asked anyone listening, "What should I do? My daughter was in the Tower. Where is she? Where is she?"

I retreated, unnerved, into the elevator and back to the tenth floor. I called Jamie again. "It's a freak accident," he repeated. "Don't worry, Mom." Mid-sentence, the power snapped off and the phone went dead. The 20-story high rise suddenly shuddered under a tide of black ash hurtling against the windows. My stomach heaved and my legs sank. I grabbed a pillow, hugged it tight and crouched in the bathtub. The walls shook like an earthquake. I prayed to the sound of biblical thunder. It was 9:59 as the South Tower rumbled to earth.

Shouts rose from the street: "Get out of the building! Get out of the building!" I grabbed my camera and purse and fled down 10 flights, racing with others covered in dust, slipping in gray powder under foot along the Battery Park promenade. Police helped us into motorboats relaying across the Hudson to Liberty Park. I looked back at Lower Manhattan smothered in smoke, wondering what the future held.

Buses on Liberty Island shuttled us like evacuees to an army base and the Jersey City bus terminal. Mayor Rudy Giuliani blared radio updates that New York was "under terrorist attack," and that all bridges, roads and tunnels were shut down. My heart sped. What would happen next? Were John, Jamie and Virginia safe?

I wove in and out of the depot crowd. Our numbers multiplied in the cloudless heat. We waited for buses that never came. I was thirsty and hungry. I knocked on a funeral parlor door and asked to use the rest room. By late afternoon, I feared nightfall. Where should I go? Where would I sleep?

Without warning, someone yelled that the Jersey Path trains were operating again and going into Manhattan. Wasn't the city "shut down?" Was this a terrorist's trick? False hope? Should I stay or follow the pack?

I scurried with the herd down the escalator and onto the train. The train door slammed shut. Whatever our fates, we were all to-gether — white and black, mothers, fathers and small children, His-panics, Asians, rich and poor and bearded boys in Grateful Dead tee-shirts. We white-knuckled the overhead bars, minutes seeming like hours, linked in league as we rattled through dark tunnels under the Hudson, trusting, hoping and holding on. Talk about faith.

Miraculously, the train arrived at the station and the doors opened to whoops of joy. We cautiously climbed the stairs to 34th Street. At rush hour, the busy intersection was strangely deserted and the air thick with heat. The uptown subways weren't running. I started walk-ing north to a friend's apartment, thankful for every uncertain step.

It would be days before I could take Amtrak home, months before Jamie could return to his contaminated apartment, and longer before we would understand how much the world as we knew it had changed.

When I phoned Mrs. Peale, I was still reeling and particularly anxious to hear her perspective and reassurances. Had her faith faltered? Did it still remain rock solid? Did she question her positive beliefs?

"This is a difficult time," she agreed. "In such a time, we have to be positive; remember God is still over us all. We need to be ready to accept what comes; help as many as we can. There's never been a time quite like this one. It's awfully important that our feelings depend on God. We need a practical approach as never before. I've lived through other difficult times, and we need to pray more earnestly than ever before to live through these difficult times which are not finished yet."

No fault lines for Mrs. Peale. Her words were as certain as ever. Still guided by her husband's persuasive convictions, she cautioned: "Never talk defeat. Use words like hope, belief, faith, victory. He said, 'Change your thoughts and change the world.'" She added that her own beliefs were built on the "law of attraction — what one asks for and believes in, one gets; positive thoughts will be heard and rewarded."

If Mrs. Peale was not inclined to question, she still heard and responded to those who asked. "I had a letter today from Texas, a gentleman who had a difficult marriage of three years. It hasn't worked out; he's disappointed. He needs peace in his life. I wrote him to turn to God, and read as many religious books as he could find.

"I did not have theological training but took psychology in college. I try to be helpful; be ready to talk and encourage people in their faith. It encourages me to hear that my letters are helpful. It makes me feel God has a plan for my life."

At her birthday celebration, Mrs. Peale needed no hymnal to sing "Faith of Our Fathers." She pressed on, her assurances appealing, constant in God's plan, immovable faith, affections and calling. "I try to carry on what my husband would have been doing," she said. "I'm still at it. I still live by my husband's motto: 'Live your life and forget your age.'"

I was heartened by Mrs. Peale's unscathed convictions as she prepared for an afternoon walk within sight of the Catskill Mountains. She didn't second-guess what couldn't be fathomed or changed. "Help as many as we can," she urged. "We need to be aware of the fact that God is ready to help. We need to keep that uppermost in our minds. He will help personally in problems of everyday life. He very much wants you to ask. He will answer 'yes, no or wait awhile.'"

Mrs. Peale celebrated her 100th birthday on September 10th, 2006, testimony to a century of patience and positive thinking.

Ruth Stafford Peale died at home in Pawling, New York on February 7, 2008. She was 101.

PHOTO BY DICK SNYDER

Bishop John Shelby Spong, Jr., Theologian

I experience God as the power of love.

28

Living the Mystery

BEFORE HIS THIRD BIRTHDAY, Jack Spong found a goldfish floating at the top of the family aquarium and ran to tell his mother. She scooped up the tiny fish and flushed it down the toilet. Too soon, Jack learned that death could be sudden and meant things disappeared.

Jack Spong witnessed early the distressing disappearance of his kindly grandfather, several school friends, and his father, John Shelby Spong, his namesake who died when his son was 12.

These painful deaths may not yet have set Jack on his journey to becoming a charismatic and controversial Episcopal theologian and Bishop, but they did make him all too aware of life's sorrows and inevitable end. He yearned for assurances, ways to make sense of death's reality. "I needed to believe and embrace the Bible," Spong wrote in *Eternal Life: A New Vision Beyond Religion, Beyond Theism, Beyond Heaven and Hell.*

Jack's need to believe and make sense of life's limit would shape his years and still preoccupy his later decades. I was drawn to Spong's temporal and tolerant thoughts on Christianity and the hereafter. His interviews and manner were appealing — a rangy, gregarious cleric with a chivalrous Southern accent who wore his Bishop's blouse like a cardinal among sparrows.

In late fall of 2014, he phoned from his home in the woods of suburban Morris Plains, New Jersey. He was now retired there with Christine, his wife of 25 years, a former staffer of the Episcopal Diocese of Newark, his editor, organizer and beloved companion. At 83, Spong recalled his ongoing journey from god-fearing beginnings to an outspoken and passionate man of the cloth.

Unlike Ruth Stafford Peale's supportive childhood, Jack's was fraught with uncertainty. After his father's death, he and his older sister and younger brother were raised in Charlotte, North Carolina, by a mother widowed at 35 with less than a ninth grade education. She had no money or bankable skills. She did, however, have an unshakable Presbyterian faith that she practiced and required her children to conform to without question.

"My mother was an old-line Calvinist: anything that was fun was sinful or fattening. She was very rigid. Sunday was God's day; you did nothing on Sunday. I really couldn't stand Sunday because I couldn't stand a God who would have a day like that," he said.

"She was very strict and believed children were born in sin. It was her job to beat the sin out of them, so she was quite into corporal punishment. But she was also sweet and loving and kept our family together. It was the life she had, and she drew very firm lines so we had some security. She lived to 92 and was remarkable in many ways.

"My father (a traveling salesman) never went to church. He drank like a sailor. And he cussed like a sailor. And he smoked like a stovepipe." Spong's courteous tone harshened. "He did all the things that my church thought were evil, and when he died (of heart disease at 54) all these church people came to me and said, 'You must be happy now because your father's in heaven.' 'Til that time they'd told me that anybody who did all the things my father did, was surely going to hell. It didn't connect, so I was sort of repelled by that (attitude)."

Young Jack kept quiet and went to work. "We lived in pretty deep poverty. I started carrying newspapers at 12 to bring in 10 dollars a week and milked cows next door to bring in three dollars a week.

"When I was in school, I was one of the nerds because I didn't have proper clothes to wear. I certainly didn't have an automobile. Because of jobs, I didn't have time to participate in sports. I was just really a survivor."

His gracious tenor returned. "At 14, I met Robert Crandall, the new rector of St. Peter's Church in Charlotte. He was 32. My image of a clergyman was that you had to be 80. He was very life affirming, a Bing Crosby *Going My Way* type. He played a guitar; he had a beautiful wife; he drove a white convertible; he wore white buck shoes. He did all sorts of things that broke the stereotype.

"He and his wife had no children; they sort of adopted me. I really did need some parents so I sort of adopted *them*. I wanted to live in his orbit and do anything in the world that he felt was worthwhile. To this day, I still try to emulate this man. I wanted to be a priest; that's where that desire came from."

Besides breaking the clergyman stereotype, Bob Crandall interpreted God in more appealing and broader terms than had Jack's mother; she quoted the Bible to justify segregation and the inferiority of women and Jews. "My mother was a biblical literalist who always said, 'The Bible *says*.' Crandall said, 'The church *teaches*.' That was the first step out of the fundamentalism of my childhood."

At St. Peter's church, Spong had found a mentor, the first of many strong role models who would influence his spiritual odyssey. Here too he found a sanctuary and second home. Jack became a devout acolyte, and president of the church and diocesan youth groups. "I was a church rat. I was down there every time the place was open. I much preferred to live in that world than I did in my home. I was just very much into the church orbit."

Spong's poor grades upped to straight As and he vowed to keep going. "I was motivated to make something of my life." He would be the first in his family to attend college. He graduated from the University of North Carolina in three years and was elected to Phi Beta Kappa. He also met his first wife, Joan, with whom he would have three daughters.

With the wind in his spiritual sails, Spong answered the calling that set his future. In 1955, he received his Master of Divinity degree from the Episcopal Theological Seminary in Alexandria, Virginia. He later studied contemporary biblical scholarship at New York's Union Theological Seminary, Yale Divinity School, Harvard Divinity School and at Edinburgh, Oxford and Cambridge universities.

Over the course of his studies, Spong questioned the Virgin birth, Jesus' bodily resurrection, and the Gospels' historical accuracies. He also gained more influential mentors and role models. At Carolina, he studied Greek, philosophy and physics, and changed his mind on evolution due to zoology professor Claiborne Jones. An active Episcopalian, Jones taught that Charles Darwin, a man who did not believe in original sin, was "a thorough going evolutionist." "I didn't think you could be both," said Spong. "I'd thought evolution was some sort of godless scheme."

Prior to Seminary, Spong didn't dispute the concept of a heavenly deity. "I had not yet embraced the Copernicus revolution to say nothing of Galileo. The Bible was written from the point of view of God as a supernatural being who lived above the sky. We still say 'Our Father who art in heaven.' Heaven is clearly located above the sky which we call 'the heavens' today."

At Seminary, Spong met the prominent theologian Paul Tillich, and termed it "a life-changing experience." "Tillich redefined God.... God was not *a* being who lived above the sky and periodically answered prayers and did miracles which is what most people think God is supposed to be. He was being itself. He was the ground of *being*.

"'*He*' is even the wrong word. God is the life that flows through the universe; God is the love that makes us all more deeply human.

God is the being out of which *our* being emerges and in which we are rooted.

"None of these (supernatural) images make a lot of sense to space-age people, but that's the language of the Christian faith in its traditional form. And so we still use it." Spong found it initially difficult to connect to Tillich's more amorphous understandings of God. "To try to relate Tillich's concept of God and his religious symbols to the kind of Sunday school training that I'd had in Charlotte was almost a lifetime work. I started with his definitions and I've worked on that the rest of my life."

Spong, the inquirer, was also impacted by the work of theologian Dietrich Bonhoeffer, an ecumenical Lutheran pastor active in the German resistance; he attempted to overthrow the Third Reich while espousing responsible, ethical action against evil as the fulfillment of God's will. "Bonhoeffer said we've got to develop a Christianity without religion. Religionless Christianity is very appealing to me because religion per se is not very appealing to me."

Each new post in Spong's 45 year ministry was decisive in building his sometimes controversial beliefs and direction. First as a lay reader during college, and then in 1955, as rector of St. Joseph's Episcopal Church in Durham, North Carolina, he expanded his perspective and teaching skills while interacting with congregations that were a mix of Duke medical students, faculty and nearby millworkers. The Carolina native served as rector of Calvary Parish in Tarboro, North Carolina, and supported integration in 1959.

At St. John's Church in Lynchburg, Virginia, Spong raised textual questions in adult Bible study that dismayed fundamentalists. Over the next eight years as rector of St. Paul's in Richmond, Spong, allied with a leading rabbi, promoted a dialogue of Jewish-Christian understanding that drew an avid radio and television audience. He removed a Confederate flag from the chancel, and offered compelling, pre-service Bible classes, one of which ended with a matriarch's comment: "Reverend Spong, I don't agree with anything you say, but I love the way you say it."

Buford Scott, a parishioner with whom Spong worked on open housing, described his friend of 40 years as "a full-time student of the Bible," one who said, "'The only true sin is to fail to live up to what you're capable of becoming.' I asked him how do you know what you're capable of becoming?' He said, "You have to stretch yourself every day to be more capable than before.'"

In 1976, Spong "stretched" his priestly muscles by leaving the land of grits and spoon bread to become Bishop of Newark, New Jersey. Newark was then a city in turmoil, needful of Spong's dedication to social justice. He pitched in from the pulpit and on the streets. His inclusive "teaching ministry" — often to conservative but concerned congregations — addressed racial segregation and healthcare; he campaigned for women clergy and ordained openly homosexual priests.

Did Spong consider himself a theological rebel?

Not exactly. Spong said his activist theology and ministry were particularly shaped by "three great mentors" — the Reverend David Yates and Bishops John Hines and John Robinson. "They all lived very richly. They exhausted the meaning of today. And I think that's the way to live."

Reverend Yates, rector at the Chapel of the Cross in Chapel Hill, North Carolina, was a pacifist during World War II as well as that rare activist for desegregation in the 1940s South. "David said, 'These [black] people are the children of God, and you cannot discriminate against a child of God.' He was a man living true to his moral concerns."

Hines, "a deep Southerner" and the presiding Bishop of the Episcopal Church from 1964 to 1973, fostered African American businesses in Durham, North Carolina. "John turned the resources of the Episcopal church during the [race] riots in this country toward funding Black Power organizations. He steered the church towards a deep involvement with the black community and towards the ordination of women. He taught me that you stand up for what's right and you don't bother to compromise. You don't worry about whether you are popular or not."

And British Bishop John Robinson, author of *Honest to God*, "called Christians to live in the 20th century, to reject the simplified and outdated concept of a heavenly being in favor of Paul Tillich's existentialist God. Robinson really took religion out of the church and put it back where people could talk about it," said Spong. "He did biblical scholarship with integrity and modeled for me how it could be done.

"When Robinson died, I felt that my world had been shaken radically, and I had to be the one to rise up and take his place because nobody else was going to do it. And so I did. At least in my mind that's what I was doing."

He reconsidered. "There were a lot of people who thought I didn't have the ability, I couldn't hold a light to him but that's OK. I hope I speak to my children, to the world in which I live, but I clearly don't speak to everybody."

Far from fundamentalism, Spong's prominent ministry, theological leadership, and 22 books, (*Jesus for the Non-Religious* among them) earned him a liberal label along with 16 death threats. "I try to speak to those who have been so turned off by fundamentalism that they don't see any reason for a Christian church. No threats have come from a Buddhist or atheist," he said. "They come from Bible quoting, true-believing Christians.

"The Christianity that I grew up with just couldn't live in the world that I was increasingly beginning to live (in). You have to do one of two things: you have to give up your Christianity or you have to give up your *world*. Or, a third thing, you have to forge a brand-new relationship between the two which means in the process, you have to change the way you think about almost all Christian symbols. And in some sense, that's what I've done. And consistently for the rest of my life."

In changing his thinking, Spong clarified his beliefs as "a church person who keeps trying to redefine God, Jesus and life after death."

He quoted Jesus' reason for being: "I came that they may have life, and have it abundantly." Spong urged his readers "to live fully, to love wastefully, to be all that you can be.

"Today," he confirmed, "I am still a deeply committed Christian. I have a deep and really rich sense of God's reality and God's presence, but it is not definable. I can't tell you this is who God is or that is who God is, but I just sort of live into this mystery and I rather like what I find.

"I say, 'I walk the Christ path,' but I don't think God's a Christian. I walk the Christ path because it's the only way I know to walk into the mystery of God. And if I walk it deep enough and far enough, I will transcend scripture, I will transcend creeds, I will transcend Christianity itself. That doesn't mean Christianity is bad. It just means it's a human religion that has pointed millions of people in the direction of God and it's the path I choose to walk. But God cannot be bound by my path."

Bishop Spong paused on his path. Although retired, he still frequently preached and lectured across the US and abroad. He still wore his clerical collar, still studied and wrote weekly columns and best-selling books in pen on yellow pads in his book-lined study. Perhaps with his mother in mind, he was researching his next text — *Biblical Literalism: A Gentile Heresy* — at nearby Drew University, a small, coed college with a Methodist theological seminary.

There in rural New Jersey, Spong also clocked four miles daily on the treadmill and planned summer mountain hikes and walking tours with Christine. Spong's first wife, Joan, died of cancer after 37 years of marriage.

"I can't now imagine anything better than being married to Christine and living to 83 and still being creative and happy. She's an absolutely incredible partner. Without her," he said, "I would shrivel quickly."

Spong opposed his losses with redemptive beliefs confirmed in *Eternal Life: A New Vision Beyond Religion, Beyond Theism, Beyond Heaven and Hell:* "I believe deeply that this life that I love so passionately is not all there is.... This life is not the end of life. I experience God as the power of love. I do believe that love is eternal and I am held in the bonds of love by my family, my friends and countless acquaintances.

"I have been drawn, it seems relentlessly as a moth is drawn to a candle, into a study of death and thus into a consideration of that question to which religion seems to devote so much of its energy — namely, whether death might be a doorway to something more."

And now this student of life's end considered death, "something more," something beyond mortality, a universal consciousness, a shared mystical and eternal union with God.

"This mystical experience is what I'd call *wordless wonder.* You experience something you can't put words to but know it's beyond anything you've ever known before. Universal consciousness recognizes that you are part of everybody else and they are part of you. There's a unity that you can't begin to comprehend."

Spong's childhood fears of death and disappearance had long gone. "To me, the way you prepare for dying is that you learn how to live. The more deeply you love, the more you engage in life now, the more life turns mysterious at its core. When falling in love, you've transcended one of the greatest boundaries on our humanity and you get a taste of what might be beyond the limits of our humanity."

To the novice listening on the other end of the line, Spong counseled, "Just take what day you've got and live it. I feel like the mystery in every day is an adventure and I want to keep walking into it."

PHOTO BY ELIZABETH HOWARD

Dr. Ian Pretyman Stevenson, Reincarnation Researcher

*The idea of a second chance or umpteenth chance
wherever it may be, that's appealing.*

29

Holding Onto Hope

WHILE MY FATHER DIDN'T BELIEVE strongly in God or an afterlife, my mother was curious about reincarnation and all spiritual possibilities. She read and marked the Bible as well as books by psychic healer Edgar Cayce. She was intrigued by para-psychology, precognitive dreams, extrasensory perception and earlier lives. She'd attended lectures by Dr. Ian Stevenson, a clinical psychiatrist and scholar at the University of Virginia famed for his research on reincarnation. Dr. Stevenson became chair of UVa's Department of Psychiatry in 1957 at age 38, after graduating at the top of his medical class at Montreal's McGill University.

Also curious about the possibilities of reincarnation, I felt my mother's approval when I interviewed Dr. Stevenson in 2004. He arrived in gray suit, crest tie and tassel loafers, carrying a heavy, scarred briefcase. At 86, he remained a hardy, courtly gentleman.

We met at the University of Virginia's Division of Personality Studies located off campus in a Victorian house. The hallway was decorated with tokens from Stevenson's worldwide treks: maps of Burma and Sri Lanka, a red and black striped Kandyan drum, a Burmese shell fan. Photos from the 1970s and 1980s showed Dr. Stevenson wading in an Indian river, balancing loafers and an L.L. Bean bag; jotting notes beside a Jeep, with scant shade from the scorching sun.

Upstairs, Stevenson's office was streamlined to desk, electric typewriter, French/English and German/English dictionaries and files storing some 2500 cases of reincarnation. His replies, by turn reticent, polite and pointed, conceded that his study of reincarnation — sometimes called survival of personality after death — was ongoing and serendipitous.

As a physician, Stevenson had always been interested in personality development and the effects of mental states on the body. Studying the causes of psychosomatic illnesses inclined him to psychiatry and psychoanalysis. In the 1950s, he'd even investigated the clinical use of psychedelic drugs LSD and mescaline, then legal and considered promising.

He'd read widely on personality development and psychical research, including extrasensory perception and near-death experiences. He was especially drawn to reports of children in India who claimed memory of previous lives. "Discontent with other explanations of human personality, I wasn't satisfied with psychoanalysis or behaviorism or, for that matter, neuroscience. Something seemed to be missing," Stevenson told Tom Shroder in *Old Souls: The Scientific Evidence for Past Lives.*

Stevenson's own essay on reincarnation claims won him underwriting for his first research trip to India in 1961. "I discovered a kind of pattern emerging. I found that these (Indian) cases rather often occurred in very young children between the ages of two and four, and the children usually stopped speaking about the past life between the ages of seven and eight."

He questioned the children and their parents and found memories of death wounds that corresponded to birth marks along with unexplained illnesses and phobias seemingly related to trauma in a former life. Such discoveries made Stevenson wonder if personality mysteries might not be due to reincarnation as well as heredity and environment.

This old school scholar, driven for answers, had risked his career to travel a precarious path. He'd spent 40 years collecting evidence of children's former lives. He documented claims of early childhood cases in Southeast Asia as well in Africa, British Columbia, South America, Lebanon, Turkey, and the United States including Alaska.

Stevenson's US cases focused on American Indians of the Northwest. He also authored some 300 publications, including 14 texts, from *Twenty Cases Suggestive of Reincarnation: Body, Mind and Spirit* (1966) to *European Cases of the Reincarnation Type* (2003).

While becoming the acknowledged founder of scientific research on reincarnation, Stevenson's early research generated so much controversy among his University of Virginia colleagues that in 1967, he gave up his administrative duties to pursue research as director of the newly established Division of Personality Studies.

A decade later Harold Lief, a psychiatrist and former chairman of the University of Pennsylvania's Department of Psychiatry, wrote in the *Journal of Nervous and Mental Disease:* "Dr. Stevenson is a methodical, careful, even cautious investigator, whose personality is on the obsessive side.... Either he is making a colossal mistake, or he will be known as 'the Galileo of the 20th century.'"

I was intrigued by Stevenson's contradictory persona — a restrained, cultured academic willing to take enormous professional and personal risks. His youthful daring still showed. So there in his office stripped to the necessities, how did he, in fact, define reincarnation? How did he view reincarnation in relation to faith and an afterlife?

Dr. Stevenson spoke carefully. "It's the association of a person — I don't mind using the word soul — who has lived a previous life and then becomes embodied in a new physical form. That sounds sort of complicated, but that's what it amounts to. A soul would be the continuing element that becomes associated with successive physical bodies."

So as we age, can we count on the soul's survival? Didn't Socrates and Plato believe the mind was more important than the body?

"Yes, [survival) or a new body," said Stevenson. "We should have a new body even in the next world … there has to be a body of some kind."

Is reincarnation connected to the Christian belief in resurrection?

"I don't think so. I have an acquaintance, a Cambridge scholar, who is also a physicist and an Episcopalian priest, Church of England. He's written extensively about religion and science and he believes in the resurrection in some kind of physical form but apparently not in reincarnation. It's interesting."

Very. Is it fair to say that reincarnation implied progression?

Stevenson folded his long arms over his chest. "Well, there's the hope of progression, but it doesn't always happen. In fact, I've recently been studying notes on five or six cases in which the deceased person had certain attitudes and tastes — good and bad. The new persons remembered the lives of these persons and there'd been no progress."

"How discouraging." We laughed.

"Yes, it is a bit." Stevenson had written that six of his cases showed "a lack of moral progress in purgatory." He added, "I think one's conduct would be altered according to one's view of subsequent life, whether purgatory or reincarnation. Or extinction.

"I'd like to think people would have to take more responsibilities in their destinies. They should take more responsibility, but they don't. On my first trip to India, I visited the Ramakrishna order of Hindu monks in the North. They're all well educated and they're engaged in educational functions of one kind or another in the ashrams. Swami Muktananda asked, 'What are you doing in India?' I said, 'I've come to look at evidence of reincarnation.' There was a long silence. Then he said, 'That's very interesting. We know it's a fact in India. And we know it, but it makes no difference because we have just as many rogues and villains here as you have in the West.' That was the end of that interview."

"That's discouraging, too." One more irony.

"Well, he was realistic," said Stevenson.

Stevenson also seemed a realist, a scientist who had dedicated his research to proof of an afterlife and "moral progress," one who ostensibly didn't adhere to an orthodox faith or belief in God. "My idea of God is that He is evolving. I don't believe in the watchmaker God, the original creator who built the watch and then lets it tick," he wrote in *The Red Pill.* "I believe in a 'self-maker God' who is evolving and experimenting; so are we as parts of Him."

Ian Pretyman Stevenson was born October 31, 1918, in Montreal, the second of four children to British parents of contradictory faiths. "I wasn't really raised in any religion. Not exclusively. It was very eclectic," he said. "My father, a journalist (an Ottawa correspondent for the *Times of London*), had no religion at all.

"My mother was a homemaker very interested in religion, especially Asian religions, including theosophy. She had a very absorbing library on Asian religions. But she didn't reject Christianity; she was simply an experimentalist. I remember going to different churches with my mother, the Anglican church and once to a Christian Science church. I think with my mother, religion was a quest. Nowadays, she'd be thought of as a New Age person. They called it then, 'New Thought.'"

Had his mother's quest influenced his own?

"I don't know. Maybe. The New Age people put out a lot of rubbish, but they have an essential optimism. I like that." His smile tried to hide a hint of mischief. "They have no connected corpus of belief among New Age people, although many of them do subscribe to reincarnation. And a lot of them believe in paranormal powers of various kinds, unusual things."

Stevenson acknowledged his mother's example more directly in *The Red Pill:* "My mother believed strongly in the influence of thoughts on psychical wellbeing, and I may owe to her my initial interest."

He granted that his interests also encompassed research into near-death experiences, deathbed visions, apparitions and poltergeists. In 2005 Stevenson published a biography of Stefan Ossowiecki (1877–1944), a Polish engineer who became a well-known psychic and clairvoyant.

How had further research affected his beliefs?

"You're getting into the matter of what do I believe, and I don't like to answer that question. I think my job has been to present evidence and everybody has to make up his or her own mind.

"That seems pretty severe, doesn't it? So many people look for authority. They want people to tell them what to believe."

Guilty. It was also tempting to think of having many lives to attain perfection. If we knew our lives were progressive, wouldn't we try to better ourselves with each incarnation?

"Yes, yes. Try," Stevenson teased.

I tried again. "That would seem to imply that you do believe (in reincarnation) but you're not saying."

His smile turned sly. "But I'm not saying."

Seeming so convinced, had he any sense of his own former lives?

Stevenson debated. "To a very slight extent, yes. It's not anything I like to talk about. It is later in life. Various psychics have tried to read my past lives and none of them have agreed."

So did he assume to have an afterlife?

The eminent physician peered over his wire-rimmed glasses. "Now you're encroaching on this forbidden topic."

I laughed. "I'm still trying."

"Yes, you certainly are."

Had he now reconciled his findings with other scientific beliefs?

"What other beliefs?" Stevenson volleyed. "Reincarnation is not beyond science. Nothing's beyond science. Journal editors have sometimes been unkind to me saying what I'm doing is not scientific." In *Old Souls: The Scientific Evidence for Past Lives*, he asked with frustration, "Why do mainstream scientists refuse to accept the evidence we have for reincarnation?"

He also saw reasons for doubt. "A belief in reincarnation is warranted by the strongest cases we have, but it's never the only explanation. All of our cases have flaws of some kind. They depend ultimately on human testimony. Nevertheless, some of them are pretty good."

And convincing to some of the unlikely. Supposedly World War II General George Patton believed that his deeply engrained warrior instinct dated from previous lives; he claimed to have attacked a prehistoric mammoth, fought as a Roman legionary under Julius Caesar, as an English knight during the Hundred Years War, and as marshal alongside Napoleon in the war of 1812.

Did Stevenson think we Americans somehow felt particularly entitled to an afterlife?

"Wouldn't that promote a belief in reincarnation? It's an interesting irony," he said.

And reassuring. Did he now find reincarnation a comfort as well?

"Well, I'd certainly like to be a better person. I don't have much time left in this life to do that. The idea of a second chance or umpteenth chance, whatever it may be, that's appealing. You have to start as a good baby." Oops. More laughter.

If Dr. Stevenson desired a second chance, he approved the immediate powers of love and hope. "I've been trying in recent months to find a good definition of love. I came up with — well, nothing is original anyway — 'love is never having to say you're sorry.'" He became bashful. "Another definition of love I like is 'giving something to someone who needs what you can give without expecting anything in return.' What do you think of that?"

I liked it.

"My first wife died of diabetes with every imaginable complication. I noticed how mechanically she was treated, so often by good doctors careless in their words. So I wrote a couple of papers on preserving hope in patients. That is an unfortunate weakness of many doctors. They flee from the final scene. Some of the time, the doctor just needs to shut up. They talk about all the dreadful apparatus they can bring to bear."

As Dr. Stevenson had provided hope for his first wife, he did so again now caring for his "super wife" of 20 years after she'd had a stroke. They, like Holmes Brown, had an apartment at Westminster Canterbury, an attractive assisted and independent living community on the outskirts of town. They had no children, "a joy I missed," he said.

I was surprised by Stevenson's revelation that once a mile-a-day walker and tennis player, he'd been ill much of his life, despite his solid build and seeming good health. This still inquisitive and closet optimist feigned disbelief when I proposed that others his age might have retired.

"They did? What kept Brahms going, writing great music until he was in his 60s? I guess you do those things because you think they're of some value."

Hopefully, Ian Stevenson felt recognized for his pioneering inquiry into afterlife possibilities. We stopped on the stairs where he identified photos of his early mentors. Eileen Garrett, entrepreneur, medium and founder of The Parapsychology Foundation, underwrote his first trip to India. Chester Carlson, founder of the Xerox Corporation, was his UVA benefactor. He described Carlson as "not only a great inventor, but a great man, a great soul."

Dr. Stevenson, a man still open to time travels, knew a great soul when he saw one. He held the door for me as I wished him many more fruitful journeys ahead. "There were several times when I kept telling my wife, 'This is my last trip to India,' My wife said, 'I don't mind you going to India again, but I want you to stop saying, 'This is my last trip.'"

Dr. Ian Stevenson died at home in Charlottesville, Virginia on February 8, 2007. He was 88.

PHOTO BY BILL DOW

Harry Kullijian, Businessman, and Carol Channing, Actress

The secret to the whole thing is love.

30

Believing It's Never Too Late For Love

TALK ABOUT LOVE AND HOPE. Carol Channing and Harry Kullijian went steady in the seventh and eighth grades. In 1933 Harry was the leader of the Aptos Junior High School band, and Carol took the stage to run for class vice president. Together they made up her campaign theme: "If Carol is your vice, it's a virtue." Carol won her first audience big time.

Carol and Harry also went out for ice cream and watched Joe DiMaggio train at San Francisco's Golden Gate Park not far from where they grew up. Most importantly, Harry gave Carol her first kiss, right there at her kitchen table. While innocent — and even witnessed by her father — it was a kiss Carol would never forget. And after a lifetime apart, Carol and Harry would kiss again, this time for keeps.

In the intervening 70 years, Harry, the son of an immigrant tailor, became a successful California businessman and land developer, and Carol became "The First Lady of Musical Comedy." She'd studied dance and drama at liberal Bennington College in Vermont before exiting early to hit the New York pavements. She debuted on Broadway in 1941 as understudy to Eve Arden in *Let's Face It*. Playwright and author Anita Loos spotted Carol's talent in the 1948 revue *Lend an Ear* and later cast Carol as the flashy gold digger Lorelei Lee in

Gentleman Prefer Blondes. Carol's fame was cinched with her flamboyant rendition of "Diamonds Are a Girl's Best Friend."

In 1964, Carol starred in *Hello Dolly!* — the longest running musical of its era — as Dolly Gallagher Levi, the captivating, unsinkable matchmaker bent on bagging a rich husband.

While Dolly achieved celebrity as a supreme matchmaker, offstage Carol's romances were less than storybook. She married three times — to Ted Naidish, a novelist; Alexander Carson, a pro football player with the Ottawa Rough Riders and the father of her son, Chan; and Charles Lowe, her publicist, manager and spouse of 42 years. She divorced Lowe in 1998.

In her 2002 memoir *Just Lucky, I Guess*, Carol confessed that she spent many lonely years during and after her three marriages. She also remembered Harry Kullijian, her first love, and the affection she still held for him. They'd grown up and drifted apart. She knew he'd married and had a son and daughter, and had done well in business. She longed to see him again.

A mutual friend read Carol's book soon after Harry became a widower and coaxed Harry to call her. 'She won't want to see me," Harry thought, "but I took a chance." And Cupid struck.

I wrote Carol Channing for an interview hoping to hear her never-too-late-for-love story from her own lips. Harry called from Modesto, California, introducing himself as a first name, whatever's-on-my-mind, friendly kind of fellow. "Our story," said Harry, "is all about hope … love and respect. Our love is invigorating. It makes us feel young. It's a miracle for Carol and me to be together again."

Harry won me at *invigorating* and we set the time for an interview. Carol answered, her sandpaper and satin voice sensationally as advertised. She said she was resting, stretched between two chairs. At 85, she was an acrobat, too. Carol spoke fast, her forthrightness endearing as she admitted to seven bleak years before meeting Harry again. "I was just desperate; I was so alone. You find when you're my age, everybody's dead, and as an only child you have no family, and that's terrible."

Carol replayed their reunion. "I was sure Harry was dead. He's a year older than I am. He called and I said, 'Well, when do we see each other?' And then all of a sudden Harry walked through my gate. Two weeks later we were engaged because we knew each other so well. And we'd shaped each other at an impressionable age. He had a beautiful 60-year marriage ... in this very house in which I'm living now."

I pictured moonstruck Carol when she married Harry at a friend's house near San Francisco on May 10, 2003. She wore silk pants, Harry a dark suit. "It was wonderful when he held me in his arms. He'd even promised my parents to take care of me," she recalled. "Of course it didn't hurt that he is so beautiful. He's Armenian. He looks biblical to me, like Moses sitting on Mt. Sinai eating a fig." Eat your heart out, Charlton Heston.

"It's just chemistry and I'm unaware of what creates it. Why is it with other people you don't have chemistry?" Carol asked. "What brings people together?"

Hmmmm. "Maybe similar attitudes and point of view? The same approach to life?"

"Maybe," Carol said. "I knew when Harry was 13 years old and I was 12; he was the exactly the same as he is now. He said, 'Isn't that strange? Carol, you haven't changed one iota.' Isn't that something? My feelings for him haven't changed either."

"I think you said something profound."

"I think *you* did," Carol proclaimed.

With the steam still rising from their reunion, Carol spoke confidentially. "This is my *first* marriage. The secret to the whole thing is love. If you do just love each other, and you don't say, 'Oh I *have* to love him or 'I *have* to forgive him.' There's nothing to forgive when you finally have a marriage where *love* is involved.

"You don't say, 'Now can we afford a housekeeper?' You don't say, 'What kind of home will we live in?' You don't ask, 'How much money do you make?' None of that. You just love him. And he loves you."

Just like that. So why do we make love so complicated and take a lifetime to figure it out? If Carol's earlier marriages were only preamble to Harry, what had savvy, openhearted Carol hoped for in her previous marriages?

Carol buzzed on, engagingly honest. "I had three marriages and mostly it was because my mother in New York — when I was young and trying to get a job — said to me, 'Carol, it's 10:30 at night and you're sitting there talking to this man. You can't talk to a man alone at night in your little one-room apartment. You can't do that!' So I married him. I was terribly lonely trying to get jobs. And I just married three times for that reason."

And yet Carol's marriage to Charles Lowe lasted over 40 years. "Charles kept me working and most actors are grateful for that," she said. "We had very little time to be alone together. I was working all the time. And boy, did I learn a lot."

She hit a low note. "He wasn't interested in me. I was lonely. I didn't miss him. I spent my life going from hotel rooms to dressing rooms all the way around the world. I thought that was marriage."

According to Charles Lowe's 1999 *New York Times* obituary, Carol filed for divorce in May 1998 and said her husband had abused her, mismanaged her money and that they only had sex twice in their marriage.

Carol's good cheer swung back up. "And all of a sudden, this is my *first* marriage! You don't have to say anything. You just want to do things for each other. I notice in my husband's family, they're all very gentle and sweet with their wives and considerate. The husband tries to do the dishes even though he doesn't do them right. Marriage is a *beautiful* thing," said a lady willing to be vulnerable again late in life.

She opened a window into her new, previously unimagined existence. "It's never the same. Every day is different, to tell you the truth. It's wonderful here. We have a beautiful rose garden. We have a white fig tree and a black fig tree and an apricot tree and peaches, cherries and lemons and oranges, a walnut tree, everything. We say to each other, 'What will we have for breakfast?' And then we go out and get whatever we want, just pick it off the tree. It's heaven. Harry also cooks or we'd starve to death."

Carol's idyll included daily walks in the garden or into Modesto and back. "Walking's the best. We also have a swimming pool; that helps. Sometimes I join Harry on his 'rowboat' machine. And we dance. I taught Harry."

When not waltzing, Harry had served eight years on the Modesto City Council, and started Citizens Leading Effective Action Now (C.L.E.A.N.) to fight pornography.

On Sundays, he and Carol often sampled different Protestant churches. Harry was raised in a religious Armenian household and she as a Christian Scientist. Her father, a newspaper editor, had also been an active lecturer and editor of Christian Science publications. "I can't say I'm a Christian Scientist. I go to doctors. But the curtain goes up at eight o'clock at night and I've got to be on that stage. I think Christian Science is pretty good training; nothing's going to stop you from doing your work."

Carol didn't even slow down after nearsightedness caused her several falls into the orchestra pit. She emerged from her last nosedive having broken an arm, three ribs and a collarbone. Carol was especially proud of not missing any *Dolly!* performances, some 5,000 in the 1960s, popular revivals in 1978 and 1995 as well as 1998 tours on the road when she was under a doctor's care for uterine cancer. "That was eight shows a week, 16 in concerts. I was doing cobalt and chemo. There's nothing like sheer panic to create adrenaline. The healing process is to keep working." I felt the adrenaline still pumping via AT&T.

The winner of 10 Tony awards for *Dolly!*, including best actress in a comedy, Carol said her work cure was only amplified by the give-and-take of an audience. "You give the audience a little piece of your soul, and they give you a little piece of your soul back again by appreciating it — or applauding or laughing or crying. It builds and by the end of the show, I either feel better or I'm *healed!* My doctor said, 'Well for gosh sakes, you *are* healed."

And Carol Elaine Channing, born January 31, 1921, in Seattle, Washington, still revered the healing faith of her father and lifelong mentor. "Daddy used to say, 'God loves you the most when you're working because his healing flows through you faster.' Whatever God does, I don't know, I don't claim to know. I think all of us, whether we realize it or not, believe. We had to have one creator. Some people don't believe that, but then no doctor could put us together and make us live. Sometimes onstage I still hear Daddy saying, 'Tell it to an understanding heart. Tell it to me.' I do and it's brand-new to me. Are *you* an only child, too?"

"Yes." I felt a quick kinship.

"That's it!" said Carol. "And then you get to worshipping your father!"

We laughed, two only daughters who kept their papas on pedestals.

Carol was only 35 when her father died; he was 68. "Too soon. I never got over it. I just grieved for decades. Finally now, it's the first time I don't have to keep his picture in front of me and talk to him. But he's still with me." Carol's mother sent her off to college confessing that her father was actually half German-American and half African American but had always passed as white. Her mother said she didn't want her daughter to be surprised "if she had a black baby." Carol kept her secret until she published her autobiography at age 81, then saying she was proud of her heritage and its "great strains in show business."

Reminiscences about her father and hero now flowed easily. "We'd go for a ride to break in the new car. We'd sing all the way to San Jose and back to San Francisco. We also drove from San Francisco to Boston every summer, so we sang ALLLLLLLLL the way to Boston and ALLLLLLLLLL the way back again.

"Daddy would drive and I was next to him. Mother was in the back seat. She'd clap to what we were singing. Daddy and I'd sing and harmonize. He was able to make me sound good. My voice is high and I had thin vocal cords growing up. Oh, we loved doing it.

"We sang Baptist hymns usually. 'Amazing Grace' and 'Underneath the Everlasting Arms.'" Carol burst into song, reviving her childhood repertoire to full volume. The phone vibrated. "Oh roll Jordan roll, roll Jordan roll ... I am bound to shout to glory when this world's on fire ... Oh glory, Hallelujah!" Back came the jubilation. "We continued singing right up until he died. 1956."

And for 45 years Carol kept performing. Now with Harry at the helm, they'd soon tour her revue of reminiscences: *The First 80 Years Are the Hardest.* Carol called Harry: "Where am I booked?"

"Santa Barbara, Austin, New York," he called back. I jotted down her New York dates.

"We open in The Feinstein Room at the Regency. They charge way too much," said Carol. "You can pose as my dresser." I had my ticket.

When not performing, Carol and Harry ran the Channing-Kullijian Foundation funding scholarships for arts education in public schools. In 2007, Governor Arnold Schwarzenegger honored Carol for her contributions to arts education in California, and in 2008, she won the National PTA's Life Achievement Award for her foundation's support of children's education.

"I'm 85 years old. I have found that the hardest thing in the world to find is exactly what you have that can mean something to your fellow man. What is it that I can offer to these students? If you find yourself, you've found it," said Carol, entertainer, artist, teacher and role model.

"All we (artists) do is recreate what is already created … so it's pretty well religious work. It is in all the arts. It keeps anybody young."

If Carol's "religious work" kept her young after a lifetime on stage, she also kept to youthful hopes wherever they led. "I want to check out on a high note and not a low note," she said. "I want my tombstone to say she 'lifted the lives of others.'"

Carol's second phone started ringing. It didn't stop.

"Do you need to answer that?"

"Just a minute. Hold on. I've got to get up off this chair now." She groaned. "I can't do it …. Oh, I've got it upside down …. Oh, and now there's the doorbell."

And there was Carol tangled in phone lines, wide-eyed, and still playing for laughs. "Are you OK?" I waited to be sure. "Any parting advice?"

"I think it would be the essence of ego to tell somebody else how to live," Carol said. Whether overture or encore, she suddenly sang: "It's just love … which is all there is." She stopped. "Well, wait a minute. What's that song? Harry and I just love it. 'Ah, sweet mystery of life, at last I've found thee." The lyrics sped up. "I know at last the secret of it all. 'Tis the answer; 'tis the end of all of living. For it is love alone that rules.'

"You know that one?"

I knew that one. And I loved it.

I arranged with Harry to attend Carol's performance of *"The First 80 Years Are the Hardest"* at Feinstein's in the Regency Hotel. We met backstage just long enough to take photos that proved Carol's rechargeable batteries and coast-to-coast grin were for real. And to see that Harry was right, their marriage was all about hope.

The lights came up and the bass, drums, and Steinway hit *"Hello*

Dolly!" Carol Channing entered stage left in a lipstick-red tuxedo with mouth to match. She strutted in sequins, bumping and grinding her slim hips.

Carol wowed loyal fans with her cabaret revue, a seemingly off-the-cuff blend of songs she had made famous, Broadway patter, and saucy impersonations. She gave us her you've-got-to-be-kidding, gee-whiz gravel and gusto. She channeled "Red Hot Mama" Sophie Tucker, brassy Ethel Merman, inebriated Tallulah Bankhead, and diamond-decked Queen Elizabeth at a command performance. Carol—batty to professional purpose—animated her own Al Hirschfield caricature.

The dinner audience clapped and called for the old standards. Carol pretended amazement; her dark eyes saucered: "You *remember!?*"

We remembered and clapped for more. Carol delivered a still sexy "Razzle Dazzle" with rhinestones sparkling on her toes. She finished with Dolly Levi's rousing ballad, "Before The Parade Passes By:"

> With the rest of them, with the best of them
> I can hold my head up high
> For I've got a goal again, I've got a drive again
> I wanna feel my heart coming alive again
> Before the parade passes by. (WORDS AND MUSIC BY JERRY HERMAN)

Now perhaps her personal battle hymn, Carol sang an encore, and invited Harry to her side. He took her hand, Carol's willing partner as they soft-shoed into the spotlight. They ended in step with a gentle kiss.

Harry Kullijian died at home in Modesto, California on December 26, 2011. He was 91, on the eve of his 92nd birthday. Carol Channing died at home in Rancho Mirage, California on January 15, 2019. She was 97.

PHOTO COURTESY OF RICHARD WILBUR

Poet Dick Wilbur and wife, Charlee, on their wedding day, June 1942

"Which is to say that what love sees is true;
That this world's fullness is not made but found."

31

Cherishing a Long, Happy Union

FORGET VITAMINS. FORGET GERITOL. Carol Channing and Harry Kulijian found the best elixir of all. Just as love rejuvenates at any age, so can it safeguard a long, happy marriage. I remembered Dick and Charlee Wilbur, our Key West neighbors behind the high hibiscus. We'd met at the communal pool and lazed in the "Southernmost" shade. The Wilburs seemed a sophisticated, mysterious duo — Dick tall and straight as a Windsor, easy and elegant, formal at core, Charlee effusive and elusive, Claire Trevor to his Ray Milland.

Dick fell for Mary Charlotte Hayes Ward when they were college students, he at Amherst and she at Smith; he often walked the nine miles between campuses to see Charlee.

In *Poetry* magazine, poet Donald Hall recalled Charlee's story of first meeting Dick's family. "When the couple parked outside the New Jersey house of Wilbur's childhood, Charlee watched a young fellow skip down the stairs, dressed in tennis whites and carrying a racquet. It was Wilbur's father — and Charlee told me, 'I knew what I was in for.'" Dick and Charlee married after his graduation in June 1942. If Charlee knew what was in store, Dick wooed a coolheaded and more-than-hoped for helpmate.

Dick liked to tell the story that on their wedding night they stopped for dinner and he, then 21, was carded and denied an alcoholic drink, while Charlee, a year younger, was readily served.

During World War II, Dick was stationed with the 36th Allied Infantry Division in Europe. An army cryptographer, he saw infantry action in Italy, France and Germany. He wrote poems "to calm his nerves" and sent them home to Charlee and a few friends and teachers. Charlee forwarded her pick to an editor at the *Saturday Evening Post*. The poem was published in 1944 and caught the attention of poet Robert Frost. On return from war, Wilbur began his M.A. in English at Harvard where Frost became his mentor and friend.

At Harvard, Wilbur was also friends with French poet André du Bouchet, an associate of *Foreground*, a publication on the lookout for new talent. He recalled their association in the *Paris Review*: "André heard from my wife one evening that I had a secret cache of poems in my study desk. He asked to see them, then took them away to read. When he came back about an hour later, he kissed me on both cheeks and declared me to be a poet."

Three years later, Wilbur's first book, *The Beautiful Changes* debuted to *Poetry* magazine's acclaim: "A Remarkable New Talent." Establishing Wilbur's exceptional skills at the age of 29, *Ceremony and Other Poems* was published in 1950.

According to a Poetry Foundation critique, "These early poems show the beginnings of what would develop into Wilbur's signature grace: the brightness and buoyancy of the world, focused into formal precision. Also in evidence here are Wilbur's lifelong thematic preoccupations: classical art as a provocation to poetry; the heightened decorum of love; and the natural world as a site of study and a source of revelation."

In Peter Dale's *Between the Lines*, Wilbur considered Charlee's crucial role in his poetic career. "If I have gotten away with being a poet, it has had a great deal to do with my marriage to a woman whom Willa Muir called a perfect poet's wife — a partner, muse and friend who is even surer than I that poems are necessary."

At the 2003 Key West Literary Seminar, Dick read *"For C,"* his tribute to Charlee, his partner, friend and most trusted muse.

> Still, there a certain scope in that long love
> Which constant spirits are the keepers of,
> And which, though taken to be tame and staid,
> Is a wild sostenuto of the heart,
> A passion joined to courtesy and art
> Which has the quality of something made,
> Like a good fiddle, like the rose's scent
> Like a rose window or the firmament.

When we were neighbors, Dick had detailed their domestic harmony. "Charlee is devoted to cooking good vegetables and I raise our herbs and fruits. She's always making sure I don't drink too much." His smile implied that he wasn't averse to an accustomed sip or two. "I've always been fond of drink like my friend Peter Taylor. We have wine with certain dishes. And also if you've put in a good day's work and play, we like to spend a half hour looking at the television news and having a cocktail. We've been pretty restrained about things like that for the past 15 to 20 years. Prior to that time, I won't say we were. We're not studious about the avoidance of calories or the matter of drink. We eat a lot of ice cream; we eat a lot of things we don't see any reason now to deny ourselves." Dick and Charlee also biked to the gym and beaches.

Years later, we talked on the deck hidden among avocado and grapefruit trees while Charlee rested upstairs. Dick waited when he heard her cautious steps and watched her safe descent, cane in hand. They had then been married more than 60 years.

"I think Charlee and I are really quite surprised at how old we've gotten to be. But if one's marriage is companionable and pleasant, it is extremely sustainable. The only moments when I feel the bottom drop out of things are when I imagine being without Charlee. I would have to study it all over again, how to live in the world. And that would be quite a hard thing to do in one's 80s."

Timothy Murphy, a former student and family friend, wrote online of an intimate, late-in-life evening with the Wilburs in Cummington. Charlee was in a wheelchair having suffered spinal fractures and nearly fatal post surgery sepsis. When time for dinner, Wilbur suggested that they create a conga line to the table across the room. "Charlee disdained her wheelchair, her walker," said Murphy. "She was a woman of middle size, but Dick is a very large man, and he placed his hands on her hips, steadying the love of his life. They set out with Charlee snapping her fingers above her head, and Dick kicking left and right .... I'd (earlier) asked Dick how, given the self-destruction of so many of his talented peers, he had so spectacularly persevered. Charlee blurted, "He *married* well." Wilbur agreed.

In May 2007, I heard that Charlee had died. She was 85 and Dick was 86. Her *Boston Globe's* obituary read: "Charlotte Wilbur Inspired and Guided Poets."

I remembered Dick's anguish at the thought of losing Charlee. "I know," he said in the *Globe*, "that as I went on writing poems without deliberately aiming to do so, I began to write with her tastes and sensibilities, as well as my own. I suppose the muse is thought to be participator, but she was an unusually participating muse."

The night Dick read "For C," he tendered the hope that poetry's job was "to arm us with the words with which we can confront reality."

I hoped that poetry, now put to the test, would arm Dick against despair as he cherished his sacred union. "I think it's a great life and I feel grateful," he'd told me. "It seems to me that the world is full of wonders. My feelings are that we are in the hands of a good god so whatever happens will quite possibly be all right."

I remembered that at St. Paul's Episcopal Church on Duval Street, Dick had sat on the aisle, Charlee beside him. When it was time for communion, he took her arm in his, and in slow step, they approached the rail, knelt and prayed together.

Richard Purdy Wilbur died in Belmont, Massachusetts on October 14, 2017. He was 96.

PHOTO BY ELIZABETH HOWARD

Suzie Zuzek dePoo, Artist

What's more beautiful than a unicorn?

32

Transforming This and That

AT THE GALLERY ON GREENE in Key West, a unicorn glided like a giant mobile, catching the light and gently riding the air. It was sculpted from wire entwined with bits of china, crystal and glass once buried on the beach. Nearby were mermaids, a Madonna, and Adam and Eve clipped from tin or painted on driftwood. Enchanted, I asked about the artist and was told she was 82-year-old Suzie dePoo. She lived behind the battered wall on Dey Street and it was okay to drop by.

No one answered my knock. I peeked into a window to see a thinning, tinseled Christmas tree touching the brightly canopied ceiling, and large and small paintings checkering the walls. A calico cat stared up from the rusty glider. Others slunk between roots of giant cactus and banyans, past racks of drip-drying dishes and broken lawn chairs. Open sheds spilled chicken wire and weathered planks. Life-sized tin sculptures of jesters and guardian angels strumming mandolins crowded in a far corner. Peacocks cried from their pen. Mozart's "First Piano Concerto" blared from a boom box. I felt lost in a Fellini fun house — part garage sale, part works in progress with nods to Picasso and Botticelli.

"Hello. Suzie? Suzie de Poo?"

The screen door swung behind a small, fine-featured woman wearing a man's shirt and torn, cotton skirt secured with a safety pin. "Hi. I'm Suzie." She wound her watch. "I'm on daylight savings so it's 20 after 12, my time." She said she usually arose at four a.m. and slept year round on her screened-in studio porch.

With no questions asked, Suzie, operating in her own time zone, ushered me into her studio. Here she stuck to her work schedule surrounded by a jumble of "favorite things" — her large, tile flower paintings, porcelain pitchers and colored glassware; faded posters of "The Birth of Venus" and "Save the Florida Cougar;" doll chairs, a patchwork quilt, a splintered cross, china masks and pale photographs of a young girl practicing at the ballet barre. Rows of canvases and painted ceramic boxes hid under draped sheets. A broken crystal chandelier swayed from the ceiling.

Suzie unveiled her latest commission — a tile mural of mermaids floating with poems amidst coral, seahorses, turtles and dolphins. She laughed sweetly. "The client wanted a mermaid leaning up against a tree. And some sky and birds. I couldn't see that."

She dipped her brush into a purple quartz glaze. "Some glazes come out looking like you expect and some don't when they dry. I wonder how it's going to come out, but I just keep plugging along.... I don't really care if I sell my art. I want to do it. I love beautiful things. I love unicorns. What's more beautiful than a unicorn?"

I couldn't imagine.

We discovered a mutual love for the mythical creatures of "The Lady and the Unicorn" medieval tapestries hung in the Cluny museum. At 14, I'd visited the museum with my parents, awed by the blood-red tapestry against the stone wall, a flowered menagerie of monkeys, rabbits, exotic birds and unicorns.

Suzie said she had once sheltered monkeys, parrots, rabbits, ducks, chickens, goats and even a donkey. Now limited to a slew of cats and peacocks, she transformed discarded debris into her own fanciful creations. A Pegasus of wired beach glass pieces carried a dragonfly on its wing. Its light-catching wings reminded me of my father's novella, *The Dragonfly*.

Suzie cast such a magical spell I returned often to see her at work. She twisted stubborn copper threading into birds, fish tails, a man in the moon. She wove clumps of chicken wire into a pair of peacocks. "I didn't know what I was gonna do with the wire," she said. "I started stomping on it and just kept twisting."

And Suzie kept twisting this and that into new, imaginative works. I wondered if she'd always made art from whatever she could find. "When I was young, I did my daily chores, and then I had a warm place behind the kitchen stove where I could draw while my mother was gone off looking for a lost cow. When my older sisters had a little space left on their papers, they'd give it to me so I could draw," Suzie said. "I liked to draw and I wanted to go to art school."

Suzie was born Agnes Helen Zuzek on December 5, 1920, the youngest of five raised on a dairy farm in Gowanda, New York, near Buffalo. Her parents were Slovenian immigrants. "My mother had a pretty hard life. She used to say, 'Heaven and hell are right here.' My father was a little dictator. He never laid a hand on her, but he'd keep her up all night. She'd be sitting by the kitchen stove, he just yelling at her. Yugoslav. If the horses ran away it was her fault. One time, they didn't speak for seven weeks.

"Some women know that a guy is going to take care of them, but I always thought, 'I'm going to have take care of myself.'" Suzie joined the Women's Army Corps during World War II and rose to the rank of sergeant. She was nicknamed by fellow soldiers who mispronounced "Zuzek." She studied drawing in the army, and afterwards on the GI Bill pursued design and illustration at the Pratt Institute in Brooklyn and at the Arts Students League in New York.

In Manhattan, Suzie turned out floral patterns for a textile designer and met and married John de Poo, a merchant seaman and businessman from Key West. The first of their three daughters was born before Suzie and John returned to Key West in 1954. For 25 years, she biked to the Key West Handprints factory to design dress fabrics. Her unique "island style" floral designs were sought by many, including socialite client Lilly Pulitzer.

Suzie worked at the factory for a decade before she and John separated; she then raised their daughters on her own. "John said, 'Choose between me and the cats.' I said, 'I can't choose. I can't give up the cats.' So he left. I never asked him for a penny. I worked to support me and the girls," Suzie said with no regret. Although long parted, she and John had only recently divorced.

Like Alma Bond, Suzie was in her mid 60s when she chose a new creative course — switching from textile design to painting and sculpture. She still followed her mantra: "Art is not static, it must be created and then let go, so more art can come."

Her work was shown locally as well as across the country. In 2001, The Key West Museum of Art & History honored her with "A Remarkable Retrospective." The Key West library opens onto Suzie's ceramic mural, "Alice in Wonderland" — a lush garden of books, fruits and flowers.

Suzie also helped establish the Key West Arts Center and several galleries for budding artists. She still befriended young artists, taking in strays of all persuasions, giving many shelter in her ramshackle hideaway.

One morning we sat together in a patch of sun under the laundry line of tattered wool sweaters blowing over our heads. She handed me a review describing her work as "idyllic with no suggestion of the darker side." "He asks, 'Where's the pain?'" Suzie tapped her chest. "Well, the pain is here. That's when I do most of the work, when I'm in pain."

Her mobile phone rang. Suzie listened patiently. "OK. Come on over." She stroked the gray kitty curled in her lap. "My granddaughter. She's had a lot of problems. Drugs. A baby. She makes jewelry but needs money. They get mad at me for giving her money, but what are you going to do?"

Keep giving.

"Last year I lost…." She stopped. "My grandson was killed. He was 15 years old. He was driving the car. Of course, my daughter will never get over it. She's my oldest.

"Maybe your time is given to you and you have to go, no matter what. You wonder what did happen. I was real angry thinking what kids can do to their parents. I couldn't even cry the first day."

How had she found comfort? In her work? Faith?

"Well, I was raised Catholic. And long ago I made a promise — if this kitten would get well, I'd go to church. She got well, and I started going to church. I went when my granddaughter was three or four, but I never went back. I still say my prayers and believe in Jesus, but I don't go to church."

Did her works of Madonna and Child, Adam and Eve reflect her faith?

"Adam and Eve are the one way I can paint nudes." We laughed.

If no longer a churchgoer, Suzie's faith in all she met never wavered. A negligent client who'd never paid for a large painting or answered her phone calls, showed up with a check a year after the fact. She met him with a smile and a hot cup of coffee.

If Suzie seemed too trusting and lived in disarray, I suspected she was really a disciplined artist who consciously chose light over darkness. She understood the cruelty of time, her works reflecting the utopian, the Garden of Eden before the fall.

Suzie rewound her watch. "It's still an hour ahead. I'm on time. I have to go feed the peacocks. I was trimming trees in there earlier. I want more sunlight into the peacock yard for the little runt who hates the cold. I have to do all these chores every day — feed the animals, sweep the yard a little bit, clean a little bit of house. I like to work on the tin a lot, too. I can do it just before I feed the cats at the end of the day."

She unfolded a crumpled note from her skirt pocket. The letter, saved with a grocery store recipe for fried watercress, was sent by her eight-year-old granddaughter when Suzie was hospitalized for "tension." She read the note aloud: "Dear grandma, I'm sorry you're in the hospital. I miss you. I hope you don't get better. Love, Crystal.'" More laughter.

Suzie, then up and off again an hour ahead of me, did her work, both routine and beautiful. "Work is your salvation," she counseled. "It really keeps you going. I like hard work, any kind of work. Any physical labor charges up your batteries. I haven't got the energy I used to, you know. But, I'm lucky to have lived so long and have something I enjoy doing. Age shouldn't be a dirty word. Don't waste your time worrying about it."

With no time to lose before leaving Key West, I stopped by Suzie's to say goodbye. I gave her spring flowers and she handed me a package wrapped in newspaper. It felt fragile. I unfolded the pages one by one. There in the folds was a palm-sized dove of bent wire and beach glass buffed blue, aqua and smoky gray. "I tried to make you a dragonfly, like your father's," she said shyly. "It didn't work out, but I hope you like this."

I tried to spin Suzie off her small, sturdy feet. I carefully rewrapped her beguiling dove for the flight home. It landed in my office window, where it now catches the light.

Suzie and I exchanged postcards and on future Key West visits, I hurried to see her. I called Suzie's name and tiptoed over the banyan roots hoping to spy her amid the backyard clutter. If lucky, I found her in a far corner of the shed listening to Cuban opera and painting driftwood panels, more Madonnas or an Adam and Eve. We hugged.

Toward the end, Suzie stopped painting. I more often found her resting on the couch close to this season's shedding Christmas tree. Finding Suzie always felt like a homecoming, her still willing presence, a tiny, torch-bearing Lady Liberty, welcoming me ashore.

Suzie Zuzek dePoo died at home on July 13, 2011. She was 90.

PHOTO BY ELIZABETH HOWARD

Sol and Barbara Jacobson, Quakers

*I liked the Quaker philosophy of God being in every person;
being open to every person that you ever meet.*

33

Sharing Love and Peace

On another winter day in Key West, I crossed the street to join protesters gathered on the corner of Palm Avenue. A slightly stooped gentleman wore a handwritten sign: "No Iraq War." The light breeze ruffled his white hair. He raised his placard with the pleas of his younger compatriots: "Restrain King George," "Stand Up for Peace," "Peace is Patriotic."

He offered me a sign: "Peace Not War." Who was this genial, senior fellow standing up for peace? Sol Jacobson introduced himself, a Quaker against the impending war in Iraq. "Come to our Meeting," he invited. "Sunday at 10 in our garden." I accepted with fond memories of morning Meetings at Friends Seminary that started the school day in communal silence. By then, John's school also had adopted the philosophy and practices of the Quakers and become Tandem Friends School.

I learned that Quakers Sol and his wife, Barbara, opened their home to all visitors. Sol, now 90, had made his mark as a Broadway press agent for the likes of Katherine Cornell, Ray Bolger, Maurice Evans, George Abbott, Zero Mostel, Bette Midler and Bea Arthur.

He'd worked for the Shuberts, theater owners in New York City and across the country, publicizing some 200 Broadway shows and road tours. From 1940 to 1980, Sol promoted New York theatrical productions including *Tea House of the August Moon, Flower Drum Song, West Side Story, A Funny Thing Happened on the Way to the Forum* and *Superman.* He'd publicized *Fiddler on the Roof*—his longest running hit—from its original 1964 Broadway production to tours of the West Coast, South Africa and Norway.

Barbara, a classically trained pianist, had been the set designer when they met in 1933 at the Hedgerow Theater in Rose Valley, Pennsylvania. They remained friends and married in 1973 after both lost their spouses the year before. She was now 88.

On my first Sunday visit, I spotted Sol's "No War" sign hung on the door of their white clapboard house on Grinnell Street. Swags of colored prayer flags draped the porch. "The wind blows blessings towards you," said an early arrival.

"Sometimes the wind blows the other way, too," said Barbara, shepherding us in from the chill. She jotted attendees' names in a leather-bound journal as we took seats in a circle. Sol sat on the stairs.

As quiet descended, I wondered where to look. The louvered doors? The floor-to-ceiling heirloom mirror, the whittled ibis, calla lilies? Quiet competed with passing mopeds, barking dogs, low-flying planes. Palm fronds scratched the roof. Wind hummed in the eaves.

I closed my eyes to "coo currooooing" of mourning doves in the Spanish limes. I felt uneasy sitting in silence with strangers. I tried to picture a deserted beach, the warm waves with my feet sinking into the sand. I tried not to replay problems I couldn't solve. I wondered how Quakers achieved pacifism, how they came to internal peace. A quarter hour passed without a word. Then a man lamented the loss of a friend to AIDS. He asked that no more lives be lost to war; a woman volunteered a psalm of peace.

"Good morning, friends," said Barbara at 11.

"Good morning," we answered and joined hands. We introduced ourselves, and some signed up for future protests against the war.

Sol and Barbara served pink lemonade and Valentine cookies. I asked if I could come and talk further about being Quakers and living so long and well.

The morning we met, the sun was strong in the Jacobsons' garden — a haven of banana, sour orange and grapefruit trees, purple and lemon-shaded orchids, red crotons and shocking-pink hibiscus. The fountain sprayed and gurgled. Barbara wore a tee-shirt of Babar the elephant swinging from a parachute.

She and Sol presented a duet on their Quaker beliefs dating from the 1950s when they and their earlier spouses all lived in Rose Valley. "The Quaker philosophy of nonviolence appealed to me. I was attracted to the silence. Group meditation is a very powerful way of being spiritually moved," said Sol. "I liked the Quaker philosophy of God being in every person; being open to every person that you ever meet. They have something of the divine nature."

"Also," said Barbara, "it's wonderful to feel you don't have to have someone interpret for you to God. You can speak directly. And listen directly."

According to the Religious Society of Friends, the basis of the Quaker faith is "the belief that God endows every human being with a measure of the Divine Spirit. We gather in quiet assemblies mindful of the words, 'Be still and know that I am God.'"

How had sophisticated Sol and Barbara originally come to their unembellished faith?

Solomon A. Jacobson was born in Harrisburg, Pennsylvania in 1912, an only child named for King Solomon and raised in the Reformed Jewish tradition. "My father wanted me to be a rabbi," said Sol. "I wanted no part of it. My father was a merchant who sold men's clothing. Successfully, thank god. My mother was British. I was forced to go to Temple every Friday. I hated sermons. I'd rather have been at a basketball game with my buddies."

Sol also grew up loving to act and to write. He studied English literature at Dartmouth College. He first encountered Quaker principles in 1936 while writing publicity for the American Friends Service Committee, founded "to foster an increased interest in Quakerism throughout the United States and to draw all Friends groups into closer sympathy and fellowship."

Sol was drafted into the Army at 30 and subsequently wounded by shrapnel in his leg and hand at the Battle of Brest in Brittany. After recovery in an English hospital, Sol edited the 29th Division newspaper in Holland. In 2009, he was awarded the Chevalier dé la Légion d'Honneur, France's highest honor for war valor.

"I was still ready to tackle Hitler. My mother was part Dutch. All my Dutch relatives were killed, massacred." Sol spoke with new hurt and dismay. "Barbara's brother was a delightful guy, P.T. Captain Bob, Harvard. He was in advertising but then World War II came along. He was killed.

"I was not a pacifist, but every rifleman was a pacifist after he's been in a war. The war certainly accelerated our commitment (to being Quakers). We found out that we'd all become Quakers at the same time unbeknownst to each other."

Barbara nodded her agreement. "I was always a pacifist, although I had fights as a child. I was brought up without any religion at all." Her father was a lawyer and non-practicing Unitarian, her mother, a Baptist.

Barbara traced her Quaker faith of more than 30 years to the Gwynedd (Pennsylvania) Meeting in 1974: "Finally, perhaps the high point of my spiritual journey at Gwynedd Meeting was to know that it is possible to live on two levels at once. Both in this world and in the one with God. It is like listening to what is going on while also hearing a Schubert melody in the background; like taking part in an action while feeling the sun basking on one's back at the same time; like having God stand in silently, while one is talking with someone.

"While the periods of living on two levels at the same time are not always sustained, one can find oneself there, almost always at Meeting for Worship, where, while aware of others and oneself, God seems overarching it all."

Barbara, mother of four, not only found a spiritual community at Gwynedd Meeting, but helped start a nursery school, and with her first husband in 1967, established *Foulkeways*, a Quaker retirement village. She and Sol now lived at *Foulkeways* when not in Key West.

Barbara was appointed the first woman clerk of the Philadelphia Yearly Meeting in 1976 and delivered the opening address, "The Journey into Wholeness." After Sol's retirement, they both attended weekly United Nations sessions to inform the Friends' World Committee on issues of world peace, and in the 1980s were delegates to Friends' conferences in Sweden and Switzerland.

Barbara also worked tirelessly for the League of Women Voters, as did her mother, the first woman to run for Congress from Pennsylvania. A formal portrait of her mother hung in the master bedroom. "This was painted when she was 101," said Barbara. "She looked beautiful; she walked without any trouble; she dressed every night for dinner with nobody taking care of her except my daughter and her husband."

Barbara hesitated. "But at 101, my mother said she 'didn't like the road ahead,' so she took her own life. Pills. She picked a day — December 6. Rather than be sick and have someone take care of her, she didn't want that. It is terrible to think about, but the children all admire her very much for having done it. She was right, the road ahead did not look too good. You can't go on forever."

I looked again, staring for clues. The woman in the portrait seemed poised and serene. What trusted timepiece told her that the quality of her life was no longer worthwhile? Had Barbara at 78 considered her mother's decision when she was diagnosed with potentially fatal non-Hodgkin's lymphoma?

"No. I'm completely recovered. I'm fine now," said Barbara, shoulders back. "Being a Quaker gives you a way of looking at things. Quakers have a theory that the only person you can change is yourself. That's very sustaining, I think. Begin with you."

Bolstered by their beliefs, the Jacobsons kept adding birthdays by participating in around-the-clock activities. Sol clicked his camera at every Key West arts, library and literary event. He and Barbara also tutored as Literacy Volunteers. "One year I tutored a Haitian; another year, a Chinese. It's amazing the complex of people who migrate to Key West." He grinned. "I have a wonderful Polish student from Warsaw. I love teaching. They give you one hour of training. You plunge in. It's like swimming."

And still plunging in, the spirited teacher also liked to cook and share his fare. His special banana bread sold out at the monthly library book sales. "I have delusions of adequacy as a baker," said Sol, the vegetarian, heating up his garlic mushroom soup and whole-wheat buttermilk bread. He cut us hefty slices and tossed the salad greens with avocado and feta cheese. The spices rose; the sun slipped through the flowering vines. We closed our eyes, and I felt thankful for more than a meal.

Their recipe for resilience?

Sol and Barbara — a couple who often wore red — looked to each other already knowing their answer. "I just think it's acceptance," he said.

"It's more than that, too … enjoyment. Helping other people achieve whatever they're hoping for." Barbara smiled. "Especially if you approve of what they're hoping for."

"Our time is taken. I just feel I'm a lucky guy to be alive," said Sol, a practitioner of Tai Chi.

"So do I," said Barbara.

Sol laughed. "I can't wait to read the obituaries. I enjoy reading what other people have done in their lives. A while ago, I had an illness — an angioplasty. I go to the chief cardiologist at the University of Pennsylvania twice a year. He tells me a bad Yiddish joke and sends me home. I'm delighted I'm still here. Rather amazed. Occasionally when we're biking down the road, I think, 'Ye gods, I'm 90 years old and I'm still on a bike. Beware, motorists.'"

I loved spotting teammates Sol and Barbara cruising the crooked lanes with their bike helmets strapped tight. We met up on Tuesday mornings for bocce games at the seaside park. Barbara, agile as a young athlete, usually won. When victorious, Sol announced, "I'm staving off the Visigoths."

And the Jacobsons kept staving off the fates, their garden gate opened to friends and newcomers. Over the next six years, I looked forward to returning to the Jacobsons' each February, sitting in their garden circle, our heads lowered in silence.

Catbirds and palm warblers sang hide and seek; church bells rang; laughter trailed passersby. Sea mist and jasmine mixed in the air. If once ill at ease and a curious outsider, I now felt safe and mysteriously connected to those gathered in stillness. While not a Quaker, I closed my eyes and let go of nagging doubts that had once felt impossible to relinquish. I prayed for peace and found it.

One Sunday, a visitor spoke with gentle openness. "It's sad that we get old and die. ... But 'love never faileth.'"

On the hour, Barbara again greeted those drawn together. For a moment, we held hands and listened. "Earlier Sol and I were reading a psalm passage that praised those who 'toil on the highway.' We were thinking, 'Who do we know who does this?' Some of us might prefer to work on 'lanes' instead of highways; we toil for a time, if not forever."

If not forever, Barbara and Sol were surely among those trying and toiling, "open to every person they met," graciously sharing their choices, their peace and sanctuary. *Love never faileth.*

After seasons in the Jacobsons' garden, I felt my internal clock reset and my sorrow stilled. I missed my father but sensed that his tender presence had been received into this trusting circle. My father had now joined the communion of my wise and compassionate mentors. I felt my journey ending.

Heading home once more, I could only say thank you to Barbara and Sol for their vital time and instruction. Like that given so generously by so many, their guidance and inspiration accompanied me, providing friendship, healing, new purpose and faith in the years to come.

Sol Jacobson died in Key West on February 17, 2010. He was 97.

Barbara Jacobson died in Gwynedd, Pennsylvania, on August 9, 2011. She was 96.

EPILOGUE

Ashes and Grace

NOW PAST MOURNING, I'VE CARRIED with me the comfort and closeness of my mentors, their wisdom and encouraging examples. When I was hungry, they fed me. The greater their years, the more nourishment they gave. They showed me helpful options, acceptance and creative choices. I especially remember Stanley Kunitz' words: "I think it takes tremendous courage to live well, and that holds true at any age in life. The courage comes out of knowing that if you don't persist, you fail. The courage to be is (always) the courage to dare."

In the decade of writing this book, I more fully fathomed the tolls of aging — the loss of health and friends and the effort to jockey on to the roses. While old age was once years ahead, it's now official. I don't have to take off my shoes when going through airport security. My heart beats out of sync, and I can no longer brag that I don't need any medications. John plants a smaller garden and I go to physical therapy.

We're slow to consider an exit plan from our home of 47 years. Some friends have sold their houses and moved to condos or retirement communities. I toured one such place alone. John refused to join me, insisting that when and if needed, we'll find help. I'm pushing for Plan B — a downstairs shower and a list of helpers in hand when required.

I won't consider life without John, still funny, and irreverent, still airing his political angst and delivering his fresh-from-the-garden dinners. He is my reliable rock.

For now, I lurch on, writing for an online journal and volunteering with the International Rescue Committee refugee agency, a place to connect with new and younger people from around the world.

A while ago, I halfheartedly volunteered at a nursing home. I saw feeble and ailing old age up close and was daunted by the sight. Mercifully I was paired with a gentle, valiant man who collected poems on roses and liked to go out for egg salad sandwiches and rides in the country. When given no privacy, he chose dignity; when others decided his fate, he chose patience; when facing the unknown, he chose faith. He taught me how to say goodbye.

When doubts about my future arise, I ask myself what one of my role models would do. I hear their words and voices. I tell myself that if they aged well, maybe I can too. I embrace my mentors' internal presence along with the invaluable company of friends and family.

And in mourning my father, I finally mourned my mother as well. Somehow her death 25 years earlier had been less of a body blow, perhaps because I was younger and still in mid-stride, perhaps because she died suddenly from heart failure while we were far away in California, or perhaps because like many daughters and mothers, we had our tension points. At her death, our differences were not yet fully settled and stayed suspended.

I've come to remember my mother as the game, scrappy woman with the nervous laugh who brought medical articles to her doctors, the lady who cooked Chef Boyardee spaghetti out of the box and took notes in musty churches, graveyards and libraries to document our family history. I discovered crates of clippings and her essays that communicated a supportive wife and frustrated feminist trying to sort out aspirations at the expense of her own identity. With an architect's talent, she'd bought, designed and sold several houses. She proposed two unproduced TV series, "Dollars for Scholars," and "Hail to the Male," and produced a local radio series on finance, "Caution: Women at Work." She also wrote an entertaining, unpublished memoir about life with my center-stage father.

My mother was the faithful, compulsive connector, sending cards for all Hallmark holidays, networking, introducing and advising people who too often ignored her savvy suggestions. She was the mother who took me to play in Stuyvesant Park after persuading New York Parks Commissioner Robert Moses to clean it up. She scooted me past drunks on Third Avenue to Friends Seminary; she took me to the orthodontist and afterwards to Hamburger Heaven. A bird dog for discounts ahead of the pack, she taught me the art of bargain chic. She hosted my high school and college friends. She framed my first published article and came up with endless magazine interview ideas. She invited her grandchildren to dive into her pool and into her arms every summer day.

A few years ago, rather than wait hours in the hospital during John's hip replacement surgery, I took a walk and ended up in the nearby cemetery where my mother was buried. I seldom visited the cemetery. But on that cold day with fine rain falling, I was glad to find her gravestone in the mist, to rest against it, and finally, to cry.

I now feel my mother at work in me and value what I once resisted. She, too, has become a cherished role model. Having outlived my mother by six years, I hope to follow my father to 90.

Several years after my father's death, his ashes were still stored in the corner of my office. He'd asked that his ashes be scattered on the grounds at the University of Virginia, and I fully intended to carry out his wishes, but the day never seemed right.

Early in the winter of 2004, we arrived home from Key West and were met at the airport by Virginia and Dave. We threw our suitcases into the car as Virginia announced, there in the pickup lane, that she was going to have a baby. A baby? A baby! You could have heard me holler on Skyline Drive. John and I jumped up and down and we all huddled in a hug.

Virginia and Dave had been married seven years, and I thought maybe they'd decided not to have children. Soon after sharing their news, they showed us sonograms of a shadowy, curled image. A girl! And she would be named Lydia Grace. She arrived round, rosy, alert and ahead of schedule. A miracle!

With Lydia Grace's entrance, I felt it was finally time to scatter my father's ashes. Earlier, I'd dusted a handful under magnolias stretching to the Rotunda on the University's Lawn. On my father's birthday, I gathered with John, Jamie, Virginia, Dave and baby Lydia to scatter the rest of his ashes. It was a sleepy Sunday in January. The students were still gone on winter break.

We met at the Darden School where my father had worked more than 40 years. Surrounded by a stand of white pines, we scooped the ashes and let them fly. The gritty dust disappeared into the grass and pine needles. Jamie read the 23rd Psalm. John and the children and I held hands. Together we said the *Lord's Prayer*. Lydia Grace, bundled against the cold, smiled throughout.

At home, I scattered more ashes under our white oaks and read aloud my father's poem, "Rose." We remembered him and happy summer afternoons by "Papa's pool." Later we would decide to use my father's inheritance to build our own pool, a sunny place to love, laugh and play as he'd taught us to do.

Rose

During the past week,
outside my window,
a rosebud has become a rose.
To the cynic who finds
no magic in this fact
I say: go design me a machine
that gradually takes a bud
as tightly packed as a cigar,
and, with invisible and gentle efficiency,
twists it open, unwrapping it leaf by leaf
to make a perfect flower.
A rose is not a rose is not a rose.
A rose is a miracle.

Everard Wilson Meade, January 2, 1910–January 5, 2000

ABOUT THE AUTHOR

PHOTO BY KAREN MAUGHAM

Elizabeth Meade Howard, an award-winning reporter and former lecturer at the University of Virginia, writes on aging, health, women and families. Howard has produced educational and documentary films; several focus on remarkable women in their later years. A member of the American Society of Journalists and Authors, Howard is the art editor of *Streetlight Magazine* online. She and her husband, John, live in Charlottesville, Virginia, where they plan to celebrate many more birthdays with their children and granddaughter, Lydia Grace.

Made in the USA
Middletown, DE
13 December 2022

18413095R00195